AF695166

Illegal Drug Use Through the Lifecourse

Hidden older illegal drug users are a seldom-researched group; most research on illegal drug users instead focusses on the young or the institutionalised. To counter this trend, this book reports on a study of current 'hidden' users of illegal drugs aged 40 and over. These are individuals who have sustained illegal drug use over the long term, largely away from the gaze of the authorities, whilst living otherwise 'conventional' lives, holding down jobs, raising families and so on. Thus they have much to tell us about how illegal substances can be integrated into life over the long term, how that integration intersects with other aspects of one's existence, and how illegal drug use is ultimately shaped by changes in personal circumstances and wider social contexts. Utilising insights from the 'lifecourse perspective', the development of the participants' use over their lives is analysed and placed in social context. The book also details the nature of their current drug use. Thus, the book illustrates the place of illegal drugs in the lives of the participants and how this came to be over the decades as they also juggled work, family and the everyday minutiae of life with their use. The result is a unique look at the illegal drug use of an often ignored group of older drug users, which charts the changing role that illegal drugs have played – and continue to play – in their lives.

Dr David Moxon was formerly a senior lecturer in criminology at Sheffield Hallam University, UK. Following undergraduate studies in law and a master's degree in international political economy, David undertook doctoral research on a sociolegal theme at the University of Sheffield, being awarded his PhD in 2008. As well as his work on the 'hidden' drug use of older adults, he has focussed upon contemporary issues of criminological theorising, including the notion of 'social censure', the viability of Marxian theory in the criminological arena and consumerism and its relation to crime.

Dr Jaime Waters is a senior lecturer and course leader in criminology at Sheffield Hallam University, UK. Her research to date has focused on illegal drug use among older adults. Jaime's PhD on the topic was awarded by the University of Sheffield in 2010, following on from master's level studies at the same institution and undergraduate studies at the University of Western Ontario (Canada). She has also published work on research methodology, and she teaches on qualitative and quantitative methods.

'A fascinating book that provides important insights into a group oft-neglected by research, yet much speculated about: the aging drug user who has neither matured out of drug use nor come to the attention of treatment services or the criminal justice system. A valuable and timely contribution to the literature'.

Dr Gary Potter, Senior Lecturer in Criminology,
Lancaster University Law School

'A high quality contribution from criminology on the normality of illegal drug use, or 'deviant leisure' in the life-course of older adults, this book asks some penetrating questions of legislators and all those who support the politically selective and often absurd 'war on drugs'. Why penalise something that, in its meaning in context, is like walking the dog? Moxon and Waters adds to the growing lobby for the decriminalisation of cannabis in the UK whilst more harmful drugs such as alcohol and caffeine are freely available'.

Professor Colin Sumner, Programme Director, BA Criminology,
Head of School of Sociology and Philosophy, UCC, Ireland

Illegal Drug Use Through the Lifecourse

A Study of 'Hidden' Older Users

Dr David Moxon
and Dr Jaime Waters

Routledge
Taylor & Francis Group
LONDON AND NEW YORK

First published 2017
by Routledge

2 Park Square, Milton Park, Abingdon, Oxfordshire OX14 4RN
52 Vanderbilt Avenue, New York, NY 10017

Routledge is an imprint of the Taylor & Francis Group, an informa business

First issued in paperback 2020

Copyright © 2017 David Moxon and Jaime Waters

The right of David Moxon and Jaime Waters to be identified as authors of this work has been asserted by them in accordance with sections 77 and 78 of the Copyright, Designs and Patents Act 1988.

All rights reserved. No part of this book may be reprinted or reproduced or utilised in any form or by any electronic, mechanical, or other means, now known or hereafter invented, including photocopying and recording, or in any information storage or retrieval system, without permission in writing from the publishers.

Notice:
Product or corporate names may be trademarks or registered trademarks, and are used only for identification and explanation without intent to infringe.

British Library Cataloguing in Publication Data
A catalogue record for this book is available from the British Library

Library of Congress Cataloging-in-Publication Data
Names: Moxon, David, author. | Waters, Jaime, author.
Title: Illegal drug use through the lifecourse : a study of 'hidden' older users / David Moxon and Jaime Waters.
Description: Abingdon, Oxon ; New York, NY : Routledge, 2017. Includes bibliographical references and index.
Identifiers: LCCN 2016019701 | ISBN 9781472461568 (hardback) ISBN 9781317118961 (web pdf) | ISBN 9781317118954 (epub) ISBN 9781317118947 (mobipocket)
Subjects: LCSH: Older people—Drug use—Great Britain. | Drug abuse—Great Britain. | Drug abusers—Great Britain.
Classification: LCC HV5824.A33 M69 2017 DDC 362.29084/6—dc23
LC record available at https://lccn.loc.gov/2016019701

ISBN: 978-1-4724-6156-8 (hbk)
ISBN: 978-0-367-59599-9 (pbk)

Typeset in Galliard
by Apex CoVantage, LLC

For Isla and Bethany

Contents

Tables

Figures

Acknowledgements

This work would have been impossible without the willingness of our participants to give freely of their time and to talk openly about their lives. They welcomed us into their homes, made us cups of tea, bought us drinks, made us laugh and discussed their personal histories with frankness, often delving into some sensitive and deeply personal matters, despite their bewilderment as to why we were so interested in them. We thank them sincerely, and we hope the book does at least some justice to their stories.

We also extend our gratitude to those individuals who helped us to find our participants. Over the course of the study, a handful of people went to great lengths to assist us in locating potential participants and to encourage those who fit our criteria to speak to us by, amongst other things, patiently explaining the purpose of the study and vouching for us. Whilst their efforts were not always successful, without their assistance the difficulties we encountered in building a sample would have been insurmountable.

Finally, Jaime would like to thank the late Jason Ditton. Jason, whose gentle encouragement of a nervous and uncertain MA student from Canada (who had somehow found her way to Sheffield), is fondly remembered. Without that encouragement, things would have turned out very differently.

1 Introduction

Changing times

'Meet the silver sniffers' (Goodchild 2005), run the headlines, who are 'balding, wrinkled and stoned' (Kluger and Ressner 2006) with 'one foot in the rave' (Preston 2014). With an eyebrow often firmly raised, media outlets on both sides of the Atlantic have been eager to document an apparently new phenomenon in the world of drug use: the rise of the older user. This trend has been particularly pronounced in the US, where the lifestyles of the so called 'baby boomers' have become a national talking point and their drug use, particularly their cannabis use, has featured in publications such as *Time* (Kluger and Ressner 2006) and *The New York Times* (Kreuger 2013). As Black and Joseph put it, 'popular depictions of grey-haired pot smokers have ranged from retired empty-nesters picking up marijuana in their newly acquired free time, to free-wheeling hippies who never put away their pipes, and to older adults turning to pot to relieve health problems associated with aging' (2014: 822). In the UK, awareness of the phenomenon has been raised by television documentaries such as the Sky 1 screened *Stoned in Suburbia* (Redback Films 2005), and pieces appearing in, for instance, *The Guardian* (Ford 2011, Preston 2014), *The Independent* (Goodchild 2005), and *The Times* (Cavendish and Porter 2013). Meanwhile, millions of viewers have enjoyed online videos that went viral and drew comment from more traditional media (Hooton 2014). Whilst the tone of much of the coverage has been light-hearted, grave concerns about the public health implications of increased drug use among older people have been raised in both the US (Lazar 2010) and the UK (Roxby 2010, *Daily Mail* 2011).

The proliferation of popular interest in illegal drug use by older adults marks a sea change in attitudes, for, as recently as the turn of the century, illegal drug use was generally held to be a phenomenon of youth, and the possibility that older users existed was barely even considered. Within the academy, the consensus was perhaps best expressed by Winick's 'maturation hypothesis' (1962), which famously suggested that users 'mature out' of drug use during their thirties. This idea became something of a received wisdom and contributed to a dearth of research on older users relative to their younger counterparts. However, over recent years, a body of research evidence has steadily accrued suggesting that older illegal drug users do in fact exist and are increasing in number

(Stephens 1991, Anderson and Levy 2003, Sullum 2003, Notley 2005, Waters 2009, Hathaway et al. 2010, Fahmy et al. 2012, Askew 2013). Furthermore, in 2015, the UK government's annual report into 'drug misuse' based upon the findings of the Crime Survey for England and Wales (CSEW) included for the first time an annex on 'older drug users' (Home Office 2015a: 27).[1]

Yet it is not only the existence of older users that is finally being acknowledged. There has also been a creeping acceptance of the idea that illegal drug use can form a routine component of a 'conventional' everyday life (Plant 1975, Hathaway 1997a, 1997b, Pearson 2001, Hammersley 2011). This is so-called 'normal' drug use (Hammersley 2005, 2011) is integrated more or less sustainably into otherwise largely orthodox lifestyles and tolerated or simply ignored by others. Whilst 'the existence of normal patterns of drug use that do not verge upon or develop into the pathological remains questionable, even offensive, to many people' (Hammersley 2005: 201), the evidence that long-term users of illegal drugs can function perfectly happily as, for want of a better term, 'mainstream citizens' (Cohen and Sas 1994: 72) is increasingly providing a stark contrast to the decades-old 'junkie' stereotype that still often dominates popular discourse around drug users.

Much of the 'normal' drug use that is revealed in this body of work is 'hidden'. Historically, the bulk of drugs research has attended to those who are engaged with the criminal justice system regarding their drug use, or those who are involved in drug treatment programmes of various kinds. As a result there has been something of a blind spot regarding those individuals who use drugs quietly and unobtrusively and do not come to the attention of the authorities, and the overall picture of illegal drug use has been significantly distorted as a result. Recently, however, there has been a far greater recognition of hidden users who are not embroiled in legal and treatment structures of any kind and continue their illegal drug use away from the gaze of the authorities (Anderson and Levy 2003, Notley 2005, Shewan and Dalgarno 2005, Warburton, Turnbull and Hough 2005, Hathaway et al. 2010). Such work is beginning to serve as a long overdue corrective to the somewhat skewed view of drug use that has been encouraged by the emphasis upon those who are somehow institutionalised (Plant 1975).

This book reports on a UK-based study that sits at the intersection of these three emerging areas of current research. Its focus is the illegal drug use of *older adults*, whose use is *hidden* and *normal*. The 30 participants in the study were individuals who had sustained their illegal drug use over the long term, largely avoiding scrutiny by the authorities, whilst living otherwise 'conventional' lives that included holding down jobs, raising families and dealing with the everyday minutiae of life. As such, they had much to tell us about how illegal substances can be integrated into a life, how that integration can intersect with

1 The CSEW was known as the British Crime Survey until 1 April 2012.

other aspects of one's existence, how the role and function of illegal drug use can transform over time, and how illegal drug use is shaped by changes in personal circumstances and wider social contexts. This, then, was a modest study intended as an initial mapping exercise of what is undoubtedly a much larger unexplored continent. Indeed, to simply document this group in detail represents progress of sorts in what remains a nascent field of inquiry. It is also timely, for, as we will see, the need for greater understanding of drug 'careers' is only likely to become more pressing in the coming years.

Our contribution comes at a time when there seems to be a growing sense around much of the Western world that a comprehensive recalibration of drug policy may be imminent. That the 'war on drugs' has been a spectacular failure, neither preventing the use of illegal substances nor strangling the criminal networks that provide them, is quickly becoming an academic and popular orthodoxy. Policy developments in certain territories acknowledge this, however tacitly. For example, we have seen moves in various US states towards the decriminalisation of cannabis, and potentially full legalisation (Dickinson 2015); the legalisation of cannabis in Uruguay (Wainwright 2015); the creation of a legitimate market for coca leaf in Bolivia (Wainwright 2015); and the decriminalisation of the use and possession of 'personal' amounts of illegal drugs in Portugal (European Monitoring Centre for Drugs and Drug Addiction 2011). Whilst Russia, China, Japan, Sweden and many African states, among others, remain opposed to any significant relaxation of prohibition, it is clear that many national governments are finding ways to quietly subvert their obligations under United Nations conventions (Wainwright 2015).

In the UK there seems little prospect of any impending liberalisation, and the government still appears to be of a largely prohibitionist mindset. For example, the controversial (Bell 2015, Scott 2015) Psychoactive Substances Bill, currently passing through parliament and expected to become law at some point in 2016, targets so-called 'legal highs'. If enacted, it will become an offence to produce, supply or offer to supply any 'psychoactive substance' with the exception of named exclusions such as nicotine, alcohol and caffeine. Remarkably, not only does this open up a host of definitional issues and create a blanket ban that is designed to pre-emptively outlaw substances that are yet to be produced, but it reverses the longstanding legal principle that citizens can do as they please unless explicitly forbidden; if the bill becomes law, then all 'psychoactive substances' will be banned unless expressly permitted by the government (Travis 2015). However, on the other hand, the government's own comparative report into international drug laws (Home Office 2014a), released on 29 October 2014, brought to an end 40 years of almost unbroken official political rhetoric that only harsher penalties can tackle the problems caused by illegal drugs (Travis 2014). The report found no evidence that the tough enforcement of laws on personal possession leads to lower levels of illegal drug use. It also found much to commend a health-led rather than a criminal-justice-led approach. In the wake of the report's publication, we were reminded of the deeply contentious nature of the drugs issue in the UK when the Liberal Democrat Home Office drugs minister Norman Baker, whose party was in coalition government between 2010 and 2015, claimed that the report had been 'suppressed' for months by their Conservative coalition partners. Baker resigned from his post just a few days later on 3 November 2014, citing differences with Conservative Home Secretary Theresa May (BBC News 2014). And, predictably, the report received a hostile reception from parts of the right-wing press (*Daily Mail* 2014). Yet the very fact that such a report had been published offered some encouragement to those who favour a relaxation of the drug laws in the UK. Even if events in places such as the US are moving much more quickly, in the UK as elsewhere it is clear that the kind of kneejerk anti-drugs sentiment that Sullum (2003) memorably termed 'voodoo pharmacology' is at least being challenged, and those pushing for liberalisation are emboldened and appear to be building momentum, however slowly.

The remainder of this chapter will discuss in more detail the context and background of the research study that this book reports on. We will begin by defining the key terms of the project – namely 'older adult', 'illegal drugs' and 'current', 'hidden' and 'normal' use. Then, we will look at the evidence regarding how many older adults use illegal drugs. Following this, we will go on to examine what we already know about hidden older illegal drug users. To this end, we will explore the research that has emerged from the UK and North America, as well as consider the notion of the lifecourse and the 'drug career'. Finally, we will provide an outline of the rest of the book.

Definition of terms

There is little consensus in studies of drug use as to precisely when somebody ceases to be young. Of course, being 'older' is relative, and as a result there is a sense in which any definition will inevitably be to some extent arbitrary. For example, Hall's (1983) 'aging' users were those aged 65 and over. Miller, Belkin and Gold (1991) considered those aged 55 and over to be 'elderly', whilst Rosenberg (1995) used the age of 50 as the threshold. Boeri (2002: 1) noted that much drug research considers 'older' users to be those aged 35 and above, although along with her collaborators (2002, 2004, Boeri, Sterk and Elifson 2006) she somewhat sidestepped the issue by focussing on the 'baby boomer' cohort who were born between 1946 and 1964.[2] In the UK, the Department of Health's National Service Framework for Older People (Department of Health 2001) suggests that people 'entering old age' are those aged 50 and over, whilst Public Health England (2013) define the 'older' heroin using population as those aged 40 and over. Meanwhile, in the annex to the Home Office's *Drug Misuse* report (Home Office 2015a), 'older drug users' are considered to be

2 Baby boomers are defined by the US Census Bureau as those born between 1946 and 1964. Others favour a starting point of 1945, an end point of 1965, or some combination thereof (Boeri 2002: 291).

those aged 40–59; somewhat opaquely, the report states that 'this age range was chosen as it provides sufficient cases for robust analysis while reflecting an appropriate age for "older" drug users'.[3]

There were two main reasons underlying our decision to define an *'older' adult* as someone aged 40 years and older. The first was born of somewhat practical concerns. We had initially wished to study those aged 50 and over, for we felt that this would allow us to analyse the personal histories of people whose lifecourse had spanned the post-war shift from an industrial society of producers to one of consumers (Bauman 1997) and the associated flowering of various 'spectacular' subcultures (Hebdige 1979), each with their own particular forms of drug consumption. Unfortunately, we struggled to recruit many participants in this age bracket, as we will discuss in Chapter 2. We had, however, found willing participants who were in their forties, so the decision was taken to lower the cut-off point of the study and focus upon those aged 40 and over. This decision was at least justifiable in terms of the second reason – namely, a feeling that there was something of a 'cliff edge' in existing research whereby very few studies indeed focus on drug users aged 40 and over. Thus, as is so often the case in research, practical concerns trumped the original plan, but, given the inescapably relative and arbitrary nature of any definition of 'older', we were not too concerned. Ultimately, it is perhaps best to think of the 'older' adults in this study as simply being older than those who are conventionally studied in research of this nature. Thus, they are *older* even though they may not be *old*, although even this will be of little consolation to some of our participants who positively bristled at our classification of them!

This is a UK-based study, and so *illegal drugs* in this context means those substances that are listed as 'controlled drugs' in the Misuse of Drugs Act 1971 (as amended). Of course, this list is fluid, and the status of substances is subject to change. This fluidity has become more pronounced in recent years as the government has attempted to keep up with the fast-evolving nature of 'legal highs' or 'new psychoactive substances', which as we have already seen has

3 The annual *Drug Misuse* report is based upon the findings of the CSEW, which began asking questions related to drugs from 1994 (although much of the data is only comparable from 1996). Apart from a few questions on cannabis asked of 10–15 year olds as part of the CSEW child survey (Home Office 2015b: 2), drug questions are asked only of people aged 16–59. As the report itself states, 'the CSEW self-completion module is only asked to those aged 16 to 59 years old; therefore it is not possible to examine drug misuse among those aged 60 or over' (Home Office 2015a: 27). This is described as an 'economy measure' due to 'very low prevalence rates for the use of prohibited drugs' among those aged 60 and over (Home Office 2015b: 2) and is a long-standing position (see, for example, Roe 2005: 9). Typically only a small amount of analysis by age cohort has been carried out, with a particular focus reserved for the 16–24 cohort. In short, the approach of the Home Office has both reflected and reinforced the 'prevalent attitude that older people do not use drugs' (Beynon 2009: 9) that we have already suggested is becoming increasingly outmoded. The annex on 'older drug users' included in the 2015 report (Home Office 2015a) suggests the beginnings of a shift in thinking, however.

culminated in the Psychoactive Substances Bill. However, although one or two participants reported experimentation with legal highs, the overwhelming majority of participants used only those well-known drugs whose proscribed status, whilst often contentious, is not factually in doubt, such as amphetamines, cannabis, cocaine, crack, ecstasy, heroin, magic mushrooms, methadone, tranquilizers and LSD. For the avoidance of doubt, legal substances such as tobacco and alcohol, and prescription and over-the-counter drugs, are not the focus of this research.

We defined a *current* user of illegal drugs as an individual who had used an illegal substance at least once during the past year,[4] and a *hidden* user as one who was not in contact with either the criminal justice authorities or drug treatment agencies regarding their use. Thus, our participants were people using illegal drugs 'under the radar' of the authorities. Our main aim in attempting to recruit hidden users was to build a sample consisting of older adults who were using illegal drugs 'normally' (Hammersley 2005, 2011). We were particularly keen to speak to individuals who were using illegal drugs sustainably whilst getting on with their lives as ordinary citizens engaged in work, family and the like. Although recruiting participants whose use was hidden did not guarantee this, it seemed to offer the best chance of success. As Parker, Aldridge and Eggington (2001) suggest, it is 'problematic' users who are more likely to appear in the 'capture systems' of the criminal justice system and treatment services, and so accessing participants through these gateways was ruled out. Concomitantly, this also allowed the study to go a small way to correcting the institutional bias present in samples in most research on illegal drug using populations. We did not discount those who had been involved with the criminal justice system or treatment agencies at some point in the past, although this did not apply to the vast majority of our participants.

Normal use, although it feels intuitively straightforward, has proven decidedly slippery to grasp conceptually. For Hammersley, the term 'normal' designates a mode of drug use that is 'not unusual, rare, or restricted to deviant subcultures'. Instead, it is drug use that is 'integrated into the users' lives and, to some extent, accommodated, tolerated or ignored by society'. Perhaps most importantly, this type of use 'is normal in the sense of involving patterns of activity that are not exclusively problematic and that can be explained by normal psychological and social processes. Indeed, drug use is not always the defining feature of drug users' lives' (2005: 201). Among the many other labels that have been applied to use patterns that tend towards the 'normal' are 'controlled' use (Murphy, Reinarman and Waldorf 1989, Warburton, Turnbull and Hough

4 Typically, 'current' use is used to refer to past month use, and 'recent' use denotes past year use (European Monitoring Centre for Drugs and Drug Addiction 2004). We did not wish to eliminate those who had been unable to use in the past month due to circumstances but still considered themselves to be active users, so we sought past year users rather than past month users, but retained the 'current' label.

2005), 'non-problematic' use (Warburton, Turnbull and Hough 2005, Dalgarno 2006), 'recreational' use (Goode 1969, Parker 2005, Williams 2013), 'controlled dependent' and 'non-dependent' use (McSweeney and Turnbull 2007) and 'unobtrusive' use (Dalgarno and Shewan 2005, Shewan and Dalgarno 2005). Duff et al. (2012), meanwhile, talk of 'socially integrated users'. Other researchers have developed continuums of different types of use upon which 'normal' use can be roughly mapped. Atkinson (1991), for instance, developed a continuum consisting of seven types of use, with mere 'use' at one end and 'substance use disorder' at the other end. Zinberg (1984) distinguishes between 'use', 'misuse' and 'abuse', with 'use' defined as experimental, recreational and circumstantial and resulting in few social costs. Thus, what is here termed 'normal' use is close to what Atkinson and Zinberg simply class as 'use'. In the end, all of these terms clearly overlap to a degree, and each one comes with its own advantages and problems. Nevertheless, the idea of 'normal' use did hold a particular appeal, for it felt most redolent of the type of experience that we were seeking to capture. Beyond this, there seemed little point in adding further to the already voluminous selection of terms, or attempting to arbitrate between their competing claims.

How many older adults use illegal drugs?

Until the late 1950s, the notion of the older opiate addict was not an unusual one (Bean 1974, Rosenberg 1995). These 'early studies depicted the elderly narcotics addict as an "unsuccessful sojourner" through life' (Rosenberg 1936, 1995). However, as we have already seen, during the later years of the twentieth century, the perception that older people generally do not use illegal drugs became firmly established. Despite its narrow focus on consumers of opium derivatives such as heroin in the US, the work of Winick (1962) was one of the wellsprings of this idea. Using data collected by the US Federal Bureau of Narcotics on known addicts between 1955 and 1959, Winick sought to explain 'the disappearance of many narcotics addicts from federal records between the ages of 36 and 45' (Abrams and Alexopoulos 1998: 391). Among the reasons he suggested that this occurred were a reduction in life stresses; the death, debilitation or incarceration of the heaviest users; and the general burning out of the addiction as 'the addicts' inner fires have become banked by their thirties' (Winick 1962: 5). As we have seen, he labelled this phenomenon the 'maturing out' of drug use.

As Anderson and Levy (2003: 768) relate, numerous attempts were made to test the maturation hypothesis (Ball and Snarr 1969, O'Donnell 1969, Snow 1973, Maddux and Desmond 1981), but results proved ambiguous (Stephens 1991). Yet despite this, a tacit acceptance of the hypothesis in much of the drugs field contributed to a lack of research on older users. Alternative explanations emerged for the lack of older illegal drug users, as though this was simply a brute fact in need of theorisation. Waldorf and Biernacki (1981) suggested that users stop when they reached 'rock bottom', whilst Stephens (1991) pointed to the influence of peer support networks, support groups and therapeutic communities in promoting a sober lifestyle amongst older one-time users. The widespread acceptance of the maturation hypothesis was also partly due to its resonance with the fact that most 'volume' criminal offences are associated almost exclusively with the young (Wahidin and Cain 2006) and the perception that older people tend to be the victims of crime rather than the perpetrators (Midwinter 1990: 55).[5] Thus, with the odd notable exception from North America (Vaillant 1973, Capel and Peppers 1978, Glantz and Backenheimer 1988, Rosenberg 1995), there was a dearth of research on older users.

The idea that older drug users could be hidden only really came to prominence following the turn of the twenty-first century. As Anderson and Levy suggested, it was possible that 'rather than having "matured out" of the life, [users] remained active but hidden' (2003: 768). This position was supported by evidence from those such as Schuckit (1977: 171), who found that 'at least 5% of opiate addicts are over age 45 with 1% over age 60' but who believed that the real numbers were much higher. Whilst it is by no means certain, it seems perfectly possible that, contra Winick, older drug users existed in greater numbers than many supposed during the post-war period.

There is far greater clarity regarding the numbers of older users today. In the UK, the 2014–15 run of the CSEW suggests that 2.4 per cent of 55–59 year olds used an illicit drug in the past year, compared to 3.2 per cent of 45–54 year olds and 6.4 per cent of 35–44 year olds (see Table 1.1).[6] Of those adults aged 40–59, which the Home Office now classes as 'older users' (Home Office 2015a: 27), 3.6 per cent used an illicit drug in the past year. However, this remains well below the 13 per cent of 16–39 year olds who are past-year users (Home Office 2015a: 28). Within this group of 'younger users' the 20–24 year old cohort has the highest past year use rates, at 19.8 per cent.

However, there is growing evidence that the number of older illegal drug users is on the rise. The CSEW has tracked increases, albeit moderate and from a low base, in the proportion of older adults using illegal drugs in the past year. According to the CSEW, in 1996, 1.0 per cent of 55–59 year olds reported using an illicit drug in the past year, with 1.9 per cent of 45–54 year olds and 6.0 per cent of 35–44 year olds doing likewise. After a peak in 2003–4, these figures have remained relatively stable and stood at 2.4 per cent, 3.2 per cent and 6.4 per cent respectively by 2014–15 (see Table 1.2). The increase from 1996 to 2014–15 in past-year use measured in the 45–54 age group was rated as statistically significant by the Home Office (Home Office 2015c).

5 Over recent years the discipline of criminology has belatedly started to take the subject of ageing and crime more seriously (Wahidin and Cain 2006), and an emerging body of work has encompassed not only the victimisation of older people (Lister, Wall and Bryan 2004, Powell and Wahidin 2008) but also their own criminality (Powell and Wahidin 2006) and their treatment by the criminal justice system both as perpetrators and as injured parties (Chivete-Matthews and Maggs 2002, Wahidin 2006, Wahidin and Aday 2011).

6 Note that the annex to *Drug Misuse* does not include heroin and crack cocaine use (Home Office 2015a: 27).

Table 1.1 Proportion (per cent) of people reporting use of illicit drugs in the last year (2014/15)

Age	*Used any class A drug in past year*	*Used any illicit drug in past year*
16–19	4.9	18.8
20–24	9.4	19.8
25–29	5.4	12.5
30–34	3.4	8.1
35–44	2.3	6.4
45–54	0.6	3.2
55–59	0.3	2.4
40–59	n/a	3.6

Source: Home Office 2015c

Table 1.2 Proportion (per cent) of people reporting use of illicit drugs in the last year (1996–2015, selected years)

Age	*1996*	*1998*	*2000*	*2001/2*	*2003/4*	*2005/6*	*2007/8*	*2009/10*	*2011/12*	*2013/14*	*2014/15*
35–44	6.0	6.1	6.3	7.5	7.9	6.6	6.1	5.5	5.6	6.6	6.4
45–54	1.9	3.1	3.2	3.5	3.9	2.9	2.7	2.5	3.1	3.5	3.2
55–59	1.0	1.3	1.9	1.2	1.9	1.5	1.7	1.5	1.8	1.5	2.4
40–59	2.5	3.1	3.5	3.6	3.9	3.2	3.2	2.8	3.1	3.6	3.6

Source: Home Office 2015c

As stated in the annex on 'older drug users' in the government's *Drug Misuse* report, the increase in older users 'is likely to be due to a cohort effect, with a greater number of those who have used drugs when they were young continuing to do so as they age' (Home Office 2015a: 27). Indeed, the generation of people that experienced relatively widespread recreational drug use during their late teens and early twenties during the 1960s and 1970s are now well ensconced in middle and older age. Fahmy et al. (2012) and Beynon (2009) have made similar points, with the latter suggesting that both period and cohort effects are at work: 'Older people in the past did not use drugs because they did not use them when they were younger. Older people of today are using drugs because they did so when younger, and have done little to change their consumption as they have aged' (Beynon 2009: 9). Although this ignores the possibility that older users in the past were simply better hidden, that the number of older users is rising seems beyond doubt.

These moderate increases in drug use among older adults are occurring against statistically significant declines in drug use amongst the younger age cohorts and in overall use, although use among younger people remains far higher than use among older adults. For example, between 1996 and 2014–15, the proportion of all 16–59 year olds reporting past-year illegal drug use fell from 11.1

per cent to 8.6 per cent. In 1996, 17.4 per cent of 16–39 year olds were past-year users, compared to 13 per cent in 2014–15 (Home Office 2015a: 28). The most drug-involved cohorts also saw declines in the prevalence of use; both the 16–19 and 20–24 age categories peaked at historic highs of above 30 per cent around the turn of the century but are now back down below 20 per cent (see also Aldridge 2008). This has resulted in a slow but steady increase in the mean age of past-year users of illicit drugs, which is creeping towards 30. For those who still associate illegal drug use with teenagers and young adults in their early twenties, this is likely to be somewhat surprising (see Table 1.3).

The CSEW consistently finds that, unsurprisingly, cannabis is the most commonly used drug among older adults, with 2.5 per cent of 40–59 year olds using it in 2014–15. This represents a slight decline from a peak of 3.3 per cent in 2002–3, but is up from a 1996 baseline of 1.9 per cent (Home Office 2015a: 28). Powder cocaine use among 40–59 year olds stood at 0.6 per cent in 2014–15 (up from 0.2 per cent in 2001–02), whilst ecstasy use has remained stable and stood at 0.2 per cent in 2014–15. This compares to recent declines in cocaine and ecstasy use among 16–39 year olds (Home Office 2015a: 30).

There are other sources of evidence on the scale of illegal drug use among older adults in the UK aside from the CSEW. Fahmy et al. (2012), for example, used data from two household surveys (the 2007 English National Survey of Psychiatric Morbidity and the 2008–10 South East London Community Health survey) to describe the prevalence of illicit drug use in older people both nationally and in inner London. For those aged 65 and over, 0.4 per cent had used cannabis, the most commonly used illegal drug, during the past year, and 1.7 per cent had used it at some point in their life. Rates were higher in inner London (1.1 per cent past year use, and 9.4 per cent lifetime use). The prevalence of illicit drug use in people aged 50–64 years was found to be higher than that in 65+ year olds. For cannabis, past-year use among this cohort was found to be 1.8 per cent, with lifetime use standing at 11.4 per cent. In inner London, rates were higher, at 9.0 per cent and 42.8 per cent respectively. These figures are, according to Fahmy et al. (2012: 555), 'broadly comparable' with the CSEW, although they found greater increases in use than the CSEW was then reporting, most notably of cannabis. Specifically, Fahmy et al. found a tenfold increase in past-year cannabis use by 50–64 year olds from 1993 to 2007 and a twofold increase in 65–74 year olds from 2000 to 2007. Tenfold increases in lifetime use were observed from 1993 to 2007 for cannabis, amphetamine, cocaine and LSD (Fahmy et al. 2012).

Table 1.3 Mean age of people who had used any illicit drug in the past year

	1996	*2003/4*	*2008/9*	*2013/14*
Mean age (years)	26.6	28.7	28.3	29.3

Source: Home Office 2014b

The general picture of increasing numbers of older illegal drug users against a background of overall decline is mirrored in the treatment setting. Overall, the number of people in drug treatment is declining, as is the number of people starting treatment for heroin and crack cocaine. However, the number of people aged 40 and over in treatment is rising, as is the number of people in this age group who are 'new starters' (Drugscope 2014: 5). Older heroin users form a significant part of this (Public Health England 2013). Similar predictions have been made regarding the situation across Europe, with the European Monitoring Centre for Drugs and Drug Addiction (EMCDDA) (2008) estimating that the number of older people with substance use problems or requiring treatment for substance misuse will more than double between 2001 and 2020. This is partly due to the size of the baby boom cohort and what the EMCDDA suggests is the higher rate of substance use among this group.

As Fahmy et al. point out, 'even relatively low prevalences can represent high absolute numbers of users at a national, regional or service level' (2012: 555). Using population estimates for the UK from the Office for National Statistics (2014) and CSEW data on the proportion of people reporting use of illicit drugs in the last year, a cautious estimate of the numbers of older illegal drug users in England and Wales can be made. The figures suggest that there are around 490,000 past-year illegal drug users aged 35–44 in England and Wales, 270,000 aged 45–54, and 50,000 aged 55–59. This gives a total of around 810,000 past year illegal drug users aged 35–59 in England and Wales, and of course there are more users aged over 59 that are not captured by the CSEW. To put this in context, the Conservative Party claimed a membership of 150,000 in September 2014 (Wallace 2014), and the Labour Party 194,000 in February 2015 (LabourList 2015). By September 2015, after the Party's leadership election was won in dramatic fashion by Jeremy Corbyn, Labour's membership had risen to around 360,000 and looked set to continue growing as many 'registered supporters' who were not full members were expected to sign up (Stone 2015). Yet even this much discussed resurgence still left their membership total standing at less than half of the probable number of older illegal drug users.

In sum, it seems that in the UK we are witnessing a gentle increase in illegal drug use amongst the over-35s, and whilst older users remain in the minority they are making up an increasing proportion of the total number of users as use among younger people declines. As the Home Office itself suggests, 'this makes older drug users of particular interest, as despite their lower levels of drug use, they have not been following the overall downward trend' (2015a: 28). Indeed, if these trends continue, then the CSEW's stated position of not collecting data on the illegal drug use of those aged 60 and over (Home Office 2015b: 2) may have to be reconsidered at some point. And, as the Royal College of Psychiatrists note, the increases in drug use in the over-40 age group mean that we should anticipate a significant rise in the coming years in the number of still older people, such as those aged 65 and above, who use illicit drugs (2011: 7).

Meanwhile, in the US, a similar picture is emerging, as evidenced by a number of studies. For instance, Mauro et al. (2015) suggest that one in six middle-aged and older adults use 'substances' (including alcohol, tobacco, prescription and other drugs) to cope with stress. Han, Gfroerer and Colliver (2009) found that the proportion of users of any illicit drug among those aged 50–59 stood at 9.4 per cent, with 5.7 per cent using cannabis and 4.0 per cent using prescription drugs non-medically. Projections in the US have included a 50 per cent rise in illicit drug use among those aged 50 and over from 2.2 per cent (1.6 million individuals) in 1999–2001 to 3.1 per cent (3.5 million individuals) in 2020 (Colliver et al. 2006). Again, it is suggested that these increases are being driven by the aging of the baby boom cohort, with its higher lifetime illicit drug use rate than earlier cohorts. Schlaerth et al. (2004), who investigated illicit drug use in adults aged over 50 presenting to an inner-city emergency department in Los Angeles over a ten-month period, found that the illegal drug preferences of these older adults were broadly in line with those of the general population of users in the LA area, with cocaine being the most frequently used drug. American researchers also predict that the number of adults aged 50 or over with a 'substance use disorder' will double from 2.8 million in 2002–6 (annual average) to 5.7 million by 2020 (Han, Gfroerer and Colliver 2009). Gfroerer et al. (2003) estimate that the number of older adults in need of substance abuse treatment will increase from 1.7 million in 2000 and 2001 to 4.4 million in 2020, due to a 50 per cent increase in the number of older adults and a 70 per cent increase in the rate of treatment need among older adults.

Thus, the overall picture on both sides of the Atlantic is clear: illegal drug use among older people is on the rise. This rise is currently slow and steady rather than spectacular, and it is proceeding from a low base. Nevertheless, we should expect to see greater numbers of older illegal drug users over the coming years, and it is not beyond the bounds of possibility that we may be standing on the cusp of a major increase.

Existing knowledge of hidden older illegal drug users

It remains the case that the vast majority of research into users of illegal drugs focusses upon those in their teens and early twenties. Indeed, this trend is so marked that even studies that shine a light upon those in their mid- to late twenties and thirties (Kandel, Yamaguchi and Chen 1992, Chen and Kandel 1995) are something of a novelty. Nevertheless, as we have suggested already, over recent years, awareness and knowledge of older illegal drug users has belatedly started to develop. For example, a number of studies have included older users as defined here. However, much of this work has incorporated older users as a small part of a wider sample which also includes much younger illegal drug users. As a result, there is often little of note about the specificity of the older users' experiences (for example Goode 1970, Cohen and Sas 1994, Hathaway 1997a, 1997b, Shewan et al. 1998, Pearson 2001, Sullum 2003, Notley 2005, Shewan and Dalgarno 2005, Warburton, Turnbull and Hough 2005, Shukla 2006, Osborne and Fogel 2008, Hathaway et al. 2010, Duff et al. 2012, Askew 2013, Hammersley and Dalgarno 2013, Sandberg 2013). Other studies have restricted their attention to those using just a certain type of drug (Capel et al. 1972, Murphy,

Reinarman and Waldorf 1989, Faupel 1991, Anderson and Levy 2003, Levy and Anderson 2005, Duff et al. 2012, Chatwin and Porteous 2013, Duff and Erickson 2014). Others have focussed upon very particular subsets of older users, such as those who are institutionalised (Petersen 1978, Joseph 1995) or otherwise criminal (Bergman and Amir 1973), whilst some have a very specific emphasis; Askew (2013), for instance, looked at the manner in which 30–59 year old 'recreational' users legitimise their use, whilst Hammersley and Dalgarno (2013) looked at the life stories of those who had injected drugs in the past five years.

There is also a significant body of work that includes older users where the focus has been upon use that is regarded as 'problematic' in some way (for example Pascarelli and Fischer 1974, Green 1982, Crome and Crome 2005, Beynon, McVeigh and Roe 2007, Gossop and Moos 2008, Beynon 2009, Beynon, Stimson and Lawson 2010, Roe et al. 2010, Royal College of Psychiatrists 2011, Wu and Blazer 2011, Ayres et al. 2012, Drugscope 2014, Schoenenberger and Stuck 2014, Wadd and Galvani 2014, Crome et al. 2015). Some studies in this vein include older illegal drug users as part of a wider brief encompassing alcohol, tobacco and prescription misuse (Schuckit 1977, Petersen 1978, Glantz and Backenheimer 1988, Gambert 1992, Finlayson 1995, Abrams and Alexopoulos 1998). Often, though not always, such studies have been concerned with the idea that 'regular users of recreational drugs are also growing older and may experience more [medical] complications with ageing' (EMCDDA 2008: 2), and as a result many focus on problems of treatment and are generally largely indifferent to sociological issues. In addition, as Rosenberg noted, few studies of this type 'follow drug addicts for periods longer than one year, [resulting in] most research [providing] a fragmented view of lifestyles of the addicted elderly' (Rosenberg 1927, 1995), although there have been some studies that are longitudinal in nature (Oppenheimer, Stimson and Thorley 1979, Stimson and Oppenheimer 1982, Oppenheimer et al. 1994, Tobutt, Oppenheimer and Laranjeirna 1996). This issue is compounded by the fact that longitudinal drugs research of a more sociological bent has, to date, tended to start when the user was very young (generally still in school) and followed use patterns into the late twenties or early thirties but not beyond (Chen and Kandel 1995, Aldridge, Measham and Williams 2011). Thus, so far, there is little knowledge of how patterns of use develop in later life.

As a result of this, knowledge of older illegal drug users is patchy at best, and knowledge of what we have termed 'hidden' older illegal drug users is almost non-existent, despite the compelling evidence that this type of user is increasing in number. There are, however, a handful of studies worthy of consideration here. We will look first at those that have emerged in the UK, before turning our attention to North America.

UK studies

Pearson's (2001) ethnographic work on 'normal' drug use centred on two pubs in London and built upon the idea of normalisation (Parker, Aldridge and Measham 1998). Pearson carried out his work over a seven-year period, developing 40 consistent contacts (28 males and 12 of their female partners) along with a fringe network of a further 30 across a number of friendship groups, aged from the early thirties to the mid-fifties. His sample were predominantly white working-class men who chiefly used cannabis and, to a lesser albeit increasing degree, cocaine. He found:

> A crucial feature of these men's lives (and those of their wives, partners and girlfriends) is that they did not think of themselves as "drug users"—it is merely something that they do, or do not do, as an ancillary to other aspects of their lives, whether work or leisure—and who only rarely, if ever, gather together for the purpose of consuming drugs. This was not a "drug subculture" in which drugs were a central feature of people's lives; rather these were people for whom drug use was a peripheral but "normal" aspect of life.
>
> (Pearson 2001: 173)

On the basis of these findings, Pearson claimed:

> The use of drugs was normalized within these adult networks not in the sense that everybody used drugs all the time, but that the use of certain illicit drugs in certain ways was seen as an entirely routine aspect of everyday life. [Illegal drugs] have become a routine and "normal" aspect of life among people who are mainly otherwise law abiding and hardworking fellow citizens.
>
> (Pearson 2001: 192)

Pearson felt that his research subjects were not a unique case and that what he had found was not some transient and short-lived phenomena. Instead, it seemed to him that his subjects heralded a sustained shift in cultural attitudes towards drugs, especially cannabis. As he put it, this was 'not merely some momentary youth cultural phenomenon' but a sign that 'in the new century the age structure of recreational drug use will consolidate around a much wider spectrum than previously' (Pearson 2001: 195). More recently, Chatwin and Porteous (2013), who looked at long term cannabis users and constructed a sample with an average age of 46, made similar findings. Over the years, changes in circumstances had led to changes in their subjects' patterns of use, including periods of complete cessation, but they always had found ways to sustain or restart their use. And, like Pearson's research subjects, Chatwin and Porteous's were 'a fairly conventional group of adults who happen to be regular and long term cannabis users as well as parents, partners, employees and friends' (2013: 250–1).

As one would expect of any assortment of 'fairly conventional' individuals, hidden adult drug users do not form a uniform bloc but are a diverse group with a range of experiences and attitudes. This was explored by Notley (2005), who interviewed 40 hidden, non-problematic users, aged between 25 and 58 years of age (with a mean age of 36), 'who continue to use drugs into adulthood, incorporating illicit substance use into their lifestyles' (2005: 280). Notley identified four distinct groups within her sample, each with different approaches to and understandings of their use. First, the 'archetypal users' were older (usually over 40) and predominantly users of cannabis, although they did occasionally use other illegal drugs. They had strong legal and political views about illegal drugs in general and their own drug use in particular, and were likely to be involved, or have been involved, in alternative subpopulations in relation to their drug use. Drug use for this group was either an integral part of their everyday life or an occasional reconnection with the past. 'Realistic users' were those regular cannabis users who also used other drugs on occasion. Drug use for this group was generally a matter of cost-benefit analysis. They had in place strict controls in order to maximise the potential benefits and minimise the costs of their use. They led predominantly 'straight' lives, only dipping into drug use at designated times or places. 'Searchers' used drugs as a vehicle for self-discovery and enlightenment and saw their use as an integral part of self-understanding and development. Their use was more sporadic, although it encompassed a variety of substances. It tended to be closely controlled, but there were occasional binges. Finally, the illegal drug use of 'traders' was based upon 'narratives related to buying and selling'. Many were ex-dealers with extensive knowledge of the black market and had a varied drugs repertoire as part of an involvement in drug using subcultures. Their use tended to be heavier and more problematic when compared to individuals in the other groups. For traders, 'drug use is subjectively viewed as a consumption choice within society, which they see as relatively lacking in boundaries and rules' (Notley 2005: 287). Notley saw her groups as illustrative of the great diversity in the subjective experience of drug use. Perhaps more importantly, her work showed that 'for some drug users at least, the pattern of use in later life may become one of more considered, controlled use of a restricted range of substances, in certain settings only, as opposed to complete abstention' (2005: 288). Furthermore, 'the typified image of the helpless and inadequate "victim" of drug use could not be said to apply—without exception the sample members were industrious, engaged with "straight" society and managed their lives successfully' (2005: 289).

Shewan and Dalgarno (2005) studied 126 long-term heroin users who had never been in specialist treatment for drug use. The age range of their sample was 19–48, and the mean age was 28.5. They suggested that heroin, generally regarded as one of the most destructive illegal drugs, could be used in a controlled, 'unobtrusive' manner for an extended period of time (see also Warburton, Turnbull and Hough 2005). In explaining this, Shewan and Dalgarno suggested that the importance of 'set' (Zinberg 1984) was difficult to overstate. They argued that the 'addicted set' 'could be characterised by a narrowing of the repertoire of choice available to the drug addict, either subjectively or objectively: subjectively in that the addict believes he or she is addicted (Eiser 1982, Eiser and Gossop 1979), objectively in terms of the social pressures which come to surround the addict (Orford 1984, Cohen 1990, Davies 1992, 1997) and indeed the tangible legal sanctions (Cohen 1990)' (Shewan and Dalgarno 2005: 46). However, even taking into account the role of drug pharmacology in the process of addiction, they suggested that, with an alternative 'set', these issues can potentially be avoided and long-term unobtrusive use engaged in. For the members of their sample, heroin use over a sustained period of time did not appear to have been a barrier to, inter alia, educational, employment and family prospects. Perhaps predictably, Shewan and Dalgarno's work was extremely controversial and provoked a sometimes hostile reaction. Shewan responded to critics by stating in a newspaper interview:

> The important thing about the study is that it shows while there are heroin users with problems, there are also heroin users without problems. These people are mostly ordinary people—they are not the Keith Richards of the world—and there could be an element of good fortune in the group studied. The concept of controlled drug use is still a largely unexplored area of drug research and these results should be treated with caution, as heroin is certainly not a safe drug. Drug research should incorporate this previously hidden population to more fully inform theory and practice, and psychological and social factors have to be taken into account when looking at how to deal with any form of addiction.
>
> (Andalo 2005; see also BBC News 2005, Cramb 2005).

Despite the relatively low mean age of the participants, Shewan and Dalgarno's work demonstrated that the sustained and controlled use of what is generally seen as an extremely harmful substance is possible. When read alongside the findings of Pearson, Chatwin and Porteous and Notley, it is clear that not only do a number of older adults continue to use illegal substances but their use does not necessarily interfere detrimentally with other more conventional pursuits. Indeed, the hidden illegal drug use of older adults is often a routine and quite unremarkable aspect of their lives.

North American studies

There has undoubtedly been a more consistent interest in older illegal drug users in the US than there has in the UK. However, the vast majority of this work has focussed upon dependency and the 'misuse' of drugs, with a particular emphasis on prescription misuse. In recent years a series of works by Boeri and her various collaborators (Boeri 2002, 2004, Boeri, Sterk and Elifson 2006, 2008, Boeri et al. 2011, Boeri and Tyndall 2012, Whalen and Boeri 2014) has started to address this bias. Boeri's earlier works on the subject (2002, 2004) focussed upon 'baby boomers' residing in Atlanta who were current users of heroin or methamphetamine. Following Faupel (1991), she developed a ninefold typology of 'phases' based upon the roles the drug user maintained and the user's own sense of control. Amongst her many findings, she showed that being physically dependent upon drugs (including particularly demonised substances such as heroin) did not necessarily prevent one from maintaining other roles. Later work saw her develop a refined typology consisting of four 'phases' ('controlled' users, 'marginal' users, 'hustlers' and 'junkies') (Boeri, Sterk and Elifson 2006). Those individuals who were in the 'controlled' user phase enjoyed control over their drug use and were able to maintain legitimate and conventional social roles. 'Marginal' users also managed to maintain legitimate and conventional social roles, although they were beginning to lose control over their drug use. These findings were complementary to the contemporaneous work of Shewan and Dalgarno (2005) in the UK. Boeri, Sterk and Elifson (2008) have also argued that 'early onset' older adult heroin users with lengthy drug-using histories differ in important respects from 'late onset' users (with the dividing point taken to be 30), for instance in terms of their ability to control their use and navigate both the drug world and mainstream society.

In Chicago, Anderson and Levy (2003) interviewed 40 street injectors aged 50 and over who were not receiving treatment for their drug use. Anderson and Levy's respondents lamented the demise of the 'old school' drug-using subculture of the 1960s and 1970s. This moribund ideological system was 'replete with a proscribed set of behaviours believed to govern how and with whom illicit drugs should be purchased and consumed'. It stood in marked contrast to the 'practices and normative expectations of today's illicit drug world with its emphasis on high volume marketing, violence and predatory behaviour' (Anderson and Levy 2003: 764). In a similar vein to the findings of Preble and Casey (1969), Anderson and Levy's respondents 'described drug users in 1969 as a community bonded by common interests and cooperative partnerships with other addicts to raise money for drugs and drug paraphernalia. Heroin use formed the core of social interchanges, and drug acquisition absorbed much of the user's time' (2003: 764). In recent times they had become 'wistful for what they remember with nostalgia as the more fraternal drug culture of the past', and increasingly found 'that they must now conform to the social demands and practices of the new' (2003: 764). With the erosion of the old school, Anderson and Levy suggested that these older injectors had become 'marginal among the marginal' (2003: 769). Their attempts to deal with this, by continuing to present themselves as 'poised' as the old school demanded, and refusing to assimilate with the dominant values and norms of the 'new school', were only partially successful in the face of loneliness, stress and a fear of victimisation. In a similar vein, an analysis of the norms, values and beliefs associated with illegal drug use was the focus of Black and Joseph's (2014) work. Indeed, they criticised Boeri, Sterk and Elifson (2006) for failing to provide more of a cultural analysis of the baby boomers (Black and Joseph 2014: 825). For their part, Black and Joseph suggest that the growing use of marijuana amongst this cohort has been encouraged by pro-marijuana attitudes and norms acquired through culture and a perception that marijuana use is a low-risk activity.

There has also been a flowering of interest in illegal drug use among older adults in Canada in recent years, with a particular focus on marijuana. McKim and Mishara's work (1987) was something of a pioneer in this regard, for despite its medical focus it did include recreational use. More recently, Osborne and Fogel (2008) conducted research with 41 adult Canadians; the average age of participants in the mostly middle-class sample was just 29, although the oldest participant was 61. The study found that marijuana use among the sample was generally of a controlled nature. The drug was used, amongst other things, to enhance leisure and relaxation, manage stress, and improve concentration. There have also been suggestions in Canada that moderate, controlled use of cannabis is 'normalised', even amongst adult users (Osborne and Fogel 2007, Duff et al. 2012, Duff and Erickson 2014).

Of course, there are always inherent difficulties when taking research findings from a different context and applying them to one's own. The research that has emerged from North America must be viewed in this light. Nevertheless, there is a clear sense that not only do hidden users exist in the US and Canada but they are capable in certain circumstances of sustaining illegal drug use over a long period and integrating it into otherwise conventional lifestyles. Boeri's work, along with the research emerging from Canada, provides strong evidence for this. Meanwhile, Anderson and Levy, despite their focus upon a very particular subset of users, demonstrate the far-reaching impacts of social change on groups of users, something that we will be reminded of time and again in the coming chapters.

Drug use and the lifecourse

A further development over recent years has been the emergence of a body of work that focusses upon drug use over the 'lifecourse'. Studies of the lifecourse have been around in one form or another for quite some time, and there is considerable variety in their nature. Their lineage can be plausibly traced as far back as the Chicago School's urban sociology of the inter-war years, and certainly to Mills (1959), who linked personal biography with history and outlined their intersections with social structure. These and other scholars saw how existing social theory was ill equipped to deal with the rapid social change of the twentieth century and its tumultuous effects upon people's lives. Later scholars, drawing upon these influences, saw 'leading theories of human socialisation and behavioural change . . . as ahistorical and mutually exclusive' and as failing to account for the relationship between macro and micro levels (Grenier 2012: 28–9). It was in response to this that work explicitly focussed upon the lifecourse emerged, with formal advancements of the perspective beginning in the 1970s and 1980s.

At their broadest, lifecourse studies utilise

> a multidisciplinary paradigm for the study of people's lives, structural contexts, and social change. This approach encompasses ideas and observations from an array of disciplines, notably history, sociology, demography, developmental psychology, biology, and economics. In particular, it directs

> attention to the powerful connection between individual lives and the historical and socioeconomic context in which these lives unfold.
> (Mitchell 2003: 1051)

Giele and Elder define a 'lifecourse' as 'a sequence of socially defined events and roles that the individual enacts over time' (1998: 22), although any such sequence does not necessarily follow the same linear pattern as others. For Grenier (2012: 8) a 'lifecourse' is 'an overall trajectory across the entire period of one's life' and can thus be distinguished from a 'lifecycle' (concerned with stages of maturation and development) and a 'lifespan' (a psychological perspective which is concerned with the timing of developmental tasks). As Grenier (2012: 21) suggests, 'the lifecourse is a general concept used to refer to a holistic view of life, with studies of the lifecourse the domain of varying multi- and interdisciplinary efforts' (see also Clausen 1986).

Grenier (2012) has argued that studies of the lifecourse can be divided into three distinct, albeit overlapping, types. The first, and best known, is what has come to be known as the 'lifecourse perspective'. The lifecourse perspective is prominent in US social studies and is a 'relatively defined approach . . . that tends to remain unquestioned' (2012: 19). The 'lifecourse perspective' refers to a body of work with a specific methodological approach, influenced chiefly by the work of Elder (most notably 1974, 1975, 1985a, 1985b 1994, 1998). This body of work dominates other work under the lifecourse rubric even though, despite its own protestations to the contrary, it tends to focus upon individuals at the expense of larger structures and historical trends (Grenier 2012: 29). Though many expositions of its 'key principles' exist (see, for example, Mitchell 2003), it is generally held that the notions of historical time and place, the 'timing' of lives, linked or interdependent lives and human agency lay at its heart (Elder 1985b, 1994). Despite some methodological eclecticism, it is also primarily concerned with longitudinal data, and a battery of techniques to analyse such data have been developed (Mitchell 2003).

The second strand of work, identified by Dannefer and Settersten (2010), has been the development of 'institutional' approaches to the lifecourse which have emerged in Europe as both a challenge and a complement to Elder's more 'personological approach'. Whilst the latter focusses upon individuals and later life outcomes as a result of early lifecourse experiences, the former is more alive to the idea of the lifecourse as being shaped by institutions and even constituting an institution in itself. Such work tends to envision the lifecourse as a social and political construct. Dannefer and Settersten (2010) trace the emergence of the institutional approach to work by Cain (1964), Riley (1971) and Riley, Johnson and Foner (1972). This work called for the consideration of the lifecourse as a social institution or as a feature of the social structure: 'In this strand of thinking, institutions and structures shape ideas about what is appropriate across the lifecourse, and organise experiences into expectations of age—and stage—based norms' (Grenier 2012: 29–30). The notion that life events can occur 'on – and off – time' (Neugarten 1976) has thus been a crucial element of this work.

The third strand of work is what Grenier (2012) has termed the 'critical' approach to the lifecourse. Work of this type has been concerned with the study of ageing more generally, and the contextualising of experiences through the lifecourse. It is less defined by a particular methodological approach or outlook, and concomitantly less self-contained as a body of scholarship, than the more prominent 'lifecourse perspective' (Grenier 2012: 21). Studies in this critical strand include, for example, those which highlight the constructed nature of the lifecourse (Holstein and Gubrium 2000) and analyse negotiated identities across the lifecourse (Hockey and James 2003). Such work focusses on structural, sociocultural and interpretive aspects of experience (Grenier 2012: 35). Critical work in this vein, according to Grenier (2012: 34), can help correct the individualised focus of much of the 'personological' lifecourse perspective and add a constructivist and interpretivist edge to the 'institutional' approach. She sees critical work as offering the best chance of forging a meaningful link between macro and micro levels, through analyses of individual experiences and their intersections with social structures that do not sideline agency.

The distinctiveness of the baby boomers' lifecourse has been one of the key themes to emerge from this body of work. The specificity of their experiences is in large part due to the fact that 'the post-war baby-boomers were the first generation to live through a time when a mass consumer revolution transformed popular taste and lifestyles' (Edmunds and Turner 2002: 31). As Metz and Underwood put it,

> the boomers are more individualistic than their parents, who experienced the collective solidarity of wartime; they are more anti-establishment and non-conformist, less deferential, less trusting of those in authority, less attracted to organised religion. The boomers are the first generation of the age of affluence, who have come to expect individual wants and needs to be satisfied and have been encouraged to define themselves by personal choices.
>
> (2005: 43)

Indeed, as Gilleard and Higgs propose, it is possible to argue that the boomers have plotted a 'new and distinct course through adult life . . . one marked by change, challenge and transformation. . . . The baby boom generation broke the mould of the modern life course' (2002: 376). On the other hand, it is important not to overstate the boomers' radicalism and contrarian nature. As Judt writes, 'European teenagers of the late 50s and early 60s did not aspire to change the world. They had grown up in security and modest affluence. Most of them just wanted to look different, travel more, play pop music and buy stuff' (2006: 349). As this suggests, the boomers tend to polarise opinion, and they have been depicted in both positive and negative terms

(Phillipson et al. 2008). Concerns that first emerged in the 1980s regarding generational inequality; the instability of pensions, social security and health care; and what is often seen as their 'unhealthy zeal for consumption' (Phillipson et al. 2008: 5.1) have been raised once again more recently.[7]

In one form or another, there is an increasingly prominent trend for the notion of the lifecourse to feature in studies of illegal drug use. For example, a number of works have focussed upon the notion of the drug-using 'career', sometimes implicitly, but often explicitly. Such works frequently take their cue from Becker (1953, 1955, 1963), who famously described the process of 'becoming a marijuana user'. He saw marijuana use as a learned behaviour, with users learning to smoke the drug in such a way that it produced real effects, then learning to recognise those effects as being a result of drug use, and finally learning to enjoy the effects. Thus, Becker was less interested in the motivations behind use than the social learning processes involved in becoming a user. He proposed a sequence of stages that the cannabis user passes through, from being a beginner and then an occasional user, before becoming a regular, systematic user with a deviant identity, partly dependent upon a network of fellow users. Forms of social control became less effective as the user passed through each stage. As such Becker's central contribution, according to Osborne and Fogel, was the idea that marijuana users 'did not share a particular psychological trait that predisposed them to a specific criminal behaviour, but were rather average people who had learned to derive "pleasure" from a substance that "moral entrepreneurs" had designated illicit' (2008: 541). One can clearly see the seeds of a 'career' approach to drug use in Becker's work.

There have subsequently been many deployments of the 'career' concept in drugs research. The drug career is generally seen as something that individuals engage in simultaneously with other life careers. Some of these intersecting careers are complementary to each other, whilst others are conflictual (Marshall and Levy 1990). Even heroin use has been seen in career terms, especially 'within milieu offering limited alternatives for meaningful occupation (e.g. Agar 1973, Johnson et al. 1985)' (Hammersley 2011: 413). Faupel (1991), for instance, saw long-term heroin use as constituting a career in the manner of a conventional occupational career. He defined a 'career' as 'a series of meaningful related statuses, roles, and activities around which an individual organizes some aspect of his or her life' (1991: 24), and suggested that careers are identifiable across all types of activities, including drug use. He saw the pattern of a career

7 Note that in the UK, the post-war 'baby boom' was far less pronounced than in, say, the US or Canada. Indeed, Sandbrook has argued that in fact there was 'no real baby boom in Britain' (2005: 388; see also Falkingham 1987: 18). Nevertheless, as Phillipson et al. argue, 'the symbolism of the rise in the birth rate was at least as important as its demographic aspects. The "boom" may have been relatively small but it was significant as compared with the decline in fertility characteristic of preceding decades – this creating a sense of panic across many European countries. . . . Hence the emblematic nature of the boom . . . as a marker of post-war revival was substantial' (2008: 6.4).

as being dependent upon the availability of the drug and the underlying structure of the user's life. As Carnwath and Smith suggest, Faupel's utilisation of the notion of career allowed for the consideration of 'issues such as career entry, career mobility and retirement, providing a different perspective from that of a battle against pharmacology' (2002: 80). Similarly, Stephens (1991) argued that the 'street addict role' became a blueprint for living for many street heroin users, and entailed full commitment to a 'deviant career'. Levy and Anderson (2005) looked at the drug careers of dependent street users and found that patterns of drug use and methods of drug procurement had shifted over time as the users tried to accommodate the social and physical processes of growing old (2005: 254–5). This included attempts to come to terms with the marginalisation that Levy and Anderson had already documented in their previous work, as we have seen (Anderson and Levy 2003). Other work in this vein has depicted developmental progressions along relatively linear career paths. For instance, Waldorf (1973) traced the transformation from initial experimentation to chronic drug-use patterns, Hser et al. (1997) focussed on the careers of dependent users in treatment, whilst Fagan and Chin (1991) viewed the drug career as a sequence of stages that include 'initiation, escalation, maintenance, discontinuation, and, in some cases, renewal' (1991: 313). Hirsch, Conforti and Graney (2001: 32) plotted a potential pathway through three stages following one's initial contact with drugs. This involved experimentation, followed by integrated use, excessive use, and on towards the possibility of addiction. However, 'at each stage, dissimilar paths can be taken that will send the user on a different trajectory' (Boeri 2002: 70). Similarly Murphy, Reinarman and Waldorf (1989) found a variety of 'career use patterns' amongst their sample of cocaine users. Their findings 'suggest that while serious abuse potentially exists, addiction is not a uniform outcome of sustained use and that long-term controlled use is possible' (1989: 427). In addition, Sampson and Laub's (1993) theory of age-graded informal social control and its effects on criminal offending, which has been influential in the expansion of so-called 'developmental' or 'life course' criminology and the notion of the criminal career, has also been applied to illegal drug users, despite concerns about its 'individual-oriented' nature (Lander 2015). Williams (2013), for instance, drew upon the theory as well as notions of risk in her exploration of drug-using careers. She suggested that adult recreational users tend to be competent risk managers and are generally in control of their drug use.[8]

As well as this work on drug careers, there is also an increasing body of scholarship that focusses more explicitly on the lifecourse and illegal drug use.

8 Because sustained drug use 'is usually described in terms of pathology instead of a subjective experience and identity with meaningful roles and activities' (Boeri 2002: 67), some remain uncomfortable with the idea of describing it as a 'career'. Hser, Longshore and Anglin, for example, question the usefulness of the career concept in discussions of illegal drug use, as unlike drug use a 'career' is generally seen as something to be encouraged (2007: 516).

Much of this is North American in origin and has roots in the 'lifecourse perspective'. Boeri (2002), for example, applied the lifecourse concepts of transition and trajectory to the drug use of the baby boomers, and out of this developed her 'phases' of drug use. Boeri has also contributed to the development of measures designed to evaluate 'the discontinuous patterns of drug use trajectories over the lifecourse of older drug users' and techniques that allow for their visualisation (Boeri et al. 2011: 89; see also Whalen and Boeri 2014). Van Gundy and Rebellon (2010) used lifecourse concepts in their debunking of the 'gateway hypothesis' often applied to marijuana, whilst Jessup et al. (2014), on the basis of a sample including older adults, assessed how significant life events can affect drug use. Other applications of the lifecourse perspective to drug use include work by DeWit, Offord and Wong (1997), Hser, Longshore and Anglin (2007), Hser, Hamilton and Niv (2009), Lopez, Kreuger and Walters (2010) and Wachsmuth et al. (2016).

There have also been a number of more 'critical' (Grenier 2012) works on illegal drug use and the lifecourse. For instance, Measham, Williams and Aldridge (2011) have shown how key transitions in the passage to adulthood such as leaving the parental home, gaining employment, forging intimate relationships and entering parenthood can have significant impacts upon the illegal drug use of young women. Meanwhile, Lander's (2015) follow-up study of drug-using women in Sweden took an explicitly 'critical post-structural' approach to the lifecourse, with the concept of 'life schedules' at its heart. Life schedules, for Lander, are socially constructed, normative guidelines that order the progress of individuals through the lifecourse. Following Halberstam (2005), Lander suggests that life schedules are inherently class coded, based as they are upon a middle-class perspective that privileges supposed respectability and normality: 'The heteronormative life is clearly presented as both *right* and *normal*. The *other life*, that which askew and does not follow the straight line of normality and progression that the life schedules proclaims, is not uncommonly regarded and described as immature, problematic and/or unhealthy' (Lander 2015: 274). Those who do not follow heteronormativity and continue to use drugs as they age, including the women in Lander's sample, help to reveal in their acts of dissent 'the nature of prevailing norms and conceptions regarding ageing, gender and drug use' (Lander 2015: 270).

Outline of the book

The next chapter will critically discuss the methodological approach adopted for the study. It will aim to provide an honest account of what proved to be a rather challenging and protracted research endeavour, and as such a large part of the chapter will focus upon the issues encountered with recruiting participants through snowball sampling. Following the second chapter, the rest of the book will offer an exploration of some of the results of the research. Chapter 3, 'Past', will look at the history of the participants' use, going all the way back to their initial experiences with illegal drugs. This chapter will outline the contingent nature of illegal drug use for our participants; for them, drug use has always been conditional upon other, often insecure, aspects of life. The notion of 'transitions' as developed in the lifecourse literature is of value in understanding this. Yet transitions themselves can only be properly comprehended in light of the 'permanent liminality' that characterises post-industrial late modern society. Chapter 4, 'Present', brings us up to date by detailing the current drug-use patterns of the sample. It will outline the participants' current drugs of choice, their source of drugs, the frequency and consistency of their consumption, the set and setting of their use, and their reasons for use. The chapter will also discuss the participants' current feelings as to the impact that illegal drug use has had on their lives. Building on the argument put forward in Chapter 3, we will propose that our participants, having lived through the bumpy macro-transition to vertiginous late modern neoliberalism, have used and still use illegal drugs at least in part as a coping mechanism, a source of comfort in an often bewildering and always insecure liminal world. But drug careers themselves are also subject to these disruptive forces, and so the respite they provide is always provisional and conditional upon their wider circumstances. Finally in Chapter 5, 'Future', we will offer some thoughts on the prospects for the participants' illegal drug use, as well as on the outlook for illegal drug use amongst older adults in general. The participants' future intentions regarding their drug use will be discussed. We will then consider the issues of illegality and normalisation, both as they affected our participants and in a wider sense. The chapter will also consider the limitations of the present study and offer some suggestions for the direction of future research in the area, before concluding with a summary of the arguments made in the book.

2 Methodology

This chapter will detail the research methodology employed in the study. The aim is to provide an honest account of what proved to be a somewhat 'messy' research process (Bell 2004). To begin with, the background to the study will be discussed, before we move on to examine the process of constructing the sample using so-called 'snowball sampling'. As sample building proved to be the most problematic aspect of the research process, this section will make up the bulk of the chapter. Following this, the research instrument, a form of semi-structured 'life story' interview, will be considered, before the ethical implications of the study are addressed. Finally, we will introduce the participants who did agree to take part in the research, and explore some of the demographic features of the sample.

Background

The roots of this study lie in research for a PhD (Waters 2009) that commenced in the early years of the twenty-first century. This work was inspired by a sense that there were a considerable number of older illegal drug users who were continuing to use drugs quietly and under the radar whilst getting on with working life, family life and other 'conventional' pursuits. As discussed in Chapter 1, at the outset of the research the individuals who were of interest were those whose experiences with illegal drugs coincided with the post-war shift from an industrial society of producers to one of consumers (Bauman 1997) and the associated flowering of various 'spectacular' subcultures (Hebdige 1979). It was felt that such erstwhile hippies, punks and so on, whose drug use had begun in the 1960s and 1970s, might well have interesting tales to tell about how they had sustained their use over the long term, how they had integrated it into their lives, and how their use had changed as they grew older. Once the PhD had been completed, new contacts continued to offer fresh leads to potential participants. With a nagging sense that the PhD research had merely scratched the surface of the subject, the authors joined forces and decided to continue with the study and attempt to further develop the understanding of this relatively ignored group of users.

As we will see, enormous difficulties were experienced in the recruitment of participants, and the study took many years to bring to fruition. The glacially slow progress of the research was not entirely down to this, however. By the time it was decided to continue the study following the successful completion of the PhD research, both authors were holding academic positions in the 'post-1992' university sector in the UK. In this environment, the pressures of increasing teaching loads and administrative duties make completing research of any kind an arduous task, largely reliant on the use of whatever spare time one can engineer for oneself. Furthermore, a curiosity-driven, exploratory study of this type which is not primarily directed toward the development of policy or an easily measurable 'impact' of some kind is something that is highly unlikely to be funded. Ironically, this means that we may not have fared any better in a 'research-led' institution. As Winlow and Hall have trenchantly argued:

> The overarching problem in the field of social research is that the desire of funders to discover basic "empirical facts", which are always restrictively themed and often pre-empted in the main objectives of the research programmes themselves, influences the theoretical and methodological frameworks of the social research that produces those facts. Social research becomes trapped in a vigilantly policed tautological loop, and thus the complexity of social life is rarely investigated with any honesty, fine detail, or theoretical sophistication. In the act of producing data, researchers are treated rather like gun dogs, flushing out and retrieving game so that the hunter can pop it in his bag and go home. Further down the line when it comes to analysis, funders often encourage researchers to boil down their findings to basic bullet points and extract all "superfluous" contextual, critical and theoretical discussion from the final reports. Mindful of the requirements of funders, researchers are forced to . . . dilute, miniaturise and tightly focus their critique, dig up basic empirical data and construct narrowband policy-friendly analyses that the rhizomatic politico-cultural network to which their financial benefactors belong might find useful.
>
> (2013: 9–10)

So, we plodded on, engaged for years in what felt like the Sisyphean task of endlessly chasing contacts that generally proved to be understandably unwilling to speak on the record, but at least free of externally imposed deadlines and the need to satisfy the requirements of a funder. We worked in our own time and, when we were able to find someone who *was* willing to speak, at our own expense. Indeed, the process of writing up the research was greatly aided by the fact that one of our number left a permanent academic post and so, perversely, had more time to devote to the task.

Sample building[1]

At the outset of the research project, the decision to utilise a form of 'snowball sampling' seemed a relatively straightforward one. Snowball sampling is generally regarded as a highly effective sampling technique that enables the study of populations who are difficult to reach or 'hidden' (Atkinson and Flint 2001), and it is also considered an appropriate methodological tool when focussing on sensitive or private matters (Biernacki and Waldorf 1981: 141). Snowball sampling has been used with some success in the study of illegal drug users, particularly younger users (Kaplan, Korf and Sterk 1987, Avico et al. 1988, Griffiths et al. 1993, Ditton and Hammersley 1996, Hammersley, Khan and Ditton 2002, Notley 2005, Potter and Dann 2005, Shewan and Dalgarno 2005), although not unequivocally (Goode 2000). It has also been used to build 'community based' samples of drug users (Cohen and Sas 1994). The potential of snowball sampling to provide an effective means of building a sample of hidden older illegal drug users without relying on institutional referrals made it the obvious choice for this research. Those not involved in treatment programmes or embroiled in the criminal justice system were, in our estimation, far more likely to be using drugs 'normally', and snowball sampling held out the promise of accessing such individuals. However, the construction of the sample proved far from straightforward. This section will explore the reasons for this.

According to Noy,

> a sampling procedure may be defined as snowball sampling when the researcher accesses informants through contact information that is provided by other informants. This process is, by necessity, repetitive: informants refer the researcher to other informants, who are contacted by the researcher and then refer her or him to yet other informants, and so on. Hence the evolving "snowball effect".
>
> (2008: 330)

As Biernacki and Waldorf suggest, 'the method is well suited for a number of research purposes and is particularly applicable when the focus of study is on a sensitive issue, possibly concerning a relatively private matter, and thus requires the knowledge of insiders to locate people for study' (1981: 141).

Snowball sampling can be used as the 'main vehicle through which informants are accessed' (Noy 2008: 330), as well as alongside complementary techniques of accessing hard to reach populations. Indeed, Noy suggests that snowball

1 This section borrows heavily from Waters (2015). See Waters, J. (2015). 'Snowball sampling: A cautionary tale involving a study of older drug users', *International Journal of Social Research Methodology*, 18(4): 367–80, reprinted by permission of Taylor & Francis Ltd, www.tandfonline.com.

sampling is often employed as an 'auxiliary means', which allows researchers to 'top up' their samples and access new participants when other sources have dried up. The regular use of snowball sampling in this auxiliary manner has seen it remain 'somewhat at the margins of research practice' (Atkinson and Flint 2001). As such, snowball sampling is quite often considered to be a relatively informal method 'that is plain and rather commonsensical so as to avoid systematic reflexive consideration' (Noy 2008: 330).

Where snowball sampling *has* been contemplated in a more systematic manner, there has been considerable debate over precisely what it is and how it relates to other similar sampling techniques. Goodman (2011) notes that snowball sampling as originally conceived was designed to aid the study of social networks in easy-to-reach populations, and began with a random sample (Coleman 1959, Goodman 1961). For Goodman, the snowball sampling of hard-to-reach populations (beginning with a convenience sample) was a later development and represents a technique that is distinct from the early social network studies. Becker's (1963) famous work on marijuana users can be considered one of these later studies, whilst Atkinson and Flint (2001) trace the roots of this type of snowball sampling back to participant observation studies such as those of Whyte (1955) and Patrick (1973). Heckathorn (2011), whilst agreeing with the distinction drawn by Goodman, also draws particular attention to the further distinction between snowball sampling and what he terms 'respondent driven sampling' (RDS). The latter, developed by Heckathorn over a number of years (see Heckathorn 1997, 2002, 2007, Salganik and Heckathorn 2004, Volz and Heckathorn 2008), has gone through a number of iterations with the aim of refining a method for providing total population estimates and eliminating bias from what begins as a non-probability sample.[2] RDS is also highly prescriptive of the manner in which participants are recruited (Semaan, Lauby and Liebman 2002, Magnani et al. 2005, Semaan 2010). Semaan terms the highly structured referral process 'participant-driven recruitment' (2010: 64). For example, in RDS-based studies, participants have been issued a limited number of vouchers to give to potential new participants who are implored to turn up to a research 'shop front' where their eligibility can be determined and the research carried out.[3]

The result of all this is some considerable imprecision and terminological overlap. This is not aided by the regular use of the terms 'chain referral sampling' or 'network sampling' as umbrella categories intended to cover all or

2 Note that Biernacki and Waldorf also talk of sample control in non-RDS snowball sampling as a means of generating samples which 'in qualitative terms, if not in rigorous statistical ones, reflect what are thought to be the general characteristics of the population in question. . . . Control over the referral chains is not only selective, but is also based on *theoretical* considerations' (1981:155–6, emphasis in original).

3 The number of vouchers is limited in order to prevent over-recruitment by those who are more socially connected, and to enable the precise tracking of recruitment to allow population estimates and elimination of bias (Hathaway et al. 2010: 3)

some of the various methods referred to in the paragraph above; see, for example, Honigmann (1982) and Patton, who discusses what he calls 'snowball or chain sampling' in his exhaustive outline of 'purposeful sampling' strategies (2002: 237). This is not the place to attempt to tidy up this complexity (see Magnani et al. [2005], Goodman [2011] and Heckathorn [2011] for such attempts). However, it can be suggested that, contra Goodman, there is no logical reason why snowballs beginning from a convenience sample should *not* be used to study 'easy to reach' as well as 'hard to reach' populations if that is amenable to the research aims and objectives. It is also probably the case that Heckathorn's quest for scientific objectivity and legitimacy through the use of RDS is less relevant in a post-'linguistic turn' European context. Furthermore, the need to estimate population size and eliminate bias are not relevant for every piece of research, and as a result a more modest version of snowball sampling can happily co-exist alongside the more structured RDS, with each being utilised where appropriate.

More broadly, there is a sense in which attempting to pin down once and for all the precise meaning of terms such as these is doomed to failure. Whilst such precision might well be desirable in an ideal world, the terms in question are now used so interchangeably and to refer to different sampling techniques that attempts to anchor their meaning post-facto are in effect defeated before they are even started. It would seem far more important for each researcher to clearly and rigorously outline the sampling technique they are utilising. In this way, arguments about terminology can be relegated in importance, and research judged on its own merits rather than on some perceived terminological abuse.

For this research, 'snowball sampling' was intended in the sense of Goodman's 'hard to reach snowball sampling'. A non-probability, convenience sample of a hard to reach population was sought from which to snowball. There was no desire to estimate total population size or eliminate bias resulting from the nature of the initial sample (as in Heckathorn's RDS). Various initial contact points, chiefly friends and colleagues, were contacted in order to locate potential participants to start off the sampling process. In addition, information about the research was sent out to as many people as possible to advertise the research and its need for potential participants. Colleagues also sent out 'feelers' to their own friends and contacts in the field of drugs research. Six to ten initial participants from which to snowball were sought, on the assumption that this would provide a strong base to work from. Once participants had been located and interviewed, the researchers asked these participants if they knew of any more potential participants; the researchers then chased up these leads. The participants were *not* asked to 'deliver' subsequent participants (as is common in RDS) due to a lack of resources (specifically the lack of a 'shop front'). In addition, due to the highly sensitive nature of the research topic, it was felt that it was more appropriate for the researcher to be the one in control of the evolving sampling chains so that discretion could be assured. The use of 'privileged access' (Griffiths et al. 1993) or 'indigenous' (Power 1994) interviewers was also considered, but this was not pursued due to a lack of suitable and willing candidates for the interviewer role. The lack of resources at the disposal of the project would have also rendered this option difficult; Griffiths et al. (1993), for example, recruited a team of 23 interviewers for their Department of Health–funded study of heroin users, all of whom were paid.

Thus, the idea underlying the brand of snowball sampling employed here was that the researchers would identify and interview a number of suitable individuals who were either friends or colleagues, or had been identified by friends and colleagues. Then, after hopefully building a reliable and trusting relationship through the interview process, these initial interviewees would themselves be asked to recommend friends and acquaintances that matched the research criteria. The researchers would then chase these leads up. As Biernacki and Waldorf suggest, a chain can be continued until it either comes to a natural end or reaches a saturation point (1981: 156).

In effect, two of Zinberg's recruitment techniques for snowball sampling were utilised. In Zinberg's work, 'researchers described the project to friends and colleagues who had some professional or personal contact with drug users, asking them to spread the word about the research and to refer to us anyone who might possibly be considered [appropriate]', and 'subjects who went through the interview process were asked to refer other drugs users who might be interested in participating' (1984:8). Through the repetition of this process, sampling chains (or recruitment networks) such as that in Figure 2.1 can be constructed.[4]

Used in this manner, snowball sampling 'has proved useful in generating samples of individuals who it would be difficult, if not impossible, to access in a more conventional way' (Griffiths et al. 1993: 1619). Furthermore, Noy suggests that 'sampling procedures in qualitative research are not instrumental means whose sole purpose is to enable access to knowledge. Instead, these procedures entail knowledge *in and of itself*'. He argues that snowball sampling

> is *essentially social* because it both uses and activates existing social networks. Attending to this dimension, ties the sampling procedure to other aspects and phases of the research. That is, when viewed holistically, different research facets amount to a gestalt where each facet contributes synergistically to the overall research design, which, in turn, can potentially generate an organic and "thick" type of knowledge, knowledge that is so valued in the qualitative social sciences.
>
> (2008: 334)

That said, there are a number of methodological issues with snowball sampling. Perhaps most obvious is that it is heavily reliant on the researcher. Creating 'snowballs' can be an incredibly time consuming and labour-intensive process

4 Note that the chain illustrated in Figure 2.1 was constructed as part of a RDS-based study. It is included here to illustrate what an ideal snowball sampling chain *could* look like.

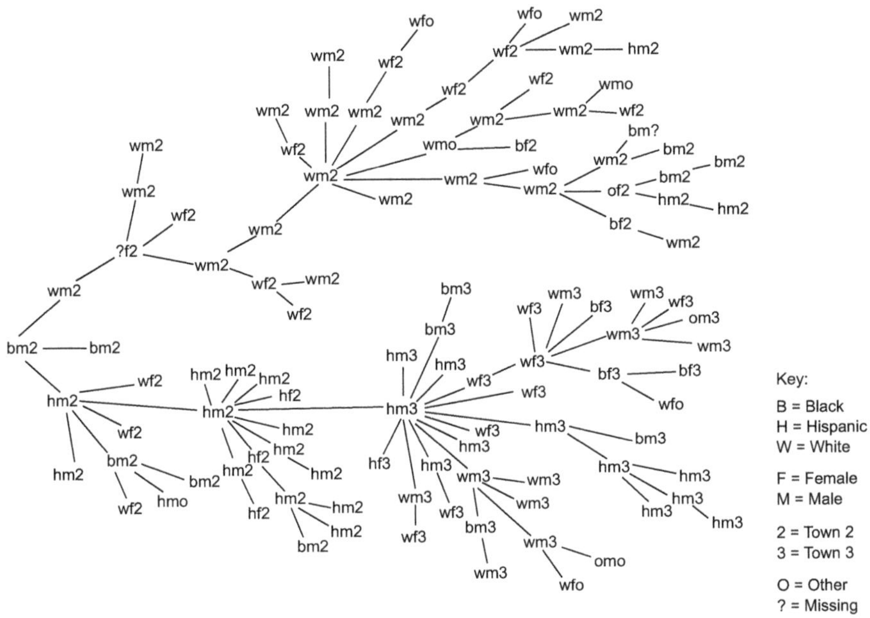

Figure 2.1 Example of a recruitment network

Source: Heckathorn (1997: 178)

Figure from Heckathorn, D.D., 'Respondent-driven sampling: A new approach to the study of hidden populations', *Social Problems*, 1997, 44(2), 174–99, by permission of Oxford University Press.

that is dependent almost exclusively on the researcher's resources and contacts in the first instance (Griffiths et al. 1993, Faugier and Sargeant 1997). Therefore, it is inevitable that the quality of the research 'may be heavily influenced by the quality of the researcher' (Griffiths et al. 1993: 1619). This is not necessarily a weakness, for an able and well-resourced researcher may be able to produce a sizeable sample and high-quality research using this method. However, even an able researcher with few resources may find it difficult to build useful samples. In such cases, the reality of snowball sampling may be that it 'does not inevitably lead to an inexorable growing mass of contacts. Rather . . . what it often produces is a slow and uneven accretion of additional data points' (Lee 1993: 66).

Another issue with snowball sampling is that of distortion. Given certain starting points, it may be that the participants in a chain share similar characteristics. For instance, they may be entirely male, or of a particular ethnic background, and so on. This may be an unavoidable consequence of asking participants for referrals in certain cases. As Griffiths et al. have argued in relation to academic studies of drug users, 'middle-class drug users may be over-represented in such studies as they often exist on the fringes of the research community and therefore provide roads of access into the behaviour by exploiting existing friendship networks' (1993: 1618). Not only does this make it difficult to generalise findings, but it also tends to over-emphasise the cohesiveness of the group under study (Griffiths et al. 1993, Atkinson and Flint 2001) whilst simultaneously overlooking isolated individuals who are not connected to networks, even where those individuals possess the desired characteristics (Van Meter 1990). Large sample sizes can go some way to alleviating these difficulties, and large samples with representative proportions for various demographic factors have been achieved through snowball sampling (Pollok and Schlitz 1998). Yet, conversely, it may be more likely that members of large chains will share similar and unique characteristics not shared by the wider population. Thus, as Atkinson and Flint (2001) suggest, 'there may be a case for initiating several discrete chains with fewer links, particularly where any inference about a wider hidden population is considered important'. Of course, the issue of distortion is one of the reasons for the development of RDS. As this research was largely exploratory, the issue of distortion was not considered to be of paramount importance; far higher on the list of priorities was simply the construction of a reasonably sized sample.

Biernacki and Waldorf (1981) suggest that there can be difficulties with, amongst other things, finding respondents and starting referral chains, verifying the eligibility of potential respondents, controlling the types of chains and number of cases in any chain, and pacing and monitoring referral chains and data quality. Indeed the problems do not halt once chains have been started. Even when potential respondents are successfully located, they may be unwilling to participate for various reasons, especially in research of this nature (Wright et al. 1992, Notley 2005). It may also prove difficult to locate further potential respondents in the first place. This could possibly be because 'gatekeepers' (be they contacts who know of potential participants or participants who know of potential further participants) may be protective of their friends and acquaintances and actually hinder access (Groger, Mayberry and Straker 1999). Again this is more likely where sensitive matters are at stake. It is also important to note that 'some groups may themselves consist of highly atomised and isolated individuals whose social networks are relatively impaired' (Atkinson and Flint 2001), and such groups may not be especially amenable to the creation of snowballs. This was particularly pertinent in this research, as we shall see.

What happened?

Unfortunately, building the sample proved to be an exercise fraught with difficulty. Despite much time spent talking to contacts and distributing information about the research, it quickly became clear that recruiting willing participants would be challenging. Thus, the decision was taken early in the PhD process to lower the minimum age of the participants from 50 to 40. This was done reluctantly as it somewhat diluted the original aim of focussing upon those born in the immediate post-war years, but as willing individuals in their forties had been found, pragmatically there was little option but to lower the minimum age. In addition, as suggested in Chapter 1, the decision was at least justifiable in terms of the 'cliff edge' beyond which little drugs research looks at those aged over 40. Even following this decision, the PhD phase of the research resulted in only a handful (nine) of initial interviews. Only two of these initial interviews actually led to a subsequent interview and could therefore be considered as 'snowballs', or at least the beginning of snowballs. However, these subsequent interviews did not lead to any further interviews, meaning an abrupt end to the sampling chain. These 11 interviews formed the primary data for the PhD, and were buttressed by secondary analysis of datasets from the Crime Survey for England and Wales (at that point still known as the British Crime Survey).

With the PhD completed, as noted above new contacts continued to offer fresh leads to potential participants. With the second member of the research team on board, efforts to build a bigger sample were redoubled. Yet even though locating suitable individuals was generally relatively unproblematic, persuading them to be interviewed was far from easy. Eventually, two further interviews, sourced through academic contacts, were conducted, but these too led to no further interviews. Something of a lucky break led to the final batch of interviews. A student of one of the research team was involved in an organisation campaigning for the reform of cannabis laws. She agreed to help publicise the research once it had been approved by the relevant committee in her organisation. An advert was then placed on the organisation's private Facebook page, with information about the research and a link to a previous article. This led to a further 17 interviews, conducted over a period of just over a year, but once again no snowballs.

Comments that were posted on the private online forum of the campaigning organisation (hosted on Facebook) in response to the research advert were indicative of the kind of suspicion that we faced at every stage of sample building; bear in mind that these comments were posted on a forum where the research had been vouched for by a fellow member of the community in question, as well as approved by the local committee. The posts appeared within a few hours of the advert being placed.[5]

> *Respondent 1*: Whether this is anonymous or not, you are asking straight arrowed people, people who are already hiding their use of illegal substances,

5 These posts are a selection of the ones that appeared on the forum. Access to the forum was restricted to members of the campaigning organisation in question, and the posters had presumably not intended their posts to be made public beyond its confines, so we have not directly quoted from posts in order that their authors cannot be traced (Eysenbach and Till 2001, Eysenbach and Wyatt 2002). Instead, following Potter and Chatwin (2012: 236), we have edited the posts to anonymise them and to ensure confidentiality and readability, whilst attempting to maintain the meaning and style of the original. We have also removed the posters' online handles, some of which appeared to simply be their real names. Whilst the comments here capture the general flavour of the response to the advert, it should be noted that it also received 62 so-called 'likes'.

to admit that they have committed a crime. An admission here is also an admission to the police, an admission to the CPS and an admission to the courts, and don't forget that marijuana carries a prison sentence even for just possession. You should have tried to agree something like an amnesty from prosecution to protect people.

Respondent 1: That seems like an awful a lot of trust to put in a stranger.

Respondent 2: I don't think that I would trust it to be honest. That's just my personal view. It may turn out to be completely fine, you may even end up really helping someone out, but there is a chance that you also may end up being contacted by the police. Either way, if you wanted to speak then I would need absolute confirmation that everything we speak about is in total confidence. If I was to live in a country where marijuana is perfectly legal then of course I would answer any question you might have. However, in this country people have been arrested for things like selling grow equipment amongst other things. I'm just not prepared to take the risk I'm afraid. Sorry.

Respondent 3: Okay, I have now had a read of the article that is referenced in the advert that was posted, and I do think that it would be good for as many people as possible to partake. But there is still a big problem. All emails that are sent can be easily traced and don't forget we are still talking here about illegal drug use. So I'm simply not sure how this can possibly be achieved with complete anonymity. As the advert points out, many people aren't on the radar and they probably wish it to remain that way. So it's a catch twenty-two situation. Ultimately the study can only ever say what we already know, including the politicians who are the real criminals here. Any person that pretends to believe otherwise is incredibly naive and they are kidding themselves. I'd make one final point. Lots of people live perfectly 'normal' lives and manage to maintain a lifelong drug habit, and they don't have any problems, and they don't turn to other kinds of crime. The drug of choice for these people is alcohol. Shock horror! Only the prejudiced can't see the real irony of what this research is trying to show.

Respondent 2: Is it possible that you could build an anonymous public forum, so that everyone could just log on as a 'guest user' and then they can simply fill out some kind of online questionnaire? Then we wouldn't have to leave any email addresses, no nothing. Just complete the questionnaire. That way people could just complete it on a different computer, not use their home computer, and leave no trace at all. It's just an idea.

Respondent 3: I agree. I feel like that might be a better idea.

Respondent 4: When I saw this I was going to give you the benefit of the doubt. [Respondent 1] has made a very good point though! We need more protection!!!

Respondent 5: [A different cannabis law reform group has] gained a bit of a reputation for grassing up medical users so I think a little bit of paranoia about this is fairly justified. I know we need more data about the range of drugs that are being used, harm caused, social class and that type of thing, so I do understand the need for greater cooperation with outsider communities. That said I still feel a little cautious about this and this is coming from a real advocate of free weed. I'm normally open to anyone who asks me my opinion, and this includes my doctors and the local authorities that I work with such as social services and the child protection agency.

Respondent 6: I'd just like to make a post here to say that this is completely legitimate. I've just finished my interview. The researcher did not ask for any delicate personal details at all. The study is just trying to find out about people over 40 who are using illegal drugs and how it affects their lives.

Respondent 7: I'd be afraid that the British version of the NSA would be able to get at this information and be able to use it against anyone who participates.

Respondent 8: To be honest, if you are paranoid enough to believe that you will be arrested for taking part in an interview such as this, it's a pretty good sign that you need to lay off the drugs a bit because it's clearly affecting your state of mind.

Respondent 3: Don't forget that some people here are professionals and they could lose their job quite easily at the mere mention of illegal drug use.

Ian (46, unemployed, cannabis user), who chose to participate in the study having seen the online advert in question, told us that he had discussed the advert with his friends and there was a suspicion 'that it was a ploy by the police, or something like that, [a] sting operation type of thing [laughs]. You know, I know it said complete anonymity but you know what some people can be like. . . . I mean with a few people their jobs would go if they were found out to be doing it so, they're obviously more cautious than I am at the moment. Like I said, I've made sure I haven't got anything in my house so if it did happen they could come round and search anywhere, they wouldn't find anything [laughs]. . . . It's okay, I'm not worried!'

The final sampling chain is illustrated in Figure 2.2. Out of the 30 interviews that were conducted in total, only two were the result of 'snowballing', and they in turn yielded no further interviews. The problems encountered in the construction of snowballs is graphically illustrated by comparing Figure 2.2 to Figure 2.1.

It quickly became quite clear that there *were* individuals who fulfilled the criteria for participation; illegal drug users over the age of 40 who are not in contact with the criminal justice authorities or treatment agencies regarding their use *do* exist, and they exist in some number, as we discussed in Chapter 1. Over the entire course of the research, around 100 potential participants were identified. Often, participants referred in their own interviews to others who fulfilled the criteria:

> I did tell one of my mates, good friend . . . he loves his dope, it was just this last week I did have a joint with him, chewing the fat as older men, thinking about ourselves and each other and I said I'm gonna get interviewed about smoking dope, "why, why are you doing it!" he said. Cos it's good that people are doing research on this, you know, and he, I'm

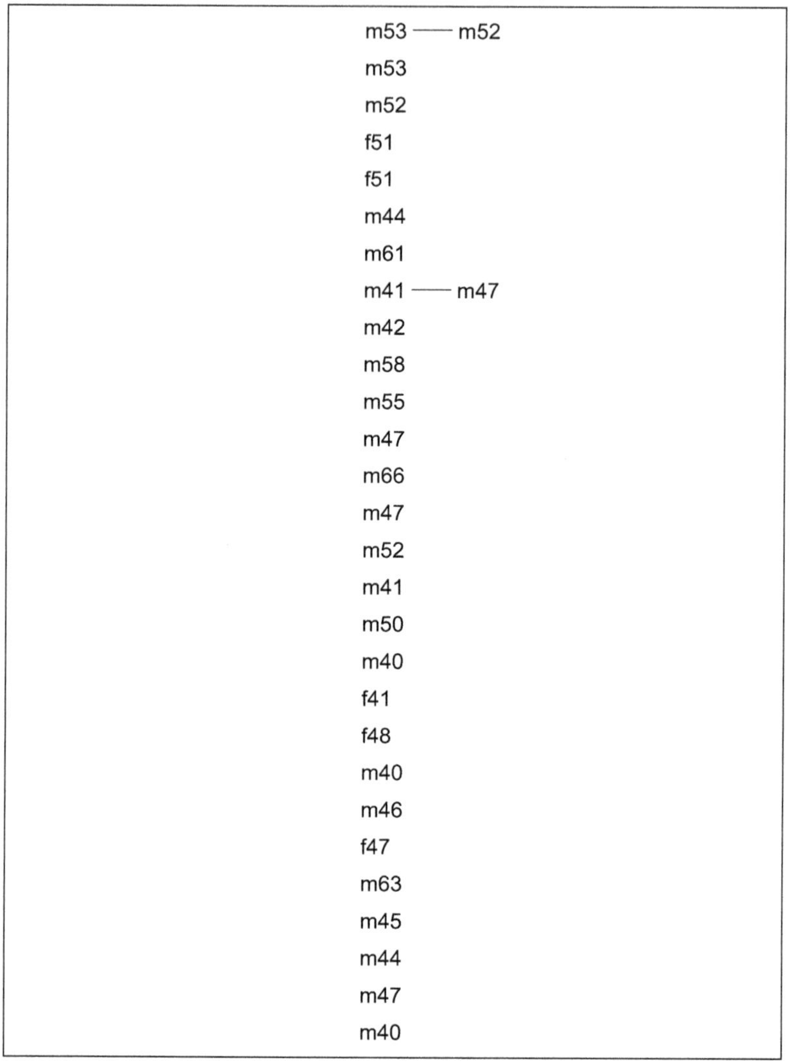

Figure 2.2 Final sampling chain

not saying he'd participate but he certainly got brought round to it you know, this is actually what we want to do, we want more of an open discussion about these things. *Winston, 58, academic, cannabis user.*

I know one other person that my brother identified when he asked me to do this and I know he spoke to me in the pub the other week and said he wouldn't do it because he was frightened that if his work ever found out he could lose his job. So you know I know he wouldn't do it, but I

> might bump into a couple, there's one that springs to mind, I'll ask my wife and if there's anybody else I'll pass them that [information leaflet] and good luck. *Ollie, 52, company owner, cannabis and occasional cocaine user.*
>
> I did talk to some friends about it and they, all the ones I spoke to just said "no" or "how much?" When I said "no money" they weren't interested. . . . They're not really prepared to take the risk of, you know, of accepting who you are, you could easily be, I don't think you're drug squad officers [laughs], you're quite nice to me, but some people are more paranoid than me, but they're just not willing to take the risk, there's nothing in it for them. . . . Go to a drug clinic you'll find loads of people over 40 willing to talk to you about their drug careers because they're sitting around in waiting rooms most of the time waiting for someone to bloody see them, so I would say your best bet is to go through a local drug agency and ask if any of the clients are willing to speak to you, but yeah, drug users who aren't seeing drug services, who are off the radar, that's where they wanna be, yeah. *Xavier, 55, researcher, polydrug user.*

Many interviewees did contact other potential participants on our behalf and also vouched for the research. Interestingly, when this occurred, some people were willing to be interviewed by the person who had contacted them, but not by the researchers themselves who were, after all, strangers. This variant on 'privileged access' or 'indigenous' interviewing was not pursued, as noted above, due to a lack of willingness and suitability on the part of the potential interviewers, and a lack of resources on the part of the project.

Ultimately, despite the intention to utilise snowball sampling, it began to feel that the research was proceeding more along the lines of what Groger, Mayberry and Straker termed 'scrounging sampling': a series of 'desperate and continuing efforts, against mounting odds, to round out the collection of individuals with relevant types of experiences we know to exist but have not been able to capture' (1999: 830).

Why did this happen?

There appeared to us to be four main reasons, some already hinted at above, as to why potential respondents were wary of becoming involved with this particular research project. These reasons were identified during the interviews themselves as well as through informal conversations with the participants and those potential participants who ultimately refused to be interviewed.

First, our intention to speak to people whose drug use was 'normal' (Hammersley 2005, 2011) meant that accessing participants through the criminal justice system or through treatment programmes would not do, as by definition individuals involved in these institutions are less likely to be using drugs 'normally', as we suggested in Chapter 1. As a result the most obvious gateways through which participants could be accessed were closed off. Of course, there is no guarantee that all hidden users are using drugs normally, but it was felt that hidden users were more likely to be using in this way. So, the hidden users that were of interest to us were not only that much harder to find, but once they had been found they were much more unlikely to be willing to speak to us; after all, the 'respondents were being asked to talk openly about a topic that they were normally accustomed to keeping hidden' (Notley 2005: 280). Thus, many of our difficulties were, frustratingly, by design. Notley (2005), in her research on adult illegal drug users, experienced similar problems with her snowball sampling and held this to be the reason for her difficulties. The perfectly understandable desire to keep their participation in an illegal activity relatively quiet is possibly also more common amongst older individuals whose drug taking careers predate the so-called 'normalisation' of many forms of illegal drug use (Parker, Aldridge and Measham 1998, Aldridge, Measham and Williams 2011). Such individuals are less likely to be comfortable talking about their drug use compared to, say, younger users involved in a more relaxed and open drug-using context.

The second reason was that older adults often have more to lose when compared with younger people. For example, they are more likely to have stable jobs, families and other ties to 'mainstream' society that could be jeopardised by the admission of illegal drug use. This was particularly the case here given the 'hidden' target population of the study. Thus, it was doubly difficult to persuade potential participants to be interviewed because their age made them less inclined to talk about their drug use *and* because they had more to lose in the event of exposure; these were individuals who were 'hidden by choice' (Noy 2008: 331). But, of course, this is one of the reasons why this group is so interesting. Even those who did agree to be interviewed for the study were generally more than happy to be hidden, and they had little interest in exposing themselves. Thus, the problems associated with accessing hidden populations were compounded in this study. Groups whose members were more blatantly stifled and suppressed may have been more willing to speak out to a researcher about their situation. Those older illegal drug users that were of interest here were content to quietly keep indulging in drug use below the radar of the authorities and their non-drug-using friends and colleagues. Anything that might have jeopardised that state of affairs was understandably viewed with suspicion.

Third, it may also be the case that the personal characteristics of the researchers played a part in the difficulties encountered. For instance, we were half the age of many of the potential interviewees. One way in which this proved problematic was that we were not part of the same peer group as the potential participants. The age gap may also have exacerbated issues of trustworthiness. Indeed, this has been raised in previous research in relation to snowball sampling (Wright et al. 1992). Potential interviewees may be more likely to trust somebody closer to their own age, with greater experience of life and possibly even drug use. They are less likely to wish to participate in an interview conducted by somebody considerably younger than them, particularly on such a sensitive issue. In addition, one researcher was a foreign national. There may well have been some apprehension on the part of the potential participants as to why a foreigner would be interested in their engagement in an illegal activity. There were also the inevitable cultural barriers which occasionally made trust and confidence rather difficult to build up. One example of this was the use of different slang terms for the same drugs, which occasionally led to awkward initial exchanges when the possibility of participation in the study was being explored, and also sometimes manifested itself during the interviews themselves (see Waters 2016). Furthermore, as a consequence of being a foreign national, one of our number had no older family members or family friends living in the research area, and as such access to the older age group was again hindered. Such connections can be important in this type of study, for they often allow for a more trusting relationship to be established between the researcher and potential interviewees.

The development of trust between researcher and researched can be critical to the success of this type of sampling method, as Berg (1988) and Faugier and Sargeant (1997) show. They suggest that trust can be slow to build and that it often only does so as the purposes and consequences of the study are revealed over time. For example, assurances of confidentiality only carry weight after a period of time has elapsed (Atkinson and Flint 2001). Noy goes further and suggests that 'the quality of the referring process is *naturally related* to the quality of the interaction: if the informant leaves the interview meeting feeling discontented, or if the researcher did not win the informant's trust and sympathy, the chances the latter will supply the former referrals decrease (and vice versa)' (2008: 334). In fact, even interactions of a high quality may not bear fruit in future referrals or participants. It seemed to us that the interviews we undertook *were* successful and participants warmed to their theme and the research itself as they progressed. After each interview we tended to leave with renewed hope that *this time* we would be able to develop a snowball. Yet each and every new contact remained cautious despite assurances from their referrer. As such, trust built up with one participant did not necessarily 'transfer' to potential new participants, and building snowballs remained almost impossible.

Snowball sampling has worked well in instances where the researcher is part of the group being studied (Duncan and Edwards 1999, Browne 2005), although of course this also raises a number of ethical questions about the researcher's role. Nevertheless, to be embedded in the social networks that are the subject matter of the research vastly increases the chances of referrals being made and a sizeable sample being constructed. In this light it is clear that our age and nationality were additional hurdles in the way of constructing snowballs. Being part of the group is also likely to have positive consequences for the nature and quality of the interaction that takes place. Here the use of 'privileged access' (Griffiths et al. 1993) or 'indigenous' (Power 1994) interviewers may have been beneficial. It should be noted with Browne (2005: 53–4), however, that there is evidence from research on focus groups (specifically in market research; see Holbrook and Jackson [1996] and Morgan [1998]) that 'where sensitive topics are being addressed people will be more open with those whom they may never meet again'. So whilst not being part of the group under study was not a barrier to successful interviews, given the nature of the research, it is likely to have hindered the construction of the sample.

This leads neatly to the final reason why snowball sampling did not work as well as hoped for in this research. Put simply, it seems to be the case that the hidden illegal drug use of older adults tends not to occur within well-defined social networks. To pre-empt one of the key findings of the study that will be discussed more fully in later chapters, it was found that older users of drugs generally indulge in the home environment, either alone or with a very small number of close confidants (see also Waters 2009, Moxon and Waters 2010). Almost all of the interviewees happily and nostalgically reminisced about the origins of their illegal drug use in closely knit social contexts such as friendship groups at school, or in relatively well-defined 'subcultural' movements such as hippy, punk and acid house. Yet it was clear that their illegal drug use for the most part no longer took place as part of any wider social milieu.

This significant change in the 'setting' (Zinberg 1984) of older adults' drug use undermined snowball sampling's effectiveness because one of its key assumptions (that the group being studied are somehow connected and this will engender referrals of potential participants from actual participants) proved to be unfounded in this case. Goode (2000: 3.12) found something similar. Thus, the steady expansion of the sample as referral follows referral from 'connected' individuals never occurred, not because hidden older illegal drug users do not exist, but because the connections between them are slight. As noted above, most participants were able to at least provide details of one or two potential participants. Yet it was clear that most of the users who took part in the research had only limited contact with other users. So, in the end, whilst snowball sampling looked like the best sampling method to address this hidden population at the outset of the research, it turned out that the nature of the group under study – hidden *and* disconnected – ultimately checked its success. Of course, it was not known at the outset of the research just how atomised the target population would prove to be.

Ultimately, despite the fact that snowball sampling is often presented as the best way to access hard-to-reach and hidden populations, particularly when sensitive matters are the focus of study, we found that it does not by itself guarantee the construction of a sizeable sample. The circumstances of our study were such that building a sample proved extremely difficult, and snowballing was unable to effectively overcome these difficulties (Waters 2015). Unfortunately, the possibility of substantially revising how participants were recruited, or even 'spontaneously innovating' in the manner of McCormack, Adams and Anderson (2012), was rendered difficult by the highly sensitive nature of the topic at hand, the fact that potential participants were largely 'hidden by choice' (Noy 2008: 331), and the lack of resources at the disposal of the project. Of course, when faced with issues such as these, the effectiveness of any sampling technique, not just snowballing, may be blunted. Nevertheless, snowballing remains an extremely valuable and often irreplaceable sampling technique, and there will be certain cases, such as this one, where in spite of its weaknesses it remains the only viable method for constructing a research sample. In the end, it is hardly surprising that 'hard-to-reach populations are hard to reach' (Goodman 2011: 350), and there is no 'magic bullet' of a sampling technique that can change this fact.

Research instrument

The research instrument utilised for the study was a semi-structured 'life story' interview. Given the cross-sectional nature of the study, and the fact that participants would be met on just a single occasion, it was felt that an interview of this type would be the most efficient way of obtaining detailed, rich information regarding the participants' drug use both now and in the past. The advantages and disadvantages of using this kind of interview are much discussed, and so what follows is a brief discussion of the most pertinent issues raised during the course of this study.

The interview was divided into two parts. The first consisted of demographic questions, using the same wording as the Crime Survey for England and Wales. The second part explored the participants' illegal drug careers and consisted of broad open-ended questions about past and present illegal drug use. The reasons behind and attitudes towards drug use were also explored, and participants were also asked about their future intentions. This latter part of the interview was loosely based on the 'life story' interviewing method (McAdams 1993), with some adaptations rendering it suitable for the purpose at hand. Such an approach has been used in drug research before, for instance by Hammersley and Dalgarno (2013). The semi-structured format was adopted to permit interviewees considerable freedom to discuss that which was of importance to them regarding their own drug use. It was also felt that this would allow the participants greater control over what they chose to reveal. As we have already seen, we were broaching a sensitive topic; participants were taking a risk in speaking to us about their engagement in an illegal activity, and affording them some control over the interview itself was one way of alleviating that risk and gaining trust. However, although a great deal of freedom was permitted to participants, the interviews did actively but sensitively seek to ascertain how drug use had been integrated into participants' lives as they grew older.

Initially the intention was to carry out all interviews face-to-face, to facilitate the building of trust and attempt to reassure the participant. Participants were asked to select their preferred venue for the interview; most chose their home, some their office, and others a quiet pub. Towards the end of the project, the decision was made to offer interviews by telephone or online videotelephony if the participant preferred. This was a practical decision made to save time and costs, but some participants stated that they would prefer to be interviewed by these methods rather than in person once they were offered the choice. Some participants opted to be interviewed by online videotelephony rather than by telephone as they wished to be able to see the interviewer. Of the total of 30 interviews, 19 were conducted in person, seven were conducted by telephone, and four by online videotelephony.

The interview was designed to last approximately an hour. Participants were giving their time for free, and so we were careful not to take up too much of it.

Most interviews did end up taking about this amount of time, but a handful were shorter (the shortest, with a particularly reticent participant, being around 25 minutes long), and many were longer (the longest clocked in at over 90 minutes). The shorter interviews saw the participants reluctant to engage with the narrative mode. In these situations it was still possible to create a narrative 'out of the bare bones of a life history produced out of brief responses to questions' (Brannen 2013); this process, as Brannen (2013) suggests, was aided by the use of field notes that gave insights into the participants and their feelings toward the subject, comparisons with narratives from other interviews and wider knowledge of the material contexts and history of the period and the subject under study.

All the interviews were recorded. One telling sign of the duration of the project was that at the outset cassette tapes were used for the recordings, as, although digital devices were becoming increasingly commonplace, it remained standard practice to use analogue recording machines. The switch to a far more convenient and user-friendly digital recorder was made part way through the project. Towards the end of the research process, to have remained with the tape recorder would have seemed wilfully antediluvian. Following completion, the interviews were transcribed verbatim (other than being anonymised and identifying features being removed or replaced). This process was carried out by the research team member that had not carried out the interview to ensure familiarity with the data. Then, analysis was carried out by hand to identify key themes.

Of course, interviews of any kind present a range of methodological difficulties. In the first place, as Maddux and Desmond suggest, the reliability of information gathered by interviews is closely linked to the 'features of the interview itself. . . . These include the place of the interview, the legal status of the subject, the feeling of the subject about giving information to the interviewer, the skill of the interviewer, and the procedure' (1975: 93–4). Furthermore, interviews that concern an individual's life history can be especially problematic. Indeed, it has been argued that researchers should not take voluntary self-presentations by interviewees at face value (Douglas 1976).[6] However, past research does suggest that drug users tend to provide reliable accounts of their behaviour (Ball 1967, Maddux and Desmond 1975, Weatherby et al. 1994, Rosenberg 1997). The participants in this study did not at all seem to be deliberately misleading or obfuscatory, although clearly this assertion is merely based upon the research team's own unreliable subjective impressions and intuitions. Even if our gut feelings about the sincerity of the participants were correct, this still

6 To go beyond an unquestioning acceptance of what an interviewee says can in fact be vital in attempting to draw something of value from this type of research, as Hammersley and Dalgarno have suggested: 'A common misapprehension about qualitative research is that it cannot address issues of cause and effect. Qualitative research can address cause and effect, but it does so by using a structural logic in the data analysis, not by statistical or other comparisons. Part of this logic is not to accept people's stories at face value, but to analyse them systematically by coding what is said, to identify interrelated issues and themes that were not necessarily apparent to the participants themselves' (2013: 22).

does little to address the issue of honest but mistaken recollections. Yet there is an even more fundamental point here. Because research participants who are discussing their own lives are not disinterested observers of those lives, there is a sense in which any self-presentation is always suggestive of the way an individual has at that moment in time come to view their own personal biography and lifecourse. This applies even to accounts which are somehow inaccurate. Life events are constantly reassessed depending upon present circumstances; as Clausen argues, 'the past tends to be reviewed in terms that make it congruent with present circumstances' (1998: 196). As a result, we might argue that any self-presentation, even one which deliberately or otherwise contains errors of fact, can tell us at least something about the attitude of the participants to their history and to their present. In the end, life stories themselves are constructions, and the interviews that seek to elicit them are 'social performances' that can only ever result in partial accounts (Brannen 2013).[7]

In spite of the difficulties encountered in building the sample and the relatively low number of interviews completed in total, as we conducted the final batch of interviews we began to get a distinct impression that 'theoretical saturation' was being approached. The notion of saturation is associated most closely with the 'grounded theory' method (Glaser and Strauss 1967), and it represents the end point of research in that tradition.[8] It is reached 'when additional analysis no longer contributes anything new about a category' (Strauss 1987: 21). The stories that our participants told about their illegal drug use bore a remarkable similarity to each other, if not in their fine details, then certainly in their broad outlines. As a result, despite the difficulties in building the sample and its final size, we are confident that we have uncovered something significant about the shape of illegal drug use over a lifecourse.

Building conclusions, albeit provisional ones, from small amounts of data is perfectly in keeping with some long-established ethnographic and sociological-criminological traditions (Hall, Winlow and Ancrum 2008: 20). The aim of the work was to take a 'tentative, hypothesis-generating, exploratory look at patterns' (de Vaus 1990: 77), and of course findings from small samples such as this one are potentially *transferable* even when they are not generalisable (Marshall and Rossman 1999). Even a single interview can potentially yield important insights; after all, in the words of Bertaux, there always lies 'behind the solo of a human voice, the music of society and culture in the background' (1990: 168).

7 Indeed, it has been argued that interviews are inherently collaborative (Gubrium and Holstein 2009), or, as Reismann (2008) suggests, 'co-constructions', and that what the interviewer brings to the table can be as important as what the interviewee says.

8 Grounded theory has developed over recent decades into a popular method for small-scale, qualitative studies such as this one, and there are many different variants on the original now in use. The broad principles of grounded theory were used loosely to guide the analysis of the data in this study, but as some grounded theory tends to be highly prescriptive in terms of starting points, techniques employed and outputs, we would not claim that the study is a part of that tradition.

Ethics

Ethical considerations were clearly of great importance in this study given the sensitive and illegal nature of the topic at hand. The participants provided us with information concerning their engagement in illegal activities, which included not only the possession but also occasionally the dealing of controlled substances. Participation in the study therefore potentially opened up the participants to serious negative legal and social consequences. As a result a number of precautions were taken to safeguard the interviewees as far as possible.

It is widely accepted that, aside from a few special circumstances, participants in any research project should be properly informed about what they are being asked to undertake before they can agree to be involved. Informed consent is usually signified by having participants read and sign an information sheet, and by confirming that they understand what the research entails and that they agree to participate. However, in this case it was deemed inappropriate to have participants physically put their name to the research by signing something as formal as a consent form. Instead the principles of implied consent were employed. As Berg has suggested, 'implied consent can replace a signed consent slip when researchers conduct tape-recorded in-depth interviews. In this instance, the interviewers fully explain the nature of the project and the potential risks and benefits at the beginning of each interview. Next, the interviewers ask the subjects if they understand the information and are still willing to take part in the interview. Affirmative responses and completed interviews serve the purpose of implying consent in the absence of a signed consent slip. The benefit of this particular style of informed consent is the elimination of any record of the subjects' names' (2001:57). In this research, potential participants were given an information sheet. They were then asked if they had any questions concerning the research. Consent was then inferred if, after having read the information sheet, they were still willing to take part in a recorded interview. In this way no lasting record of participants' names was kept by the researchers.

The issues of confidentiality and anonymity also necessitated attention. The anonymity of participants could not be guaranteed as the very nature of a face-to-face interview requires the researcher to meet and speak to the participant, as well as hold some contact details, however temporarily. Telephone interviews are a little better in this regard, but still require a conversation and the passing of contact details. In addition, participants in this research revealed details of their lives that stretched back over many decades, and so anonymity was inevitably compromised.

In order to counter this, great measures were taken to assure confidentiality.[9] Zinberg has identified a number of ways in which to 'safeguard interviewees' identity' as far as possible (1984: 9). Several of these techniques were adopted.

9 See Fitzgerald and Hamilton (1996, 1997) and Israel (2004) for discussions about issues of confidentiality in research of this nature.

First, only the research team knew the names and identities of the participants. These details were not shared with anyone else. Participants were not asked for anything other than the bare minimum of information in order to arrange the interview, although some happily volunteered more. For most interviewees, we held a name, contact details and an address, but in some instances, where interviews were arranged through a third party, only a first name was known. All these details were destroyed after the completion of the research.

Second, the participants were told that they could decline to answer any question for any reason, and that they could stop the interview at any point. With one or two small exceptions where participants wished to avoid implicating others in engaging in illegal acts, all our questions were answered fully, and no participant decided to stop the interview. Of course the very nature of the semi-structured interview allowed the participants some degree of control over what they chose to reveal and how they presented their life story to us, as discussed earlier. That said, for the most part the participants seemed to enjoy the interview process and were happy to divulge intimate details regarding their life story. Indeed, at times we were genuinely taken aback at the level of openness we encountered and some of the things that were disclosed to us. After all, even where somebody had vouched for us, we essentially remained strangers to the participants.

Third, during transcription, any information (such as a name, a place or a company name) that could potentially contribute to the identification of a participant was changed so that the transcriptions could not be easily linked to an individual. All participants were also allocated a code number and a pseudonym. It is perfectly possible that relatives, friends and acquaintances may be able to identify participants from the information contained in the transcriptions despite the removal of obvious identifiers, for as we noted above the interviewees provided very finely detailed accounts of various stages in their life. Of course, this cannot be avoided in research of this nature. Thus, once again, rather than strive for transcriptions that guaranteed complete *anonymity* (a likely unattainable ideal), we instead aimed for *confidentiality* as far as possible. As a result the proper handling of recordings and transcriptions became critical in ensuring that participants suffered no negative consequences from participation in the study. For instance, there was no physical list linking identifiable individuals back to their interview. Furthermore, the slow pace of the project meant that almost all the interviews were transcribed, anonymised as far as possible and assigned a code number and pseudonym before the next interview took place, so there was no backlog of recordings awaiting transcription. Upon completion of the project, the recordings were deleted, and the transcriptions are being stored securely with a view to eventual deletion once all research outputs have been written up.

Finally, we were careful not to discuss any information that was revealed during interviews with other participants or with the contacts who had helped to set up interviews. We maintained this policy even where participants knew each other (as in the case of the two 'snowball' interviews) or where they were close friends with a contact who had acted as a 'go-between'. For those who were interested, we were willing to share our general impressions of what we had found to date.

The sample

This section will introduce the participants and provide a demographic overview of the sample. Table 2.1 provides brief details of the 30 hidden users of illegal drugs aged 40 and over who took part in the study following the somewhat fraught recruitment process.

The sample had a mean average age of 48.8, and a range of 40–66. Seventeen participants were in their 40s, 10 were in their 50s, and three were in their 60s. Given the decade-long duration of the research project, this meant that

Table 2.1 Participants in the study

Alias	*Age*	*Gender*	*Employment status*	*Current user of . . .*
Lenny	53	M	mechanic	cannabis
Matthew	52	M	self-employed civil engineer	cannabis, occasionally cocaine
Ned	53	M	unemployed	amphetamines
Ollie	52	M	company owner	cannabis, occasionally cocaine
Pat	51	F	unemployed	polydrug
Quinn	51	F	market trader	cannabis, occasionally cocaine
Roger	44	M	manager in a small firm	cannabis
Simon	61	M	researcher	cannabis
Tom	41	M	horticulturalist	cannabis
Uri	47	M	care worker	cannabis
Vince	42	M	academic	cannabis
Winston	58	M	academic	cannabis
Xavier	55	M	researcher	polydrug
Yannis	47	M	regional manager	cannabis
Zach	66	M	retired fitter	cannabis
Adam	47	M	unemployed [disability]	cannabis
Brian	52	M	company owner	cannabis
Colin	41	M	internet entrepreneur	cannabis, occasionally other
Derek	50	M	gardener	cannabis, occasionally mushrooms
Eric	40	M	consultant for relocation firm	cannabis
Fran	41	F	retired [disability]	cannabis
Grace	48	F	carer for child	cannabis
Harry	40	M	NHS support worker	cannabis
Ian	46	M	unemployed	cannabis
Jane	47	F	delivery driver	cannabis, cocaine, occasionally ecstasy
Keith	63	M	retired civil servant	cannabis
Liam	45	M	unemployed	cannabis
Malcolm	44	M	student	cannabis
Nathan	47	M	unemployed customs officer [disability]	cannabis
Oscar	40	M	volunteer	cannabis

Table 2.2 Participants' decade of birth

Decade of birth	*Count*
1944–49	2
1950s	10
1960s	12
1970–74	6

participants were born across a 30-year period, with the first-born participant being born in 1944, and the last-born in 1974 (see Table 2.2). Five females were interviewed, as compared to 25 males; clearly this is an imbalance, and findings should be read in this light.[10] There was little ethnic diversity among the participants, with all of the interviewees identifying themselves as white. The vast majority (26) identified as 'white British'; two participants identified as 'white Irish' and two as 'white other'. Participants resided in England, Scotland and Wales.

Almost all of the participants (26) held an educational qualification of some type. This included GCSEs, 'A' levels, National Vocational Qualifications, trade apprenticeships, degrees, master's degrees and PhDs. Eighteen participants held at least 'A' levels (or the international equivalent), and 12 held at least an undergraduate degree. Only four participants held no educational qualifications whatsoever.

Participants came from a wide variety of social positions, and a range of different occupations were represented in the sample, as Table 2.1 shows.[11] Over half (17) of the participants had engaged in paid employment during the seven days prior to the interview. Of those who were not currently in paid

10 Studies in both the UK and the US have consistently found that a greater proportion of current illegal drug users are male and that older males are more likely to use illegal drugs than older females, however 'older' is defined (for example Aitken et al. 2000, Plant, Plant and Mason 2002, Anderson and Levy 2003). The extent to which women's use might simply be more 'hidden' is uncertain. Indeed, several of our male participants had female partners who also used illegal drugs, but they refused to be interviewed. Plant, Plant and Mason (2002) found that female users were more likely to report adverse consequences related to their use, although Glantz and Backenheimer (1988) found that illegal drug use among 'elderly' women was generally not problematic, especially in comparison to alcohol and prescription drug abuse. However, they did suggest that this had the potential to change as younger cohorts, including more 'drug involved' women, grew older.

11 The 'employment status' given in Table 2.1 is drawn from the participants' own descriptions of what they did for a living. As Notley argued in relation to the wide range of individuals involved in her study of hidden drug users, 'it was important to introduce as much variation as possible into the sample, and thus to "theoretically sample" a wide range of experiences that could be compared and contrasted during analysis (Glaser and Strauss 1967). This need for variability during analysis had to be balanced against both achieving a sample of individuals who were sufficiently comparable to make it possible to develop a cohesive theory about a particular group, and the difficulties in obtaining that sample' (2005: 281).

employment, four were retired, one was a full-time student, one was a freelance researcher in between contracts, one was a full-time care giver for her son, one was disabled and unable to work, and one was a volunteer worker. The remaining four classed themselves as unemployed.

There was some variation in the level of household income among the participants. For seven participants, annual household income was between £5,000 and £9,999; for three the figure was between £10,000 and £14,999; for four it was between £15,000 and £19,999; for another four it was between £20,000 and £24,999; for two it was between £25,000 and £29,999; for one it was between £30,000 and £34,999; for one it was between £35,000 and £39,999; for a further one it was between £45,000 and £49,999; and for six it was £50,000 or more. In addition, there was one participant whose income varied so greatly from month to month (from £5,000 to £24,999) that an annual figure could not be reliably identified. Over a third (11) of the participants had a household income approximately equal to or greater than the national average.[12]

Seven participants were married and lived with their spouse, whilst three were cohabiting with a partner whom they were not married to. Four participants were divorced and living with a new partner, and one was separated from a long-term partner but was now living with a new partner. In total, exactly half (15) of the participants were living with a partner. Of those who lived alone, nine had never married, five were divorced and one was separated from a long-term partner. Nine of the participants had children living at home with them, and a further four had children living elsewhere (either on their own or with a former partner). The remaining sixteen participants had no children.

Eleven participants resided in semi-detached houses, whilst eight lived in terraced houses and two lived in detached houses. The remaining nine participants resided in flats, of which three lived in flats converted from housing. Seven participants owned their home outright, with a further five in the process of paying off a mortgage on their property. One participant was in a shared ownership arrangement, and one lived rent-free in the partner's home. The majority of participants (16) rented their accommodation, either privately or from a local authority.

Over two-thirds (21) of the participants felt that their general health was either 'very good' or 'good'. A further five considered their health to be 'fair'. Only three participants felt that their health was 'bad', and one participant felt in 'very bad' health. Just over a third (12) of participants identified as having a long-term illness or infirmity. This included a range of physical and mental ailments, including arthritis, chronic obstructive pulmonary disease, complex regional pain syndrome, visual impairment, depression, post-traumatic stress disorder and anxiety. Interestingly, identifying as having a long-term illness did not preclude participants from rating their overall general health as 'good' or even 'very good'.

12 This takes into account the timing of each interview and the changing level of annual household incomes over the period of the research (see Office for National Statistics 2015).

As Table 2.1 clearly shows, cannabis was the drug of choice for the overwhelming majority of the participants.[13] Only one member of the sample (Ned) did not use cannabis at all, and for the bulk (21) of the participants cannabis was the only illegal drug they used. Yet, as we will see in the next chapter, most participants had enjoyed a more varied drugs repertoire in the past, and cannabis had often been settled upon only after years of experimentation and periods of heavy polydrug use. In addition to using illegal drugs, half (15) of the participants also smoked tobacco, and a further two lived in a household where somebody else used tobacco. The majority (26) of the participants also drank alcohol. Of these 26 drinkers, seven drank daily, eight drank weekly, six drank monthly, and five drank less frequently than once a month. Just over half (17) of the participants had visited a pub during the last month, and five had visited a club. The drinkers among the sample consumed anywhere between one and 20 units of alcohol in a single drinking session.

Summary

This chapter has detailed the methodology of the project and outlined the difficulties we faced when attempting to build a sample of hidden older illegal drug users using the snowball sampling technique. We began by discussing the background to the project and its roots in a PhD study, and the difficulties of continuing what was essentially a curiosity-driven piece of research without funding in the context of the contemporary university system in the UK. Next, the problems we encountered with the use of snowball sampling were explored, before we discussed some of the issues with interviewing and the degree to which it is able to yield robust data in a research study of this nature. We then looked at some of the ethical issues associated with the project, particularly around ensuring the confidentiality of the participants who agreed to speak to us about their engagement in an illegal activity. Finally, we provided brief details and a demographic overview of the 30 participants who agreed to be interviewed for the research.

The project as a whole has been an intensely frustrating one, years in the making, and constantly on the point of collapse when it seemed that no more participants would be forthcoming. However, those moments when willing participants finally began speaking to us about illegal drug use over their life-course have, we hope, just about made the effort worthwhile. We turn now to those participants and their stories.

13 The 'current user of' column in Table 2.1 is a subjective interpretation by the authors of how best to describe the participants' current (past-year) use. Note that the term 'polydrug use' can be used in a number of different ways. Ives and Ghelani (2006), for example, draw a distinction between simultaneous polydrug use (SPD), where individuals use two or more substances at once, and concurrent polydrug use (CDU), where individuals use different single substances on separate occasions (see also Boeri et al. 2008, Askew 2013). They suggest that most drug use falls into their CDU category, especially if alcohol and tobacco are included in the category 'drug'. Here, we considered participants to be polydrug users if they had used more than three types of illegal drugs at any time (simultaneously or concurrently) over the past year, as we wished to reserve the term for those with the most varied repertoires.

3 Past

Lives spent with illegal drugs

In this chapter we explore the histories of our participants' illegal drug use careers. To begin with, we look at the participants' initial experiences with illegal drugs, before discussing what happened in the immediate aftermath of this. Then, we will investigate the 'experimental' phase of illegal drug use that most participants underwent, where their drugs repertoire widened and where their use became heavier. As we will see, this often took place as part of their engagement in a subcultural movement. Finally, the chapter will turn its attention to the notion of 'transitions'. We will suggest that the participants' drug careers have been largely contingent upon their other circumstances at any given time. Transitions (and 'turning points') affecting occupational statuses, jobs, places of residence, family situations and health have all played a role in shaping the trajectories of our participants' drug careers. We end the chapter by suggesting that the transitions experienced by our participants can be properly comprehended only in light of the notion of 'liminality'. This refers to the sense of radical uncertainty that subjects now face as they make their way through a lifecourse that has lost its normatively ordered sense of stability and direction and leaves them feeling constantly in limbo. In this way we can begin to see the waxing and the waning of illegal drug use over their lifecourse as an inevitable outcome of our participants being repeatedly forced to adjust to an unpredictable series of transitions and turning points.

In the beginning

In general, the participants told a relatively uniform story about their initial engagement with illegal drugs. With one or two exceptions, the age that participants first used illegal drugs and the type of illegal drugs that they first experimented with was reasonably consistent. Moreover, the general nature of the participants' initial experiences was remarkably similar.

As Dalgarno (2006) suggests, simple curiosity tends to be one of the main drivers of initial experiments with illegal drugs. This was the case for a good number of our participants, with Tom (41, horticulturalist, cannabis user), for example, remembering that 'partly it was an appeal because of the illegality and unknown which made it more interesting'. Often, having friends who had dabbled with drugs fostered the inquisitiveness of participants, as in the case of Pat (51, unemployed, polydrug user) who '[was] curious actually, . . . there was this lad that I knew was a drug user and I knew him quite well and I just asked him one day if I could try it, that was it'. Indeed, the influence of friends tended to be significant. Nathan's (47, unemployed customs officer due to disability, cannabis user) experience was typical:

> I was with a couple of friends of mine, one of my friends had a mother who was a nurse, and she used to smoke a bit of cannabis and he knew where she stashed it, and we'd all heard about it, we'd all spoke about it, a bit of pot here, a bit of pot there, I'd seen a couple of Cheech and Chong movies by then, yeah, [name of friend] said "I'm going to go and get a bit of that".

Similarly, Eric's (40, consultant for relocation firm, cannabis user) exposure to some of the literature and film that dealt with drug use had provoked his curiosity:

> I'd sort of read a lot of the Hunter S. Thompsons and the Cheech and Chongs, and [seen] *Easy Rider*, that sort of thing, so it was very much the subculture that I was quite interested in.

Roger (44, manager in a small firm, cannabis user) and his friends were particularly inquisitive, and prior to their first experience with cannabis they took matters into their own hands with some rather unusual experiments:

> We used to get the insides of banana skins and dry them in the oven and roll those into cigarettes, cos we were told that worked. . . . We'd skive off school and go to someone's house where the parents were working and try, we were obviously drunk, booze as well, you know, it was all part of the same thing. It was just the rumours doing the rounds, that if you scraped the insides of the banana skins, dried them and smoked them, they'd get you high. So, I don't even know if it's true. . . . The problem is, it was a load of 15 year old lads, sat down with booze inside them as well, you can convince yourself of anything can't you. So I obviously don't know, you'd have to check with the drug agency![1]

1 These experiments can likely trace their inspiration to a satirical article in the March 1967 edition of the underground newspaper the *Berkeley Barb*. The article claimed that dried banana skins contain the (fictional) psychoactive substance 'bananadine'. Although the original article was intended to raise questions about the ethical basis for banning psychoactive substances, it was believed by many to be true (Stevens 1987: 336). Indeed, William Powell reprinted the 'recipe' in *The Anarchist Cookbook* in 1970. Its inclusion in this infamous collection quickly led to it becoming more widely known.

As Roger's tale makes clear, other legal substances were also used 'under age' by our participants before the time of their first encounter with illegal drugs. Three participants mentioned that they were already smoking tobacco by the time that they first used illegal drugs, and six were drinking alcohol. Others were not quite sure whether their illegal drug use predated their use of tobacco and alcohol, although it is perhaps reasonable to assume that for a good number of the participants, alcohol and tobacco use did come first, not least due to the fact that these substances tend to be easier to access. Malcolm (44, student, cannabis user) recalled that his initial experiences were with solvents and magic mushrooms, before he progressed to illegal substances. Adam (47, unemployed due to disability, cannabis user) also began by using magic mushrooms.[2]

As Agrawal and Lynskey (2009: 4) have suggested, most current older users of illegal drugs are likely to have been using over the long term, as initiation of use in mid or late life is rare. According to the Home Office, 'almost all older adults [who have used illegal drugs at some point in their life] reported first taking drugs before they were 40: 97 per cent of older cannabis users, 96 per cent of older cocaine users, and 95 per cent of older ecstasy users started before this age. This suggests that older drug users are those that have taken drugs over their adult lives, or at some point over their adult lives, and are now continuing to do so as they age' (Home Office 2015a: 30).[3] Indeed, for most participants in this study the first time they used illegal drugs was in their mid-teens, as Table 3.1 shows. This is an unsurprising finding, and is consistent with received wisdom and previous research (for example, Warburton, Turnbull and Hough 2005). Just a couple of participants had used illegal drugs before becoming a teenager, with the youngest, Nathan (47, unemployed customs officer due to disability, cannabis user), starting at 11. Three of the sample used illegal drugs for the first time in their early 20s, with Ian (46, unemployed, cannabis user) being the oldest at 23. Although there is some debate regarding the age at which a new user should be classed as a 'late onset' user (Lynskey, Day and Hall 2003, Boeri, Sterk and Elfison 2008), on most measures even Ian would not fall into this category.

2 Prior to the 2005 Drugs Act, fresh (not prepared) psilocybin mushrooms were not illegal. Section 21 of the 2005 act amended the Misuse of Drugs Act 1971 so that *both* fresh and prepared magic mushrooms (such as the 'liberty cap') became Class A drugs. As Malcolm's and Adam's first experiences of magic mushrooms predated this, we have not counted them as their first experiences of an illegal drug.

3 The Crime Survey for England and Wales has also found that 'older adults who have ever used drugs tend to have first taken drugs at a later age than younger adults'; for example, they note that 'the most commonly reported age for first taking cannabis for younger adults who have ever used cannabis was 16, and 18 for older adults who used cannabis'. Note that these findings were taken from the 2011/12 run of the Crime Survey for England and Wales (the most recent time these questions were asked); they concern only cannabis, powder cocaine and ecstasy ('the three most prevalent drugs'); and they refer to those individuals who have 'ever' used these drugs (and are therefore not necessarily current users). Of course, it is also important to note that younger adults will not yet have had the opportunity to start drug use at all ages, due to their current age (Home Office 2015a: 30).

Table 3.1 Age of participants when they used illegal drugs for the first time

Age	*Count*
11	1
12	1
Teen	2
13	4
14	3
15	5
16	3
17	3
18	4
19	1
20	0
21	1
22	1
23	1

Note: Some participants responded with two ages upon being asked when they had first used illegal drugs; Colin (41, internet entrepreneur, cannabis and occasional other drug user), for example, stated that he was '15 or 16'. Where this occurred, the younger age was used. In addition, two respondents could not recall precisely when their first use occurred but knew that it was during their teenage years, hence the 'teen' category in the table.

Table 3.2 Type of drug used by participants when they used illegal drugs for the first time

Illegal drug used	*Count*
Cannabis	26
LSD	3
Amphetamine	1

Table 3.2 outlines the first illegal drugs used by our participants. Cannabis dominates, as one would expect. As we will see in Chapter 4, cannabis remains the drug of choice for most of our participants to this day. However, there were exceptions, with three participants using LSD first, and one (Ned, 53, unemployed, amphetamine user) using amphetamine.

As well as this consistency in the timing of the participants' first experiences and the substances that they used, there was also a sense that the nature of that first experience was reasonably similar in the majority of cases. Participants generally reported that their first dalliances into illegal drug use were relatively unplanned and spontaneous and felt somewhat insignificant and trivial; initiation into illegal drug use was not a moment that seemed to be charged with any special significance. As Quinn (51, market trader, cannabis and occasional cocaine user) put it, 'it was just one of those things, nobody actually said "oh try this", it just happened. Do you know what I mean? Just sort of came from nowhere really'. In a similar fashion, Lenny (53, mechanic, cannabis user), when he was presented with an unexpected opportunity to try cannabis for the first time, simply thought, 'oh, we'll give it a go'. Ned's (53, unemployed, amphetamine user) experience was also typical in many ways, despite the fact that he was the sole participant whose first encounter with illegal drugs involved amphetamine. He recalled holding a firm anti-drugs stance at the time, and likely did not realise what a simple, friendly offer of help from a friend entailed:

> Well, I was going to an all-night dance and believe it or not I was very, very anti-drugs at the time and we were travelling over the moors, it was 12 o'clock at night and [I] started to fall asleep. Well my friend just turns around and says "well instead of falling asleep do you want to take these and see how you go on like". So I did and after that, that were it, I was totally awake having a good time, and came home the next [day], sort of fell asleep and I just took it as having a good time, that was all, nothing sinister in it at all, it just happened. Before that, I mean I'd never touched anything in my life and was very, very anti-drug and couldn't understand why people wanted to take it.

Keith's (63, retired civil servant, cannabis user) story was also fairly conventional. Having being brought up on a farm and attended a boarding school, for him 'what happened during the sixties, you know, went past me completely, I viewed it from a place from which it was unobtainable'. However, at the age of 19 whilst attending a music festival, he and a friend were invited back to a tent, whereupon their host rolled a joint and asked if they wanted to try some: 'I didn't go specifically looking, it was just an opportunity passed my way'. His first experience was not a complete success, however:

> Well the trouble was, at that time, I didn't smoke, so it was hot, dry, and I must admit I wasn't terribly impressed. It didn't help that the structure that we were sitting in was one [the host] built out of straw and he was sitting in there passing this lighted cigarette thing around and I'm thinking, this is going to go up any minute now, so hardly conducive to relaxation [laughs].

One reason why the first experience of illegal drug use was often not seen as being particularly momentous was that it tended to occur as part of the normal ebb and flow of teenage life and was usually undertaken with a friend or a group of friends rather than alone and in isolation. The fact that illegal drugs were being used for the first time was somehow less important than the fact of engaging in a collective activity with peers:

> A group of us went away for a weekend and somebody brought along some cannabis. . . . It just sort of happened, the weekend wasn't to specifically do drugs or anything, or to smoke cannabis, we were just away for the

weekend . . . and one night somebody introduced some cannabis. . . . So it wasn't, you know, I hadn't thought about doing or not doing it. *Simon, 61, researcher, cannabis user.*

I would imagine it was most people's normal [experience], being in a group of friends and somebody had a joint and that getting passed around and me taking a little toke of that. *Yannis, 47, regional manager, cannabis user.*

One or two participants did recall that they were at least vaguely aware of the potential significance of their first experience of illegal drug use, although obviously the extent to which this relies on the benefit of hindsight is open to debate. For instance, Winston (58, academic, cannabis user) recalled how even at the time of his first faltering steps into illegal drug use, he felt that it was somehow emblematic of his becoming a part of an emerging subculture:

> I think I was 17 and probably the first thing I ever did was I smoked a joint before a Pink Floyd concert . . . and was sick. That'll be the very first time I think, yeah. Sixteen or 17 I think. . . . I thought I was part of a new scene, you know, developing sort of hippie, music scene really. Bohemian, young bohemians [chuckles]. . . . As I say it coincided with the importance of seeing a major new, very psychedelic group, you know at the age of 17, it was seen as major, I guess it felt like a major turning point.

Inevitably, there was the occasional bad experience. We have already seen the concern that Keith (63, retired civil servant, cannabis user) had felt about smoking his first joint in a straw tent, and he was not alone in having a less than satisfactory time. Oscar (40, volunteer, cannabis user), for example, had felt pressure to try cannabis as everyone else among his group of friends was doing so. He said that upon trying it, 'I threw up for about 20 minutes and went to sleep. And said I wasn't doing that again!' In a somewhat similar vein, Colin (41, internet entrepreneur, cannabis and occasional other drug user) partook in his first experience inside a disused horse stable that was used as a meeting place amongst his friendship group. However, it did not go well:

> They gave me too much and fucked me up. Actually I didn't do it again for a few years. They gave me a bucket bong and they crammed it because they thought it would be funny, when you are not very used to it and you take a large amount in one go. So if you don't want kids to take drugs, give them a bucket bong [laughs], put them off for life! [It] made me turn green and cough for an hour. I didn't like it at all.

Fran (41, retired due to disability, cannabis user), despite initially enjoying her first experience which involved smoking a cannabis joint with friends whilst on a camping trip at the age of 13, had an unpleasant surprise in store:

> Rather embarrassingly, when I woke up in the morning I had actually weed myself, and I think, I'm thinking possibly that put me off it because

> I was, I was that out of control that actually I couldn't wake up to go to the toilet as such. So possibly that maybe put me off slightly you know, . . . the fact that that happened I think it put me off for a while because it probably wasn't until I was, . . .when I was 15 that I had it again.

However, the vast majority of participants enjoyed their first time and were keen to try again when circumstances allowed:

> After the experience I thought that was amazing, why hadn't I heard about this before, why is it being kept a secret from me? [laughs]. *Derek, 50, gardener, cannabis and occasional mushroom user.*
>
> Oh, it was awesome. It was brilliant. I wish sometimes that you could get back to those early days when you actually got stoned on a joint. *Eric, 40, consultant for relocation firm, cannabis user.*
>
> Around a very similar time I got very drunk and what a horrible, vile experience it was, having the room spin round and things, very sick and feeling really bad for a couple of days. And then I had a couple of spliffs, and everybody's like this is so bad for you [laughs] and it wasn't, it wasn't, it just made me feel quite okay and you know, happy, everything was a bit more colourful, but nothing much, it was just everything was a bit more vivid. And I felt quite at peace because I suffer quite a lot with anxiety and it actually made me feel really chilled which was a really nice feeling. *Grace, 48, carer for child, cannabis user.*
>
> Yeah I was, like, I was quite amazed because I was always anti-drugs before I had it, I wouldn't touch a thing like, but when I tried that it was just, [it] made me laugh, it was like kind of something I've never experienced before, something could do that, you know. *Ian, 46, unemployed, cannabis user.*
>
> Fantastic, fantastic, it made me feel how I thought we should feel anyway. We should always feel pretty happy within ourselves and that's how it made me feel. . . . I knew straight away. I knew straight away that, if ever I try anything it will be this, if ever I went for any drug it would be this. *Nathan, 47, unemployed customs officer due to disability, cannabis user.*

So, our participants' first experiences using illegal drugs were, for the most part, unplanned, spontaneous and not imbued with any wider significance, instead tending to take place simply as part of routine socialising with friends. Upon hearing our participants' accounts, one was distinctly reminded of Becker's (1953) famous argument regarding the 'sequence of changes in attitude and experience which lead to the use of marihuana for pleasure' (1953: 235). As we saw in Chapter 1, Becker's sample of novice cannabis users learned to smoke the drug in a way that produced real effects, learned to recognise those effects as resulting from their drug use, and then learned to enjoy the sensations that they had come to recognise. Here we can see our participants setting off on that same journey, with some inevitable missteps along the way. The fact that most participants enjoyed their first experience, with one or two exceptions, is perhaps not surprising given that these are individuals who are still using illegal drugs decades later. As Harry (40, NHS support worker, cannabis user) put it, 'well, I think it started a lifelong love affair!'

What happened next?

In the aftermath of their first experiences, the vast majority of participants quickly became regular users of illegal drugs. Fifteen participants immediately began using drugs around once a week or more, whilst a further 11 participants began using drugs at least once a month. The majority of these participants approached their nascent illegal drug career with relish. Take Brian (52, company owner, cannabis user), for instance:

> I loved it, I thought it was a fantastic experience. I mean in them days it was just new, you know, I mean before I'd even really experimented with alcohol, and for me it was a new door that had been opened and, you know, it was just fun, you know, I can't, there is nothing negative I can say about it. We just had some absolute belters you know, enjoyed it, we used to do it out in the fields, we used to do it indoors, you know, all we did was put music on and had a smoke and got into music and talked you know, and laughed, and it was great you know, and it was just enlightening at the time and I didn't think it would stay with me all my life but it has done.

Xavier (55, researcher, polydrug user) also took to illegal drug use with zeal and enthusiasm and seemed to instantly recognise that he had found something that would prove to be a long-term companion. He quickly settled into a pattern of regular use:

> I was absolutely stoned straight off, loved it from the moment I took it, and I've got to say if anything I felt more normal. I suddenly felt like a greater belonging in the world than I had before I smoked it, so there was no looking back after that. Within about two weeks I was a daily user.

Xavier had quickly got back in touch with his girlfriend's friend's boyfriend, an older boy, who had shared his joint with Xavier to give him his first taste. Xavier bought some cannabis from him, and the two began to frequent pubs together. This triggered 'a chain reaction of getting to know people who were into drugs' as Xavier started to become acquainted with the older boy's friends and dealers.

For Vince (42, academic, cannabis user), simply enjoying the effects of drugs was not the only attraction. In common with many others who quickly became regular users, the communal nature of the experience was also vitally important:

> I enjoyed the effects of the drug, so I suppose from that point on, you know, I sought those effects. Ah, but it was also, it was something, that a

> lot of other people do, so it was kind of as a group, a group activity if you like. So it was something probably, as well as something that I did to enjoy the effect, it was something which I think I did as a group, to be part of, to be part of the group.

Ned (53, unemployed, amphetamine user) and his friends had become involved in the northern soul scene, and their speedy progression into regular illegal drug use was intimately connected to that involvement. They became regulars at one particular northern soul 'all-nighter', and as Ned told us, 'I just enjoyed the place that much that we just kept going week after week after week and I just used to take it as a weekend recreational thing to help me stay awake and enjoy myself really'. As we have seen, Ned was unusual in that he was one of the few participants whose first illegal drug was not cannabis, and his deepening engagement with the northern soul scene ensured that amphetamine remained his drug of choice. Winston (58, academic, cannabis user), another participant who quickly became a regular user, was also unusual in that he moved away from cannabis which, as we have already discovered, he had tried for the first time at a Pink Floyd concert. Finding it difficult to smoke joints, he instead began to partake regularly in LSD, and only returned to cannabis later on. Eric (40, consultant for relocation firm, cannabis user) and his friends were more typical in that they stuck to cannabis. Eric also told the archetypal story of how illegal drug use quickly became an integral part of a night out and was closely coupled with the development of his cultural preferences at this formative time:

> It was a, sort of like, a social thing, we would go out on a weekend, when we came back from going out we would usually end up round one of my friends' houses, somebody would produce an eighth or something like that and we'd smoke it and it was great, yeah. . . . I was developing my musical tastes, my film taste, and to me I always enjoyed being stoned because it made me more aware, I would say of everything, so I loved it.

For others there was more of a sense that their drug use gradually ratcheted up in intensity over a period of time. Yannis (47, regional manager, cannabis user) spoke of a 'gentle, slow progression' into more regular use as he and his friends gradually came into contact with more users on nights out and at parties and the like as they got older. For Ian (46, unemployed, cannabis user), too, there was a steady progression from smoking cannabis 'once in a while' to eventually 'smoking it more and more and cutting out the alcohol really'. Meanwhile, others who had enjoyed their first experiences and were keen to use on a more consistent basis were unable to do so as they had only limited access to the drugs themselves and limited money with which to buy them. As a result they used occasionally when circumstances allowed. As Lenny (53, mechanic, cannabis user), one of the participants who found himself in this position put it, 'I suppose you did it if it was available'.

Just four participants did not become regular users immediately after their first experience with illegal drugs. Perhaps unsurprisingly, of these four, three

(Colin, Fran and Oscar) had endured less than satisfactory first experiences. Indeed, that Colin and Fran did not try illegal drugs again for a lengthy period of time was solely due to the nature of their first experiences. For Colin (41, internet entrepreneur, cannabis and occasional other drug user), it was around a year later that he finally tried cannabis again in the aftermath of his encounter with the bucket bong. He found that he did like the effects of the drug but even then became only an occasional user. Fran (41, retired due to disability, cannabis user) was even more affected by her episode:

> I think, I next had it again in another social situation where someone else got it in. . . . I remember having a few puffs on the joint and then the recollection of what had happened in the tent put me off so I literally had a few puffs and I decided I didn't want any more at that point because I was concerned [laughs], I didn't want to wet the bed you know. And I think that kind of stuck in my mind. . . . I had it at sort of 15, it was more of like that one-off sort of thing, and then I didn't have it again for maybe, until, until I was [pauses] in my twenties.

Oscar (40, volunteer, cannabis user), after his bout of vomiting, also paused completely for a time before he tried again. However, this pause was also down to the difficulties he had in accessing illegal drugs as well as a lack of money. A few months after he left school, these difficulties eased, and he and a friend finally became regular users. Similarly, for Liam (45, unemployed, cannabis user) a complete lack of access to illegal drugs meant that he simply could not try them again for some time, despite enjoying his first experience.

Notwithstanding these exceptions, it was clear that for most of the participants it was not long after their first experiences before they were using illegal drugs fairly regularly at the very least; in general it seemed that our participants found an appetite for illegal drugs very quickly. They progressed through Becker's (1953) developmental stages at some speed and, in his terms, were soon frequently enjoying the sensations that they had come to recognise as resulting from their illegal drug use.

Time to experiment

As Plant (1975) also found in his classic study of non-institutionalised drug users, the vast majority of our participants enjoyed what could be loosely termed an 'experimental' phase to their illegal drug use, where a range of different substances were tried and use tended to become somewhat heavier. Of the 30 people in the sample, 22 went through such a phase with a relatively clear beginning and end. In addition to this, four participants experimented with illegal drugs over the longer term. Jane (47, delivery driver, cannabis, cocaine, and occasional ecstasy user) and Ned (53, unemployed, amphetamine user) had experimented periodically throughout their drug career, albeit less so in more recent times. Pat (51, unemployed, polydrug user) had experimented throughout her life and remained a heavy polydrug user. Xavier (55, researcher, polydrug user) had enjoyed over three decades of almost unbroken experimentation and continued to explore the possibilities of a wide range of substances. Only four participants had not gone through an experimental phase: Simon (61, researcher, cannabis user) and Keith (63, retired civil servant, cannabis user) had only ever used cannabis, whilst Fran (41, retired due to disability, cannabis user) and Uri (47, care worker, cannabis user) had intermittently tried other substances on isolated occasions.

These experimental phases tended to occur relatively early in the participants' drug careers. Indeed, for seven participants, experimentation began almost immediately after their first experience. However, it was more common for experimentation to begin a couple of years or so after initiation into illegal drug use. For many participants this meant that experimentation began during the teenage years, with Vince (42, academic, cannabis user), Oscar (40, volunteer, cannabis user) and Malcolm (44, student, cannabis user), whose first experiences of illegal drugs came at 15, 14 and 13 respectively, all beginning their experimental phase before they reached the age of 16. A further nine participants began experimenting in their late teens, and another nine in their 20s. As noted above, Jane (47, delivery driver, cannabis, cocaine, and occasional ecstasy user), Ned (53, unemployed, amphetamine user), Pat (51, unemployed, polydrug user) and Xavier (55, researcher, polydrug user) did not have a distinct, bounded period of experimentation, and their experiments continued over the long term, sporadically so in the case of Jane and Ned and prolifically in the case of Pat and Xavier. Grace (48, carer for child, cannabis user) stood out as an unusual case; her experimentation, modest though it was, involving only cocaine as well as her usual cannabis, did not begin until she was aged 38:

> [I began to experiment] just out of interest. You hear so much bad press and you talk to people [who say] "but it's nothing like that, it's like this", and I just wanted to find out for myself. [It lasted] a couple of years, until I tried all the things I'd put on my to-do list [laughs]. Yes, I tried cocaine when I was 38, so 10 years ago.

Table 3.3 shows the number of illegal drugs tried by the participants, which gives some idea of the level of experimentation engaged in by the sample. Twenty-five participants had tried three or more illegal drugs over the course of their drug career, and 11 participants had used five or more.[4] Simon (61, researcher, cannabis user) and Keith (63, retired civil servant, cannabis user) had used cannabis alone.

Collectively the participants had used a wide variety of illegal drugs (see Table 3.4). Every participant had used cannabis, and two-thirds had used LSD. Ecstasy, amphetamine and cocaine had been used by between a third and a half of participants. There was also a wide range of drugs that had been used by just a handful of participants, including several which had been used by just a single participant.

4 In addition, Yannis (47, regional manager, cannabis user) did not reveal how many illegal drugs he had used, but he did state that he abandoned his experimentation with 'harder drugs' as he did not enjoy the marked highs and lows that they brought him. The number of illegal drugs he had tried is listed as 'unknown' in Table 3.3.

Table 3.3 Number of illegal drugs tried by participants during their drug careers

Number of illegal drugs tried	*Count*
1	2
2	3
3	7
4	6
5	4
5+	7
unknown	1

Table 3.4 Types of illegal drugs tried by participants during their drug careers

Type of illegal drug	*Number of participants declaring use*
Cannabis	30
LSD	20
Cocaine/crack cocaine	14
Amphetamine	12
Ecstasy	10
Magic mushrooms	9
Heroin	5
DMT/ayahuasca	2
Ketamine	1
Methamphetamine	1
Opium	1
Peyote	1
Tranquilisers	1
Other psychedelics	1

Note: The types of illegal drug listed in Table 3.4 were named as such by the participants themselves. There is some imprecision and inconsistency where participants were not specific about the substances used, or could not fully recall what they had taken (for example, one participant talked of using 'psychedelics'). Where participants were especially vague about their usage of a particular substance (as with Yannis' discussion of 'harder drugs'), this was not counted. Of course, it is perfectly possible that participants may have forgotten or even been unaware of some of the illegal substances that they had used.

In addition to this, Xavier (55, researcher, polydrug user) discussed his ongoing use of so-called 'legal highs' or 'new psychoactive substances' as a supplement to his illegal drug use. Xavier took a decidedly experimental approach to these substances too, regularly seeking out new preparations from a range of online suppliers. Interestingly, some of the other participants stated their explicit opposition to legal highs. For these participants, the lack of clarity about what they contained was a real cause for concern:

> I've never tried any of these new legal highs, I'm totally against legal highs. In fact, somebody came round here one day with a legal high, "you got to try this, you've got to try this", and I looked, "on you go, bye bye", I don't want to see it in my house, legal highs kill. So I'm dead against them. *Nathan, 47, unemployed customs officer due to disability, cannabis user.*

Of the 22 participants who experienced a relatively bounded experimental phase of illegal drug use, for the overwhelming majority this was also the time of their heaviest use. It was a period that was enjoyed, without exception, amongst closely knit groups consisting of friends, family members and partners, and it tended to see illegal drug use become an integral part of socialising:

> It was a case of anything I could get my hands on until I was 21. It was quite extreme really cos some of the lads I knew were quite extreme as well. . . . So yeah, it's virtually everything you can think of up to that age. [I was using] daily. I couldn't, I couldn't stay in, I just couldn't stay in the house at all, I had to go out every night and do something with my mates which usually involved getting off our heads on something. *Malcolm, 44, student, cannabis user.*
>
> The circle of friends I was in, of course then [their music of choice] was called progressive rock, Pink Floyd, Genesis, Led Zeppelin. . . . Yes, and all that stuff. . . . I mean cannabis smoking was common, but there was a lot of pill taking then as well, uppers, downers and all that. . . . It would be uppers, downers, speed, LSD, cannabis. It was anything that was there really. It was that, it was just available, you know what I mean? *Matthew, 52, self-employed civil engineer, cannabis and occasional cocaine user.*

As this suggests, the milieu that participants found themselves part of was often a significant contributory factor in engendering a period of heavier and more experimental illegal drug use. For instance, nine participants suggested that attending university was an important landmark in their drug career. Xavier (55, researcher, polydrug user), for example, saw his drug use 'explode' during his time at university. It increased further when he befriended a chemist who happened to have access to the university laboratories and was adept at making a wide range of psychedelics, and further still when he became a small-time dealer on campus having taken over a 'round' from a fellow student who was moving off campus. Seven participants described how becoming a regular pub goer saw their illegal drug consumption significantly increase. Indeed, Nathan (47, unemployed customs officer due to disability, cannabis user) described how he only came into contact with 'harder' drugs once he began frequenting pubs: 'all I'd ever seen prior to that was cannabis'. Adam (47, unemployed due to disability, cannabis user) began taking illegal drugs and engaged in a sustained experimental phase after he had left home and moved into a squat. Zach (66, retired fitter, cannabis user) was introduced to illegal drugs and experimented modestly whilst in the navy.

For many participants, this was a time that they looked back on with a great deal of fondness. They reminisced at length and delighted in recounting stories replete with humour and warmth. As Eric (40, consultant for relocation firm, cannabis user) put it, 'we were the right age, we knew the risks, we knew the dangers but it doesn't stop you from experimenting'. In the same vein, Roger (44, manager in a small firm, cannabis user) talked of 'a sort of joyous outburst at teenage years', and many others shared similar sentiments:

> And from then it was just like the greatest time, the greatest two years of my life, I had an absolutely brilliant time. Absolutely, from 1969 to '72, absolutely great. . . . Going to all the festivals as well then, going to all the festivals from 1969, '68, '69, I was going to festivals right through till '75. The present wife said it wasn't fair for me to go to the festivals and she couldn't at that time, you know. Cos her father wouldn't let her out, . . . she was only like 15. Festivals, great time! *Matthew, 52, self-employed civil engineer, cannabis and occasional cocaine user.*

The influence of subcultures

As we saw in Chapter 1, the 'archetypal users' in Notley's (2005) sample were likely to have been part of an 'alternative subpopulation' when they were younger. We have already hinted at the fact that a number of our own participants became involved in some of the subcultures that flowered in the post-war years, with Ned (53, unemployed, amphetamine user) deeply engaged in the northern soul scene and Winston (58, academic, cannabis user) beginning to feel part of the hippie movement even before his first experience of illegal drugs. Indeed, the 30-year span of births represented in the sample, from 1944 to 1974 (see Chapter 2, Table 2.2), meant that a great many of the well-known post-war subcultural moments coincided with the early adulthood of the participants. Our oldest participants were coming of age in the 1960s as, for instance, the hippie movement developed, whilst even the very youngest were in a position to catch the tail-end of the acid house culture that emerged in the late 1980s. Of course, many of these subcultures were inextricably bound up with the use of illegal drugs, and some have come to be intrinsically associated in the popular imagination with particular drugs of choice. For Ned, Winston and many other participants, involvement in such movements began to provide the backdrop to their illegal drug use and often framed their heaviest and most experimental phase of use.

Ned's (53, unemployed, amphetamine user) engagement with the northern soul scene stood out as being particularly intense, and he remains involved to this day. His drug of choice was amphetamine, which as we have seen he began using unwittingly in the late 1960s when attending a northern soul all-nighter. Amphetamine use quickly became an integral part of his routine at these now-revered events, as it was for many others who were involved in the scene (Wilson

2007). As Ned put it, 'I did try other little bits and bobs, but as far as I was concerned it just didn't do for me what amphetamines do and that's it, and if it isn't amphetamines I don't want it'.

Four participants identified as hippies when they were younger, and, as with Ned and northern soul, their sense of belonging to the movement significantly shaped their illegal drug use. Matthew (52, self-employed civil engineer, cannabis and occasional cocaine user) recalled his deepening dissatisfaction with the 'straight' world upon leaving school at 16:

> I got an apprenticeship from when I left school, and your hair just got longer and longer and longer, of course it ended up being down there [points to waist] and over a period of about two years, I sort of, I realised that I wasn't a [name of company] type of person, they were very regimented. . . . And me walking in in sandals and walking in on the site, as far as I was concerned I didn't start work till eight o'clock so they couldn't tell me what to wear, and they wanted me to wear safety boots. . . . I was rocking the boat.

After a couple of years, Matthew left his apprenticeship. This heralded a big increase in his drug consumption and, as we saw earlier, 'the greatest two years of my life, . . . I had an absolutely brilliant time'.

We also saw earlier how Winston (58, academic, cannabis user) related his very first experience of illegal drug use to his growing sense that he was part of the hippie movement. This developed further over the ensuing months and years:

> I think part of it might have been, . . . a gang of us took our 'A' Levels a year early so we had a break before we could go to university, so I remember it was that summer, the last summer of finishing school, and as I said I took LSD and that was quite something else, that was an absolute mind-blowing, scary as well as stunningly amazing, and I think after that I thought, Jesus, I'm not sure, it's so close to taking me to places I'd never thought about. I then, I continued to be really interested in the music, and hair getting longer and longer, and seeing myself as a sort of, you know, as part of the hippie freak movement. . . . There was a band called the Incredible String Band who I also did go and see subsequently. They were very much an LSD, a British LSD band, who were very influenced by sort of eastern mysticism, so I was already listening to some of that and the Doors, and Hendrix. I was massively keen on Jimi Hendrix as well as the Beatles of course and all of that, so you know I'd already heard of, you know, 'Lucy in the Sky with Diamonds' and all, knowing that that was about drugs and that, so I was attracted by that probably before I had the LSD.[5]

5 The longstanding rumours that the Beatles' song 'Lucy in the Sky with Diamonds' was about LSD have been repeatedly denied by both Paul McCartney and, before his death, John Lennon (Sheff 2000: 182).

The illegal drug use of two participants was, for a time, decisively shaped by their association with the punk movement in the late 1970s. Once again, involvement in the subculture informed the choice of illegal substances and the manner in which they were consumed, as Roger (44, manager in a small firm, cannabis user) remembered:

> My mate's older brother was the heroin addict and could get his hands on anything, so we used to just have speed to go to concerts and stuff. So actually at the time we used a lot more speed than dope, cause that was the drug we wanted. . . . You've got to remember that this was sort of 77 and we were all into punk. So although we had dope, the drug of choice was speed. [Interviewer's question: How did you initially get into speed?] Er, probably by reading about it in the NME! . . . I mean it was the sort of drug that was associated with punk music, so we wanted it. . . . It was always with mates, same mates I went to school with.

Six participants had been involved in the acid house movement. These participants were especially keen to reminisce at length about their experiences of the 'ecstasy culture' (Collin 1997) that emerged in the UK during the late 1980s. This included Brian (52, company owner, cannabis user), who was already in his late twenties, a father and running his own business when the acid house movement began to gain momentum:

> My brother introduced me to it again, and he's younger than me and we went to this party and he said "do you fancy trying ecstasy?" Well at this time nobody knew about ecstasy, it wasn't heard of, it was very underground, and it was very new and pure, you know there was no criminal fraternity involved at that stage, and we were intrigued and of course we smoked cannabis anyway and we decided to indulge and see what happened. Well I'll never forget my first ecstasy trip. It was absolutely amazing, I mean it's very hard to explain the feeling that it gave you, certainly euphoria, empathy, unconditional love, and the energy to want to dance. It's made music sound completely different you know. You started to hear things that you never heard in a record before. And we just thought we'd found nirvana, we thought "wow, this is it". You know we found something that is utterly amazing. So it was our drug of choice to be honest with you for about five years and most weekends we couldn't wait to go to a club. They were called warehouse raves in them days, you know, they were sort of festivals, sort of in the middle of nowhere all in an old warehouse, called acid house raves in them days, and we used to get a phone number and then you had to ring somebody and then another phone box and until somebody told you where it was. And you had about 10,000 people converging in one space and everybody was doing the same drug, all doing ecstasy and it was just an incredible feeling of oneness, you know, and that, that was something that I particularly liked about it, it brought down all barriers and you were able to communicate and

> say things to people that you probably wanted to say for years and you never, never felt that you could. So ecstasy broke down barriers.

The communal aspect of the acid house experience was particularly important to Brian who, with a regular group of between 20 and 25 friends, began regularly seeking out weekend parties. However, the drugs soon began to lose their edge as they became increasingly impure, and the pressures of parenthood gradually began to limit Brian's scope for recreation:

> I mean we could get away with it in the early days because they were young, they could be babysat, but when they start becoming sort of, sort of eight, nine, ten, they want more time, and weekends really with the kids, so I think because your family is growing up and you want to spend more time with them, it just petered out, you know, I don't think it was a sort of conscious choice to say right let's stop everything, it's just gradually petered out.

Nevertheless, Brian's encounter with ecstasy encouraged him to pursue a relatively late experimental period of illegal drug use, 'because once I experimented with ecstasy and realised that you could have six hours of fun in this little pill, I wanted to try everything else. You know, it was like, well hold on a minute, if that's good I want to try that'.

Xavier (55, researcher, polydrug user) was another participant who enjoyed memorable experiences with friends as part of the acid house subculture. His first encounter with ecstasy was, like Brian's, something of an eye-opening affair:

> I'd never danced in my life and I was sitting at a bar in '89 in a rave club and my friend and a couple of other guys, they'd discovered it a few weeks earlier and they dragged me along. I said "I'm not into nightclubs, I did all that when I was younger". . . . I'd had enough of them. They said "no this is different, you've gotta come, you've gotta come". So we all went and we all took an ecstasy tablet and I said "look, I can't dance, I've got two left feet, I'll just sit at the bar and you lot go off and dance". . . . I'm sitting there at the bar and all of a sudden after 20 minutes the ecstasy starts coming on and these waves of energy start running through my body and this music's starting to pump and all of a sudden they put on a record, Boy George produced it, I forget the guy's name now, anyway the record was called *Everything Starts with an E*,[6] . . . and just as this ecstasy hit my brain this record went, "everything starts with an e" and it went du du du du du du, it started off, and I mean literally my body and my brain

6 *Everything Starts with a E* was a record released in 1989 by E-Zee Possee that came to be seen as one of the defining anthems of the acid house movement. It was produced by Jeremy Healy and Simon Rogers. Healy and Boy George set up the More Protein label specifically to release the record as other labels refused to do so due to its controversial nature, although it was initially supported and distributed by Virgin Records.

> disconnected and my body went onto the dancefloor and started dancing, and this was the first time I'd ever danced and I didn't stop dancing for about seven hours. In fact when I went home the next day I was dancing all round the fucking house. I couldn't stop. It was like it had taken me over. So for a period of about three years, from about '89 to '92, I just took loads of ecstasy. I absolutely loved it. I couldn't get enough of it.

Fascinatingly, some participants embraced a number of different subcultural movements as earlier ones withered away and new ones flowered into being. This included Roger (44, manager in a small firm, cannabis user), who moved on from his early days as a punk who favoured amphetamine and dabbled for a time in the acid house scene and experimented with ecstasy. For Quinn (51, market trader, cannabis and occasional cocaine user):

> LSD was just sort of . . . late '60s, '70s. . . . The cocaine and the ecstasy were more clubbing, we were out clubbing, you know every weekend, we'd be down at the club, dancing. . . . That era, sort of late '80s, '90s, with a totally different crowd of people, . . . not the hippie kind. . . . Before, it was like long skirts and beads and jeans, you know what I mean.

However, by no means did all the participants welcome new subcultural movements and the modes of consumption that went along with them. Tom (41, horticulturalist, cannabis user), discussing the emergence of acid house and ecstasy use, remembered that by that time he was 'an entrenched cannabis user . . . , with not very much interest in the drug of that age'. This was partly because he did not like the idea of using a 'synthesised manufactured chemical' and partly because of his concerns about the potential long term consequences of using a substance with such a profound effect. As a result, despite being attracted by the idea of a 'communal shared tribal experience', he 'completely opted out from it'.

Notwithstanding concerns such as these, it was evident that even those participants who did not explicitly identify with a particular subcultural scene were nonetheless making choices about illegal drug use in a context where subcultures exerted a significant influence on the tastes, fashions and mores of the time. For example, Ollie (52, company owner, cannabis and occasional cocaine user), whilst not considering himself to be a hippie, 'was kind of brought up in what you might remember as being the hippie era really and dope smoking and LSD or acid were probably the two drugs of choice in those days. You're looking at the mid '60s. So it was kind of an era thing'.

The end of the experimental phase

For the overwhelming majority of the participants, their experimentation with various substances and relatively heavy use patterns was transient. Over time, most of the interviewees came to favour one particular drug of choice over others, and they adopted a more restrained pattern of use that fit with their changing circumstances that included, for example, the assumption of greater responsibilities in their working and family lives. The willingness and ability of the participants to find ways to integrate illegal drug use with their circumstances at any given time undoubtedly helped them to sustain their use over the long term, as we will see in the next section. In addition, during their period of experimentation, participants had also tended to discover something about their own personal tolerances of various substances:

> I think [I was at] the point when I realised that it had some pretty, I had fairly low limitations if you want. And doing this stuff . . . very carefully if I was going to do it [was necessary]. . . . I'm not particularly interested in experimentation [now]. I think I probably defined the boundaries and I think I know what it is that I like. And so it would be pretty unlikely I think that I'd experiment [today]. *Vince, 42, academic, cannabis user.*

Furthermore, with the exception of Ned (53, unemployed, amphetamine user) who as we know remained involved with the northern soul scene, none of the participants any longer identified with a subcultural movement. Xavier (55, researcher, polydrug user) for one sensed that his days of subcultural involvement and experimentation were over: 'I've been a hippie, a punk and a raver and now I'm a fucking old man!'

In sum, most of the participants in the study went through a distinct experimental phase that occurred relatively quickly following their initiation into illegal drug use. A small number of participants continued to experiment over the longer term, and an even smaller number did not experiment at all. Most participants had tried a number of different illegal drugs, and as a whole the sample had used a wide range of substances. Experimental phases of use tended to occur in relatively bounded contexts within tightly knit circles of friends, for example during time spent at university, or as part of one's involvement in a particular subculture. But, as circumstances changed and personal preferences were developed and increasingly finely tuned, the experimental period began to draw to a close for the bulk of the participants. Thus, we can see for the first time how transitions in and out of particular contexts and settings had significant effects on the illegal drug consumption of our participants. It is to this issue that we now turn in greater detail.

Transitions in drug careers

The concept of 'transition' has become central to work on the lifecourse (George 1993). Transitions have been defined as 'changes in status (most often role transitions) that are discrete and relatively bounded in duration, although their consequences may be observed over the long term' (George 1996: 250). Scholars of the lifecourse see transitions as being 'embedded' within 'trajectories' (Elder 1994: 5), which are 'pathway[s] or line[s] of development over the life span'

(Laub and Sampson 1998: 227). Trajectories constitute 'long term patterns of stability and change that can be reliably differentiated from alternate patterns. . . . Trajectories often include multiple transitions' (George 1996: 250), and they provide the context for and shape the meaning of each discrete transition. Examples of common transitions include the birth of children, marriage, entry into the labour force, and retirement. A trajectory may include an occupational or educational career, family life, or other similar long-term pathways. Transitions are not to be confused with 'turning points', which constitute another important notion in the lifecourse literature. Turning points are 'a time or event when one took a different direction from that in which one had been travelling'; this marks them out from transitions as the latter do not entail a substantial change in direction even where they lead to changes in activities and priorities (Clausen 1998: 202–6). Similarly, Sampson and Laub see turning points as 'an alteration or deflection in a long-term pathway or trajectory that was initiated at an earlier point in time' (2005: 16). Hareven and Masaoka (1988: 274) have suggested that turning points are best regarded as processes that take place over time rather than as discrete moments. As Carlsson puts it, 'what makes a turning point a turning point, "rather than a minor ripple", is the amount of "sufficient time" that is spent "on a new course" (Abbott 1997: 89, Laub and Sampson 2003: 39)' (2012: 3).

A growing body of research into drug use has utilised the notions of transitions, trajectories and turning points (Boeri 2002), especially when focussing on 'problem users' or 'addicts' (Hser et al. 2007), or on the factors that can lead to desistance. For instance, Cloud and Granfield (2004) noted that certain turning points in other aspects of life appeared to assist drug and alcohol addicts to overcome their addiction without recourse to treatment. Turning points including the assumption of responsibility for children or the death of loved ones who abused drugs often provided powerful motivation to terminate addiction. Jessup et al. (2014) found that for long-term alcohol and other drug users who had been in treatment, life events such as becoming a parent, grandparent or caregiver encouraged abstinence and reduced drug and alcohol intake, whilst the death of a loved one had a more ambiguous effect. Meanwhile, as noted in Chapter 1, Boeri et al. (2011) and Whalen and Boeri (2014) have developed techniques that facilitate the measurement of the continuities and discontinuities that are found within trajectories, and even allow for their visualisation.

For our participants, transitions and turning points in other lifecourse trajectories had substantial effects on their drug careers and often led to shifts in their use patterns. As has been suggested in previous research, drug careers and the transitions within them can be incredibly complex and multifaceted given the way that they interact with other facets of a user's life (Simpson 2003). Upon experiencing a transition or a turning point in, say, their working life, a participant would invariably undergo a related transition in their drug career as they realigned their illegal drug use in order that it remained compatible with the new circumstances that they found themselves in (Chatwin and Porteous 2013).

Two observations are important here. First, perhaps the most striking motif to emerge from the interviews was that the participants' illegal drug use, without exception, was shaped by their circumstances in other aspects of their lives. To put it another way, illegal drug use did not dominate their lives but was contingent upon other aspects of it. Second, given that the participants' illegal drug use was influenced so fundamentally by what was going on elsewhere in their lives, all the participants experienced periods of heavier and lighter use, ebbs, flows, lulls and explosions. Indeed, some had gone through periods of complete cessation and eventual resumption. This supports previous research on similarly sustained illegal drug careers which suggests that, for the most part, patterns of use change over time (Warburton, Turnbull and Hough 2005, McSweeney and Turnbull 2007, Chatwin and Porteous 2013).[7]

As we have already hinted, as participants gradually began to face increasing demands and assume greater responsibility in their lives, the experimental phase enjoyed by so many began to peter out and a more sustainable pattern of illegal drug use was pursued (Vervaeke and Korf 2006). Even where participants considered drug use to be an extremely important facet of their lives, and even where drugs were consumed daily and with great enthusiasm, that drug use was always vulnerable to the next transition or turning point. We saw many examples of transitions and turning points leading participants to reduce their drug use significantly. Yet this was not the whole story. Where altered circumstances allowed it, illegal drug use was often engaged in with a renewed appetite. Thus, there was no sense that drug use inevitably and uniformly declined over the lifecourse. Instead, drug use was continually reassessed and reconfigured in the light of changed conditions in the aftermath of a transition or turning point. The direction of such reconfigurations was always uncertain, and different participants responded to similar transitions and turning points in different ways. Sometimes this led to a decrease in use, sometimes to an increase, and sometimes to a more subtle shift in use patterns.

The history of Matthew's (52, self-employed civil engineer, cannabis and occasional cocaine user) drug career provided an excellent example of how transitions and turning points in other lifecourse trajectories can significantly impact upon illegal drug use. As we have seen, Matthew, along with his prog-rock loving friends, began to use illegal drugs regularly after leaving school at 16 and winning an apprenticeship at a chemical plant. However, his increasing identification as a hippie and dissatisfaction with working life saw him leave his apprenticeship after a couple of years, and there followed an experimental phase of drug use as he became a regular attendee at music festivals during the late

7 Note that we suggest that our participants' drug careers were, in the main, subject to transitions and *not* turning points. This is because even where participants had stopped using illegal drugs for a time, as they were current users the overall trajectory of their drug career had not usually been fundamentally altered by the temporary cessation of use. In Carlsson's terms, when our participants did stop using, they generally did not spend 'sufficient time' on this new course to render it a turning point 'rather than a minor ripple' (2012: 3).

1960s and early 1970s. His drugs of choice at this point were cannabis, speed and LSD. He briefly moved to London, but when the rent on his flat was increased he was forced to move out to a 'quiet, sleepy, country town', where he met the woman who would become his wife. Cut off from friends and with no car, his use immediately declined. Cannabis became an occasional indulgence, and the other drugs he had enjoyed fell completely out of his repertoire: 'I went from really regular use and never thinking about it, to "I've run out, oh well", and it'd be like two, three or four weeks before I'd get, you know, a little bit of smoke'. Following a further short-term move, he eventually went to work on a farm. This represented a major transition and led to period of just under a decade where he did not use illegal drugs at all: 'It wasn't available, it wasn't peer pressured, you know what I mean. I'd literally made a complete break from friends. . . . When we were up there, it was just, there was nothing there. I mean I was out in the middle of nowhere'. His first child was born during this period.

By the turn of the 1980s Matthew had become 'fed up with working for . . . a pound an hour, 20 hours a day, you know what I mean'. He got a job on a nearby building site and moved back into the town:

> So I moved from the farm back into the town and even then, I mean, I was there for two, three years before anything came along and then it was just very casual use more or less. . . . The stopping and the starting of it was more or less just to do with the fact that I moved. . . . If I was moving into an area [where cannabis] was really, really available, then I'd smoke it, if I moved somewhere it wasn't, I didn't. That was it.

His move into the building trade set him on a trajectory that eventually led to his current occupation as a civil engineer. His second child was born during this period, and this also tempered his drug use somewhat. Yet, following a further move to another town in the mid-1980s, his use gradually began to increase as his children grew older. He still resided in this town, and his current use was reasonably steady. He generally smoked cannabis daily, but his use did become heavier if he was undergoing a particularly stressful period at work. However, he did cease smoking cannabis completely for a few months following a takeover of the company he worked for. His new bosses introduced a drug-testing policy, so, erring on the side of caution, he took to drinking gin instead. Once he was confident that the testing policy was only being used for those whose performance at work was not deemed to be satisfactory, he resumed his use of cannabis and, on occasion, cocaine.

Matthew's was the archetypal story. The transitions and turning points he experienced were manifold. He had enjoyed a varied working life with some significant changes in direction. He had resided in a number of different locations under different living arrangements. He had got married and raised a family. He had seen his proximity to friends and fellow users vary considerably over time. He had worked for employers with different attitudes towards drugs.

Thus, it is unsurprising that his drug career had not followed a straightforward, linear trajectory. Each transition and turning point forced him to reconfigure his illegal drug use in order that it fit with his changed circumstances. Where this was not possible, he simply stopped using for a time. Thus, Matthew's drug use always remained contingent upon these other aspects of his life. And, whilst the fine details of each participant's story were very different, and the circumstances they found themselves in varied enormously, all were willing and able, like Matthew, to re-align their illegal drug consumption to suit each new situation they encountered. In the remainder of this section we will offer some examples of this.

Occupational transitions

Changes of job and of occupation, as we saw in Matthew's case, were crucial in shaping the participants' illegal drug use. Almost all participants had byzantine employment histories. Many had worked in several different industries or professions. Even those who had remained in a single industry or profession had usually worked for several different employers. Unsurprisingly given this history, participants had experienced a number of transitions and one or more turning points in their employment trajectories. These transitions and turning points typically had significant impacts upon the participants' illegal drug use, but the impacts were not uniform. Much depended upon the demands of what was being left behind as compared to what was being moved into. Becoming a student, for instance, often led to heavier and more experimental use as participants entered a milieu where illegal drug use was more commonplace and routine:

> I started back again, using cannabis regularly when I went to university. . . . Being a student again, you'd go to parties and there'd be cannabis there. *Simon, 61, researcher, cannabis user.*
>
> Then I went to university, and you know, regular drinking, meeting up with people, again in social situations, I never went out and bought it myself at that point, it was just a case of, it was there, other people brought it and I was just kind of going along with it you know. But yeah I remember sort of going to this house, and other people were doing it and it was just like, "oh, okay I'll have a joint, I'll join in with you", and again it was a social situation where other people were doing it. I suppose it's like going out and having a drink. When other people are drinking you do it, when other people are smoking you do it, do you know, it's that kind of thing. *Fran, 41, retired due to disability, cannabis user.*

Some, like Matthew, were forced to suspend their consumption for a time when they changed job or occupation. For example, in order to obtain a licence for his new line of work, Nathan (47, unemployed customs officer due to disability, cannabis user) had to undergo a drugs test and so he abstained for three months.

This was the only break he had ever taken during a drug career that began at the age of 11. Ian (46, unemployed, cannabis user) found himself in a similar position for a time. He worked for London Underground and then British Rail, both of which employed regular drug screenings: 'I worked for them for about three years and so I gave it up over that period, just to save my job like'.[8]

Perhaps most fundamentally, it was only through regular work that the participants realised the money to purchase drugs; for some, when work was unavailable, drug use inevitably declined. Ian (46, unemployed, cannabis user) was in this position:

> Yeah, easiest way I'd put it is when I'm working I do smoke more because I can afford to buy it. When I'm out of work like now, I don't smoke it so much . . . simply because I can't afford to buy it.

Even for those in work, a lack of disposable income could curb drug use to a degree. For example, Fran (41, retired due to disability, cannabis user) and her partner at the time stopped using in their late twenties due to concerns that they were beginning to spend too much money:

> Financially my partner was concerned, quite concerned that we were smoking too much, you know, and maybe at that time . . . , we did it regular on a Friday night but maybe at that time I was saying "you know, let's get some more on other days", and I think my partner was concerned that we were spending too much money on it so we kind of, you know we just kind of stopped doing it really, it was like okay let's take control, kind of thing, and try and be responsible and all this kind of thing. But yeah, we just stopped doing it for a couple of years.

Residential transitions

As Matthew's case clearly demonstrated, changes in one's place of residence also had the potential to beget dramatic shifts in the drug consumption patterns of our participants. House moves, which were often undertaken due to changes in employment, tended to herald a period of lighter use or even temporary cessation, particularly when the new place of residence was located in a different village, town or city from the old residence. In general it was not the change of location in and of itself that resulted in reduced use, but rather the fact that participants became isolated from established social networks of other users. In

8 There is evidence that drug careers are not always dominated by one's working life. Vervaeke and Korf (2006) found that long-term, heavy ecstasy users aged 38–55 in Amsterdam appeared to give priority to their social life, and adapted their work situation accordingly. Nevertheless, Vervaeke and Korf's respondents did employ strategies to prevent their ecstasy use from adversely affecting their functioning at work. This included working in jobs with shorter or flexible hours and tempering their ecstasy use in busy periods.

addition, the ready availability of supplies was also often lost in the wake of house moves:

> When I came down here, there wasn't any, I didn't really know people that were sort of into smoking cannabis. . . . Really it was a change of circumstance and not knowing people and not knowing people who were smoking cannabis. *Simon, 61, researcher, cannabis user.*

On the other hand, moving to a location where one already had a network of drug-using friends could promote an increase in use:

> I smoked a lot more when I went to [town A], that's for sure. And then, smoked even more when I came to [town B]. . . . When I was in [town C] it was, again, I wasn't with a lot of friends who smoked a lot. And it changed when I went to [town A] so often as not it's the people you know, socialising. That means a lot, more than anything. . . . Location, location, location! *Uri, 47, care worker, cannabis user.*

Some participants had lived and worked in a different country for a time. Such moves clearly represented considerable transitions or turning points, and in general saw illegal drug use decline, in part due to a loss of ready access to drugs, and in part due to the threat of sanctions in the host country. However, for the determined and connected participant, continued illegal drug use was possible. Eric (40, consultant for relocation firm, cannabis user), with the advantage of a 'fixer' provided to him by his employer, was able to continue his use in a variety of locations:

> Like I say, I've lived in New Zealand, Australia, the US, Canada, Kuwait, working over there on different assignments. And yeah, pretty much once you get somewhere, you're working in an industry where you can speak to local people and they will always find you a dealer. And yeah it's pretty much daily.

Periods spent abroad could also result in difficulties in obtaining supplies once participants returned home. For instance, Derek (50, gardener, cannabis and occasional mushroom user) found it difficult to source cannabis bud when he returned to the UK from the US:

> I didn't use any drugs for quite a long time when I came back to England. I was interested in getting cannabis again but I couldn't. I did know people who smoked but they were all smoking hash with tobacco and I didn't smoke tobacco so I didn't want to touch that.

Eventually, Derek relented and started to use hash alongside his friends. To his chagrin, his fears were soon realised and he found himself quickly becoming addicted to tobacco.

Family transitions

Transitions and turning points in family life also had substantial impacts upon the participants' illegal drug consumption. For example, getting together with a partner was often noteworthy in this regard. Where that new partner was not a drug user, the motivation to end use could be considerable (Boeri et al. 2011: 90). Ned (53, unemployed, amphetamine user), for example, went through a period of abstinence when he got married to a non-using partner:

> Well, I had five years not having it when I got married and obviously when things went wrong I went back to what I do best [laughs]. [Interviewer: "Why did you stop?"] Because I got married, more or less, yeah, and the girl I was marrying didn't take anything. . . . She had two children and they came to live with me and I stopped taking.

Becoming a parent was also a significant event that for many participants led to a marked decrease or even a complete cessation in their illegal drug use. As we have seen, Matthew (52, self-employed civil engineer, cannabis and occasional cocaine user) told us: '[during] the formative years of my children, I didn't really use'. Fran (41, retired due to disability, cannabis user) recalled: '[I] had a child when I was 18 so I wasn't drinking you know, I wasn't sort of taking anything, I was trying to concentrate on being a parent'.

Indeed, many participants experienced multiple transitions in their family life over a relatively short period of time. These multiple transitions, which typically saw them assume greater responsibilities, tended to check their illegal drug use markedly.

> Then I got married, bought my own house and had to behave sort of sensibly for a while, so it just dropped off the edge of my radar really for quite a long time. [Interviewer: "When you got married and had a young child, what was your use like then?"] Nothing, nil, zero. That was 1986 and it just didn't enter my particular world at that time. *Keith, 63, retired civil servant, cannabis user.*
>
> I mean I didn't really smoke [for] so long and I got married and I never really bothered, I mean for a long time. You know when the children were young I never even bothered. I sort of had a break really for a, quite a lot of years really . . . I suppose there wasn't any available and just one thing and another, you know. You know, I had family and children and stuff like that, it was just, it really wasn't the thing to be doing I suppose. *Lenny, 53, mechanic, cannabis user.*

Unsurprisingly, transitions and turning points in family life that were particularly momentous could have a profound influence on drug use. Quinn (51, market trader, cannabis and occasional cocaine user), for example, having used drugs regularly and experimented widely throughout her twenties, stopped abruptly when a personal tragedy befell her: 'I split up from this first boyfriend when I was 30 and I was on my own for quite a long time, then I actually went out with another guy who was a morphine addict. And after he'd died, I actually stopped taking drugs'.

However, transitions and turning points in family life did not always have the effect of curbing the illegal drug use of the participants. In certain circumstances, transitions could lead to an increase in use. As we have seen, Ned's (53, unemployed, amphetamine user) drug use had stopped after he got married and took on the children born to his wife whilst she was in a previous relationship. Ned then became a father to two children of his own, but the relationship with his wife was soon to end in divorce. After this, he quickly began using amphetamine on a regular basis once again. As he put it, 'then I got two more kids and everything went pear shaped and then I started again'. Meanwhile, Pat (51, unemployed, polydrug user) significantly increased her consumption and broadened her drugs repertoire when she married a heavy user: 'When I got married . . . I started using speed and that. Speed and blow, got right into blow then, right heavy. I started getting into speed and just a bit of whatever was going'.

Even having children did not necessarily reduce drug use. Brian's (52, company owner, cannabis user) and his partner's use actually increased following the birth of their children. Their relatively late experimental phase that we discussed earlier coincided with their becoming parents and was aided by the fact that Brian's own parents lived close by:

> Early thirties, yeah, most of it was probably intense for a five-to-six-year spell, and it was probably almost every weekend. I mean we had babysitters on tap with my parents . . . yeah my mum and dad always had the kids. We said "we're going clubbing", so we go out Friday night and pretty much cane it all day Friday, Saturday, and the kids would be dropped back to us Sunday evening and then you'd have a working week, you know.

However, as we also saw earlier, as Brian's children grew older, weekends were increasingly reserved for family activities, and so his heavy use on Fridays and Saturdays 'just gradually petered out'.

Whilst the intricacies of each participant's family life were unique, it was nevertheless clear that the ebbs and flows of a drug career were always intimately related to changing family dynamics. This was well illustrated by Winston (58, academic, cannabis user) when he discussed life during his twenties:

> You know I'd got a job that's well paid and all that, and I had a family, had a daughter quite young, you know, actually had a daughter at the end of my third year at university. So there was an issue then about how you balance. I sort of went into a quieter lifestyle while we were with my first partner, we brought up the babe. By the time we'd sort of split up, at probably, you know, my daughter was five when we stopped living together full on and we started seeing her, you know, two days a week or whatever. And it was only then that I started to go a bit sort of wilder again, fun

> seeking and out and about, you know. So it's interesting, [it] depends on your rhythms of family life.

Health transitions

A number of participants had developed health problems at some point during their lifecourse, and this had often impacted significantly upon their illegal drug use. Fran (41, retired due to disability, cannabis user), for example, became seriously ill in her thirties, was forced to retire on medical grounds, and stopped using illegal drugs for a number of years as she was taking a range of prescription medications in order to control the pain that she was suffering from. However, her prescription medication was not a success:

> I'd been taking nine tablets a day, every four hours, for seven years, and I was more ill than my symptoms made me. . . . Every day I had nausea and headaches, every single day from taking the medication, you know, my health was declining basically, so I just wanted to stop taking the medication. I got to a point where I couldn't physically put a tablet in my mouth anymore because I had all these thoughts in my head about everything that was going on. I just thought, basically, I would be on medication for life because of my issues and . . . I thought I'm going to, I want to do something different, I don't want to be taking this medication and make myself even more poorly, and that's what I did.

Her solution to this problem was to begin using cannabis again in what she now regarded as a fruitful attempt to manage her pain. Although Fran was not alone in seeing her patterns of illegal drug use change markedly in response to health issues, she was unique in that those issues had led her to completely stop using illegal drugs, before subsequently motivating her to begin using once again. Thus Fran's case brings the uneven and unpredictable effects of transitions and turning points on drug careers into sharp relief.

Furthermore, in some cases health problems had led participants to perceive of their continuing illegal drug use in very different terms. For instance, Ian (46, unemployed, cannabis user) had been diagnosed with osteoarthritis, and Nathan (47, unemployed customs officer due to disability, cannabis user) suffered a serious spinal injury at work that forced his early retirement. In the aftermath of these events, both men continued to use cannabis, and their patterns of use and levels of consumption did not change significantly. However, they had found cannabis to be a very effective tool of pain management and as a result reconceptualised their use as being primarily for medical reasons. As we will see in Chapter 4, this was not uncommon.

Multiple transitions

Previous research has suggested that multiple and intersecting transitions can often have significant effects upon an individual's lifecourse. Transitions which, in isolation, could be easily managed can prove extremely disruptive when they are faced simultaneously with or in close proximity to other transitions (Baltes and Baltes 1990, Carstensen 1992, Baltes 2003). For our participants, as we have already seen in relation to family life, multiple transitions tended to engender very pronounced and rapid changes in their drug use. Winston (58, academic, cannabis user), for example, identified a number of transitions experienced over a relatively short period of time in early adulthood that contributed to striking increases in his level of cannabis consumption. He moved out of his parents' home to attend university, and then, at the end of his first year of undergraduate studies, moved out of halls of residence into a shared house with friends. These residential shifts were accompanied by his increasing involvement in a peer group for whom cannabis was the choice leisure option, his desire to limit his intake of LSD after some slightly uncomfortable experiences, and his growing association with what he described as the 'hippie freak' subculture. Winston's account again reminds one of the process of becoming that Becker (1953) famously described:

> Towards the end, I guess, of the first year at university, we were in a hall of residence. Although we thought we were really hip it was actually quite a controlled environment really, and then it was really only when we all moved out and got a student house and then we really became cool dudes, you know, and, and marijuana became a sort of vital aspect of the whole, of what it was to be who you were, you know, in that student life. . . . Well again, it was because of having friends who were smoking, and as I knew I had to learn how to sort of enjoy it, I was keen, I was keener to start getting into marijuana rather than having LSD too often, let's put it that way, you know. And we didn't drink a lot of alcohol either, that was seen as uncool by then. You know, [we] very rarely went into pubs, partly because we thought people were looking at us even if they weren't, and you know on the odd occasion they probably were because we looked, you know, we did look the part, you know, very long haired, unconventionally dressed.

Later in Winston's drug career, the manner in which he managed transitions and incorporated drug use into his changing circumstances continued to be influenced by his subcultural milieu and his strong political views. For instance, upon becoming a postgraduate student, Winston became heavily involved in the alternative information centre movement, giving out advice on issues such as squatting and drug busts. He also contributed to underground, 'alternative' publications, 'so I guess I increasingly sort of tried to attach my recreational substance use to a broader sense of the movement, political or social movement'.

In a similar fashion, but with the opposite effect, Uri (47, care worker, cannabis user) noted that the perfect storm of his drug-using associates moving out of the area, greater responsibility at work, and the inevitable biological decline of the body in his early thirties all contributed to a general reduction in his consumption:

> Well, some people moved away, my work got more serious, things to do. I was busy then, I guess I just slowed down a bit. Thirty-five and I can get stoned with a few joints rather than you know, going out till two in the morning being stoned. Ah, you know things change, people change, and people slow down. I can't think of anybody who's still doing that actually.

The cumulative effect of several transitions over a period of time could, unsurprisingly, have major effects on the participants' illegal drug use. Vince (42, academic, cannabis user), for example, took a lengthy and almost complete break from illegal drug use having endured a difficult period during his late teens:

> I think I found it was affecting my life in quite negative way. You know, you know, sort of my exams for schooling, my psyche as well, you know, I was getting kind of depressed and alienated and so on. And I felt that it would probably be a good idea to pack all of that in. So I had a bit of a crisis I guess, you know. I stopped when I was 19 and I don't think I had it again for several, several years. Although occasionally, I think occasionally, yeah occasionally over those years, you know I would indulge now and again. But very, very occasionally, and I didn't start again until 1996, I think. Yeah, 1996. Yeah, so it's quite a long time in between time, and I very, very seldom indulged.

However, after a further series of transitions that occurred over a relatively lengthy period of time, by his early thirties Vince had arrived in a position where he felt able to increase his use significantly:

> I think I felt that my life was you know, a lot of things had changed in my life and I was in a different place. And I was actually just enjoying life at the time. It's actually very hard to put my finger on exactly why, but it was always just a feeling about that was something I wanted to do. I don't think I ever, ever stopped, I don't think I ever stopped enjoying the effects of it. I always knew it was something that I liked, I just knew there were costs and something that had to be managed and so I left it alone for a long time because I also felt that I needed to achieve some things in my life and that this was gonna prevent me from doing that. But then about 1996, I'd finished my degree, gone back to university and finished the degree, I'd been married for a few years, I was living back in [town] after being away for a long time and it actually just felt like something I wanted to do at that stage. I didn't, I wasn't really part of the culture at all, I didn't really know. I did know some friends who were drug takers but I didn't sort of associate with them very much. . . . So, I was having a lot, I grew some, I was smoking it daily and enjoying it greatly! Because you

> know, I was in the right place sort of mentally and psychologically as well to enjoy. There weren't other things that were conflicting. I didn't have any very serious pressures at the time.

We can see very clearly in this passage how Vince's return to regular drug use was not the result of one particularly momentous transition or turning point, or the outcome of an especially disruptive set of multiple transitions, although clearly such events can have significant impacts on drug-use patterns. Instead it was the result of a series of transitions, in and of themselves all fairly routine, the cumulative effect of which made illegal drug use an attractive proposition once again.

Linked lives and transitions

The notion of 'linked lives' has become another important tenet of studies of the lifecourse (see, for example, Lang and Carstensen 1998). It captures the idea that an individual's lifecourse is closely bound up with the lifecourses of others, and, as a result, the transitions and turning points that individuals experience, and the manner in which they are handled, are closely related to the nature of these intimate relationships. As Grenier has put it, 'together, a focus on linked lives, and the relational and emotional significance of these connections, allows for a more complex interpretation of . . . people's narratives that challenge transition as an individually experienced event' (2012: 138). In this light it was unsurprising that the way that transitions and turning points affected the illegal drug use of our participants always made most sense in the context of their relationships with significant others in their lives. For example, as we have already seen in the case of Pat (51, unemployed, polydrug user), participants often saw an increase in their own consumption of illegal drugs when they met a new partner who was a regular user. This also happened to Fran (41, retired due to disability, cannabis user). Her drug use became significantly heavier immediately after she left university as her new partner was from a family of regular users:

> I started going out with a guy and his family, his brothers and sisters, they all smoked weed basically. So I guess, I'm trying to think, maybe I was about 23 then. So yeah, I met these people and then I sort of became a regular weed smoker if you like, you know because I was with people who regularly smoked and yeah, I was probably around 23 then.

However, perhaps the most obvious manifestation of linked lives was when participants reported that transitions and turning points in *somebody else's* lifecourse had affected their own drug career. Adam (47, unemployed due to disability, cannabis user), for example, described how the period of experimentation that he had enjoyed whilst squatting came to an abrupt end: '[It was] a chain of events. You see I fell out with my parents, sort of left home, went out squatting for five years by myself, doing what I wanted, and then my mum got ill and I thought I'd better go back home'. From that point on, he became a user of cannabis alone. Liam (45, unemployed, cannabis user) had lived in the US as a child and joined the US Army at a young age, but his friends took a different path that would ultimately influence his own drug career: 'When I went to the army, my friends went to university and found drugs'. After coming out of the army at the age of 21, he reconnected with his friends and resumed his drug use: 'So when I came back from the army there was a lot of things going on. . . . I hit Colorado and I just started using cannabis quite recreationally'.

Drug careers, transitions and adaptability

Of course, the stories that our participants told about their drug careers were incredibly diverse and complex in their small details. Each participant, located in a material context unique to them, faced different transitions and turning points at different times, and each one reacted to these shifts in idiosyncratic ways. As a result, one drug career often looked very different from another. However, there were certain consistencies. For instance, it was clear that our participants did not fit 'the standard addiction narrative [that] predicts ever-increasing consumption of the drug of choice over time' (Chatwin and Porteous 2013: 244). Furthermore, as we have seen throughout this section, the ebbs and flows of each participant's drug use were closely related to the transitions and turning points that they experienced in other facets of their life. As Ollie (52, company owner, cannabis and occasional cocaine user) perceptively suggested, the fluctuations in his own drug career could be put down to the impacts of 'different time, different place, different people'. Drug careers did not constitute autonomous trajectories with their own unfolding logic but were largely determined by the direction of other trajectories and the changes that occurred in them. Thus, for every participant, their pattern of illegal drug use was subject to constant reconfiguration in response to their immediate situation. At times this process was barely perceptible, whilst in the aftermath of a transition or turning point in some other domain of life it was marked. Indeed, that all the participants had been able to sustain a drug career over the long term illustrated not only the importance of drug use to them (see Chapter 4) but also how adept they had been at bending their use to fit with circumstantial changes that were often far beyond their direct control. Their lengthy drug careers were a triumph of adaptability.

Transitions in late modernity: permanent liminality and sustained illegal drug use

According to Grenier, 'typical understandings of transitions across the lifecourse are derived from the stages of development, with childhood, middle age and late life marking expected stages, and roles defined in relation to family, work and society' (2012: 8). Indeed, as Mitchell suggests, the conventional view of transitions and trajectories is 'that progress along trajectories is generally age-graded such that some transitions can be viewed as more "age appropriate" while others violate normative social timetables by occurring "too early" or "too late" (Hagestad and Neugarten 1985)' (2003: 18). Halberstam (2005) and Lander (2015), as we saw in Chapter 1, add that 'life schedules' also tend to be inherently class-coded, based upon a middle-class perspective that values supposed respectability and normality. Among the many examples of transitions that are typically seen as being 'off-age' (Mitchell 2003: 18) or 'not follow[ing] the straight line of normality' (Lander 2015: 274) are leaving home at a very young age and becoming a teenage parent.

However, as the above discussion of our participants' drug careers suggests, the idea of neatly defined stages of development and 'on' and 'off' age transitions conceals the complexity and unpredictability of the lifecourse trajectories that subjects experience in the real world. Indeed, it could be quite plausibly suggested that our participants, simply by virtue of their continued illegal drug use, had failed to make one of the supposedly typical 'on-age' transitions that is expected of them, for they had not 'matured out' of their drug use as they grew older (Lander 2015). One is reminded in particular of Ned (53, unemployed, amphetamine user), who was still deeply involved with the northern soul subculture he first engaged with during his teenage years. As he put it, 'soul music's kept going for the last 30 years so I suppose I have [laughs]!' Meanwhile, we have also seen how, for instance, Vince (42, academic, cannabis user) returned to cannabis in his thirties and Brian (52, company owner, cannabis user) became involved in the acid house movement when already a parent and running his own business. Indeed, there were countless examples of participants resisting the 'straight line of normality' and violating the timetables proposed by conventional 'life schedules'. Often this occurred in relatively mundane ways, such as when participants entered or exited the labour force or 'typical' family roles at unusual times (Grenier 2012: 9). Ultimately, the conventional notions of trajectories and 'life schedules' would seem to be of only limited utility in attempting to make sense of the actual life histories and drug careers of our participants.

As Hser, Longshore and Anglin suggest, any analysis of trajectories, transitions and turning points must attend to the way in which they are shaped by broader historical contexts and social structures (2007: 517–8). Consequently, such an analysis must pay heed to the highly disruptive socio-economic shifts of recent decades that have significantly refashioned life in the Western world. These shifts have generated a huge literature which explores a number of now-familiar themes. The relative stability of modernity – with its bounded national markets, Keynesian state machinery committed to welfare principles, relatively good prospects for secure lifelong employment, and broad consensus on norms and values – is being progressively eroded (Moxon and Waters 2010). Spurred on by processes of globalisation and the promotion of neoliberalism by national governments and suprastate bodies, the major industries of modernity have contracted, and organised labour has been rendered largely impotent. The so-called 'precariat' (Standing 2011) is growing rapidly, and, as Bauman has argued, contemporary working life 'is saturated with uncertainty' (2000: 147). Market principles have expanded into once sacrosanct areas of civil society, and an aggressive individualism and consumerism has emerged. In such a context, the axes of work, family and community often no longer provide fixity of condition or a stable basis for identity formation, and 'ontological insecurity' abounds (Giddens 1990, 1991). The decimation of the so-called occupational communities that grew up around specific industries in specific places, 'where interaction in work spills over into non-work time, and where workers and their families are relatively self-enclosed, so forming the main reference group for those who belong' (Warwick and Littlejohn 1992: 27) has been particularly problematic in this regard.[9] Although it may be that the core Western capitalist value of 'entrepreneurial individualism' remains firmly entrenched (Hall, Winlow and Ancrum 2008: 131), former normative certainties about the lifecourse are dissolving, and existence is marked by an increasing economic and ontological precariousness. Individuals are no longer restricted by tradition but are instead confronted with a plethora of life choices and a demand to create meaning and identity for themselves as they negotiate these choices. This process of self-actualisation is placed on the political agenda through the notion of 'life politics' (Giddens 1991). Of course, uncertainty, insecurity and remorseless – often cataclysmic – change have been part of the very fabric of capitalism from its outset. What can be termed 'late modernity', however, has catalysed these processes and resulted in what Young (2007) called the 'vertigo' of living and working in contemporary conditions.

It is becoming increasingly apparent that these contemporary socio-economic shifts are threatening some of the foundational concepts that have been developed in the lifecourse literature. The very ideas of 'on' and 'off' age transitions and the notion of a neat, linear progression through the lifecourse via a series of standard, widely shared and precisely timed stages, are redolent of the relatively ordered and stable social world of post-war modernity and are becoming increasingly outmoded as the material underpinnings of that world are steadily worn away. The transitions that typically marked the lifecourse during the years of post-war modernity have been revealed as socially constructed passages through a particular material context. Indeed, we have argued previously (Moxon and Waters 2010) that the lifecourse trajectories of our participants were characterised not by a predictable sequence of transitions but instead by 'broken narratives'. In place of the orderly progression of the modern lifecourse, our participants had experienced abrupt and unplanned shifts in circumstance, instability and volatility. The effect of this on the drug careers of our participants, as we have seen, was profound.

The notion of 'liminality' has been posited as a potentially useful way of thinking about transitions in light of these changed circumstances. Its roots lie in the

9 The classic examples of occupational communities were those that grew up around the coal mining industry (Bulmer 1975).

anthropological work on rites of passage by van Gennep (1960), first published in 1909, which was later taken up by Turner (1967, 1969). Liminality originally denoted the ambiguous period during a ritual when participants were in a kind of limbo between their pre-ritual status and what would become their post-ritual selves. In Turner's phrase, the liminal period was an 'interstructural' one. But, as Thomassen has suggested, 'liminal experiences are not always solely embedded in a ritual structure – liminality, applied to a broader social science and historical perspective, can also refer to events that simply happen, and happen *to* us'. Indeed, in its broadest sense, liminality 'is about how human beings, in their various social and cultural contexts, deal with change', from the highly personal, such as falling in love, to collective events such as natural disasters (2015: 40–1).

Thus, in recent times liminality has come to be seen as a concept referring not only to the specifics of the ritual situation but to processes of change in general, and the disruption, uncertainty and feelings of 'in between-ness' that individuals experience when going through such processes. Indeed, Thomassen (2009: 16–7) has outlined how the concept of liminality can be applied to both time (single moments, longer periods or whole epochs) and space (specific thresholds or more extended ones such as border lands, or even whole territories or countries). Furthermore, 'liminality is also applicable to single individuals, larger groups and entire societies' (Thomassen 2015: 48). Whilst many liminal experiences occur in settings where much else remains 'normal', there are circumstances where personal and societal liminality have converged to produce something akin to a 'pure liminality' of particular intensity (Szakolczai 1998), such as during times of war.[10]

Hockey and James point out that van Gennep's 'overarching concern' was the stability of society, and for him the ritual and the ceremonial were means of ensuring that transitions were regulated in a manner that ensured their orderly and predictable nature (2003: 24–5).[11] According to Thomassen,

> if moving into liminality can best be captured as a loss of home and a ritualised rupture with the world as we know it, any movement out of liminality must somehow relate to a sort of home-coming, a feeling at home *in* the world and *with* the world, at the levels of both thought and practice.
>
> (2014: 17)

10 For an excellent history of the concept of liminality, see Thomassen (2009, 2015). Much later in his career, Turner (1982) developed the idea of the 'liminoid'. He argued that in modern consumer societies liminal experiences have been largely replaced by 'liminoid moments', 'where creativity and uncertainty unfold in art and leisure activities' (Thomassen 2015: 47). The liminoid moment is optional and represents a playful, fantastical break from the normal. As Thomassen points out, the liminoid differs from the liminal for it does not involve a change of status or the resolution of personal crisis and as a result lacks the sense of transition that is a key feature of liminality. Nevertheless, it has become a well-utilised concept in a range of disciplines (Thomassen 2015: 47).

11 This notion was less evident in Turner's notion of liminality. He saw liminality as a time and space where social structures were suspended and open to scrutiny and dissection. Thus, for Turner, liminality held out the possibility of structural transformation (see 1969: 156).

In pre-modern times, a range of coping mechanisms were available to the subject which allowed them to insulate themselves from the uncertainties of liminality and achieve a sense of being 'at home' which lent a relative if precarious stability to social life. As Little et al., drawing on the work of Giddens (1990), suggest, pre-modern peoples

> balanced their profile of risk with tradition (which gave them links and continuity with their past), close bonding with their families and social circles (which gave them a place in the present and some assurance about the future), and religion (which gave them some promise of a future beyond the disturbing boundedness of life).
>
> (1998: 1492)

Such coping mechanisms are increasingly unavailable to the atomised consumer-citizen of late modernity, despite the dangers of such a situation. As Thomassen warns,

> no culture would be foolish enough to devise a ritual sequence that stops at the liminal. Without a return to normality and background structures that one can take for granted (at least until they are shaken again), individuals go crazy and societies become pathological. Human life ceases to be meaningful in perpetual liminality. And yet, there is an extent to which this is exactly what happened in one specific transition, the one that lies at the heart of social theorising: the transition to modernity.
>
> (2014: 216)

To an extent, the Keynesian state apparatus of the post-war era helped to keep liminality as unleashed by modernity in check. However, the convulsions of late modernity have seen these safety mechanisms purposely disassembled or left to atrophy (Little et al. 1998: 1491), and the liminal, once stifled and suppressed, has been freed. As Thomassen has suggested, 'liminality somehow came to occupy a more and more central place within the space of modernity, a process which is currently accelerating to the point of absurdity' (2014: 11). The incessant change that characterises late modernity can be seen as involving the routinisation or, as Thomassen puts it, the 'institutionalisation of liminality' (2015: 54). Furthermore, the effects of the liminal are increasingly felt not only in an experiential sense but also in the arena of contemporary thought where fear, anxiety, scepticism and doubt, each 'quintessential liminal sentiments', have come to dominate (Thomassen 2014: 14). Indeed, it has even been suggested that modernity has created a kind of 'permanent liminality' (Szakolczai 2000; see also Little at al. 1998) with little prospect of any kind of resolution or 'home-coming'.

It is in this light that liminality can be seen as 'a prism through which to understand the contemporary world' (Horvath, Thomassen and Wydra 2015: 1), a concept whose time has come. A growing body of work is emerging that utilises liminality to provide better understandings of a range of disparate phenomena. Horvath, Thomassen and Wydra have suggested that in addition to 'in-between' situations, the notion of liminality can also assist in the understanding of 'conditions characterised by the dislocation of established structures, the reversal of hierarchies, and uncertainty about the continuity of tradition and future outcomes' as well as 'sudden irruptions of existential crisis in people's lives, loss of meaning, ambivalence and disorientation' (2015: 2–3). Malksoo (2015) discussed the notion of 'perma-war' and the endless security concerns of contemporary life in terms of liminality. Reynolds (2007) identified the emergence of a liminal generation in Ireland which has lived through the social transformation from modernity to late modernity. Szakolczai reads the current vogue for identity politics as an attempt to escape the 'spinning wheel of permanent liminality' (2000: 217). Thomassen's understanding of the housing market crisis of 2008 that had catastrophic consequences around the world suggests that liminality is inscribed into the very logic of the operation of neoliberal capitalist markets, and is thus scarcely possible to escape:

> From the prevailing economic rationality, the crisis is connected to the fact that prices go down, and that the market is 'stuck'. The fact that enormous numbers of people and families have literally lost their homes should and must not be neglected, but in economic terms, this is not exactly where the nature of the crisis resides. When the market is stuck, it means that fewer people are selling and fewer people buying. In other words, people stay where they are, and keep living in their houses, and less money is generated. The very fact that this is automatically seen as a crisis *is* the real crisis, a clear indication that contemporary culture is problematically *oikophoic* at its core. But this is the rationality, and governments constantly run behind it as they desperately try to introduce reforms that will inject new energy into the housing market.
> (2014: 223)

Thus, it seems that we live in an economic system that *requires* liminality and the incessant insecurity, upheaval and dislocation it brings, in order to generate the money, capital and growth that it depends upon to legitimise itself. The late modern subject must therefore exist through countless vertiginous 'periods of uncertainty, anguish, even existential fear' and continually cope with 'a feeling of the abyss or the void' (Horvath 2013: 2). Indeed, Szakolczai has suggested that

> human life is not possible and worth living without some degree of stability, meaning and a sense of home. Liminality is indeed a source of renewal, a restoration of meaning, the pouring of fresh wine into old bottles. But if there are no proper "bottles", the fermenting power is diluted and lost. If everything is continuously changing, then things always remain the same.
> (2000: 217)

Transitions have previously been conceptualised as liminal periods of 'being between' (Spencer 1990, Hockey and James 2003), or, in Turner's words, 'betwixt and between' (1967). However, when transitions are seen as taking place within an epoch of permanent liminality, in a social world that lacks stability and normative consensus, then the shoots of a reconfigured understanding of them become visible. It makes little sense to see transitions as brief liminal interludes that herald entry into a fresh period of stability or the emergence of a new, durable identity. Instead, transitions simply bookend sustained periods of liminal uncertainty. Whilst this does not strictly conform to the anthropological use of the term, which emphasised the temporary nature of the liminal phase and the reaggregation of the 'liminar' (Beech 2011) into a new social position upon its completion, it offers a potentially useful way of looking at the convulsive, turbulent social world of late modernity. In this world, upon entering a new phase in one's life following a transition, the knowledge that another transition is likely around the corner means that every aspect of the lifecourse is shot through with a nagging background anxiety, and what seems solid, fixed and immutable today can melt into air tomorrow. Thus, it is the seeming inevitability of transition that fuels the liminal nature of the contemporary lifecourse. Of course, in some senses this is not too different from the experience of modernity in the post-war era of the welfare state; after all, even then people experienced transitions such as changing jobs, moving houses, getting married, becoming parents, getting divorced and so on. However, what has changed, as we have seen, is the sense that the normative paths that guided individuals through modernity are eroding. So, the inevitability of transitions and turning points has increased just at the point where their likely nature and direction has become less certain. As a result the significance of the transition has been transformed. Whereas they once marked a moment of liminal uncertainty in a lifecourse that was at least relatively normatively ordered, now transitions simply provide staging posts between longer, more chronic bouts of insecurity.

Whilst there have been attempts to theorise illegal drug use in terms of late modernity (Collinson 1996, Parker, Aldridge and Measham 1998, Parker, Williams and Aldridge 2002, Manning 2007: 21–6), the nascent understanding of drug careers in the context of the significant transformation of the social world described above is ripe for further development. Of course, as Hammersley (1989) has argued, research subjects themselves may not be best placed to fully understand the context within which they live. Nevertheless, a good number of our participants did recognise and reflect upon some of the symptoms of the shift to late modernity as they discussed both their drug careers and their lifecourse more generally.[12] For example, several participants expressly lamented the demise of the industrial lifeworlds that they grew up and began their working lives in:

> You go there now and you look at the place, and you think "god, it's awful!" I mean run down. We lost all the petrochemical industry, all the

12 In general, participants did not recognise these developments in the terms provided by sociological theory, which, after all, is of interest only to a relatively small number of people working in a somewhat hermetic professional environment.

> steel works. We lost all the little employers that were there, there used to be masses and masses of specialist employers that used to use steel and cast iron. They were all there and getting a job really wasn't a problem, you know what I mean, cause it was absolutely booming, there was a lot of money to be made. Since then, the steel works have just about shut up, I mean it's disgraceful when I go down there and look at it now. *Matthew, 52, self-employed civil engineer, cannabis and occasional cocaine user.*

Of course this lament was quite possibly fuelled in part by nostalgia for a lost youth. However, there is also a clear sense of loss for the built environment and for the more normatively ordered and certain world of the post-war period in which Matthew grew up ('getting a job wasn't really a problem'), what it represented and what opportunities it offered ('there was a lot of money to be made'). Others made reference to the emergence of what Tom (41, horticulturalist, cannabis user) described as an 'ephemeral consumer culture', and often not in particularly enthusiastic terms. As Tom himself put it, 'I've got great pity for the children of Thatcher, people who have known nothing but the kind of consumerist expectations that people have had in the last couple of decades'.

Our participants did not only recognise some of the convulsive social changes of the past decades, but they had been touched by them in a range of ways. As we have seen throughout this chapter, the increased likelihood of transitions and turning points of an unpredictable nature in a social world where the old normative codes are being rendered progressively redundant had profoundly affected the participants' lifecourses and, therefore, their drug careers. Our participants were unable to feel certain that their circumstances at any given point would endure, and thus they seemed to exist permanently 'betwixt and between'. They assumed the status of 'liminars' (Beech 2011), subject to the uncertainties of liminality but, unlike those engaged in the ritual processes documented by van Gennep and Turner, with little prospect of being fully aggregated into a role of any stability or durability. Malcolm (44, student, cannabis user), for instance, became caught up as a young man in the cycles of employment and unemployment that were a simple fact of his line of work, and this had serious implications for his drug use:

> I was working as a painter and decorator and I'd been laid off in November and I'd lost touch with a few of my friends. I was just sitting around playing computer games and smoking cannabis and I was bored. There was a lad who I knew who lived down the street who'd been addicted to heroin for years, and he knocks on the door and asked me if I'd give him a lift to score some heroin, and I was like "yeah, okay, but can you get me some weed?" and he was "yeah, okay". At that point in my life in my mid-twenties, whereas with cannabis now I believe if I wanted to stop I could just stop, like that, I know I could, but when I was in my early twenties I believed that it was really, I was really addicted and dependent on it and I started

> panicking when I couldn't get any. So that particular night I took some heroin for the first time. I was 24, and I only did it the once, and then I thought no, you know, because I watched *Grange Hill* when I was a kid, [adopts public information film style voice] "oh god" you know, "the evil drugs". And about a year later, 25, 26, I'd found work again and I'd been laid off again. It used to be quite a common thing, they'd take you on for the summer and lay you off in the winter, and again I was bored and I was really, really, I felt really depressed and stuff, probably bored with nonclinical depression, and I sat and I thought that year previous how nice heroin actually made me feel. I mean it's a nasty drug obviously but people forget how nice it actually feels, it's beautiful, and so I went down to my mates', said "I can't stand feeling like this, get me a bag, get me a bag", and then I got addicted to heroin and I was addicted to heroin from the age of about 25 to the age of about 30.

Malcolm's was a rather extreme case where the impact of his unstable employment was particularly stark. For others, the impact of enduring liminality and manifold transitions on their drug career was more understated but still profound. For example, even the drug career of Xavier (55, researcher, polydrug user), whose prodigious and consistent polydrug consumption was unmatched by anyone else in the sample, had not been immune from the uncertainty wrought by liminality. Xavier had been employed in a number of different jobs, often on short-term contracts, and had made some significant cross-country moves in order to take up new positions. As he put it, 'I've never tried to stop, no, the more drugs I can get the better'. But it was clear that as he moved from contract to contract and job to job, and faced significant transitions in his family situation, his drug use was reconfigured in sometimes quite subtle ways. For example, a job in an academic establishment saw a slight reduction in his consumption: 'During that period I mainly only used amphetamines and cannabis so it was a fairly stable period for me. I did the job properly. There were no complaints, I was well liked'. One research position involved working with heroin users, and this led to him trying heroin. Another assignment during the acid house era saw him fall in love with that particular subculture, and he began using ecstasy, as we have seen. In addition, he recalled periods that 'were forced on me' when he could not get hold of drugs immediately after moving to a new town or city:

> Yeah, usually periods where I had to move from one job to another and I ended up in strange towns, I was in [town A] for six months, couldn't get any drugs. When I first moved here I lived in [town B] for four months before I moved to [town C], couldn't get any drugs. When I first moved here I couldn't get any for two or three weeks.

Thus, whilst Xavier's drug career seemed initially to provide the only constant in a capricious lifecourse marked by liminality, on closer analysis it actually reflected quite faithfully the different phases and circumstances that he had experienced. At no point during his lifecourse could Xavier have anticipated with complete confidence the direction that his drug career would take, because the twists and turns in his other life trajectories were entirely unpredictable in a way that might not have been the case in a more stable social world. And, although none of the other participants consumed drugs with quite the appetite of Xavier, the liminal natures of their own drug careers, forever vulnerable to the next transition or turning point in some other insecure aspect of the lifecourse, were similar. As Tom (41, horticulturalist, cannabis user) put it:

> Say if you've decided you're going to work in that career and then if the market disappears or is supplanted . . . , your market's gone and you've got to retrain. So [drug use is] really adapted to modern life in that sense, that kind of uncertainty and openness to change.

Ultimately, then, the drug careers of our participants, durable as they were, seemed to constantly exist in a state of limbo, and in doing so they served as a microcosm of the growing sense of liminal uncertainty that marked the society of which they were but a tiny part.

Summary

This chapter has looked at the history of our participants' illegal drug use. It began by looking at the participants' first experiences of illegal drug use, which tended to be unplanned, spontaneous occasions with friends. Unsurprisingly for a group still using illegal drugs to this day, most first experiences were enjoyable. Following this, the vast majority of participants became regular or at least occasional users of illegal drugs in the weeks and months that followed. Most participants also went through an experimental phase, generally quite early on in their drug-using career, which involved taking a wider range of substances and often using more heavily for a time. This phase tended to see the participants use drugs with friends in relatively bounded contexts, such as at university or as part of involvement in a subculture. Finally, the notion of transitions in drug careers was explored. It was suggested that the participants' illegal drug use was contingent upon other aspects of their lives such as work and family, and that these took priority over illegal drug use. When circumstances changed, patterns of use generally followed to fit in with the reshaped contours of a participant's life. It was suggested that these transitions need to be understood in terms of our present condition of permanent liminality (Szakolczai 2000), where the normative certainties that characterised lifecourse trajectories in the post-war years have been shattered and the lifecourse has become progressively more differentiated and racked with insecurity. In these radically uncertain, vertiginous (Young 2007) times, individuals tend to be confronted with an increasing number of transitions and turning points of unpredictable nature and direction. Drug careers like those of our participants, always contingent upon other increasingly shaky aspects of life, are thus subject to repeated reconfiguration if they are to endure, now more than ever. These themes will be developed further in Chapter 4, which will focus on the current patterns of illegal drug use among our participants.

4 Present

Living with illegal drugs today

This chapter will detail the role that illegal drug use plays in the life of the participants today, thus bringing the story that we began to tell in Chapter 3 up to date. Six facets of the current use of the participants will be explored: the participants' drugs of choice, their sources of drugs, the frequency and consistency of their consumption, the set and setting of their use, their reasons for use and the effect that they feel illegal drug use has had on their lives. We will see how the participants have managed to integrate drug use into their present circumstances, and encounter their generally sanguine and relaxed attitude towards it. We will also examine how illegal drug use has become of value to the participants in assisting them in their attempts to cope with various stresses and strains that are exacerbated by late modern conditions. And, in line with the argument made in Chapter 3, we will suggest that the relief that illegal drugs currently provide to our participants can never be taken for granted, vulnerable as it is to transitions and turning points in other aspects of life, particularly given the emergence of so-called permanent liminality (Szakolczai 2000) as one of the defining features of the contemporary social world.

Drugs of choice

Cannabis is comfortably the most commonly used illegal drug in the UK, with 6.7 per cent of 16–59 year olds using it in the past year according to the 2014–15 run of the Crime Survey for England and Wales (Home Office 2015a: 3). In comparison, powder cocaine, the next most commonly used drug, was used by 2.3 per cent of 16–59 year olds during the same period (Home Office 2015a: 3). As a result it was not surprising that cannabis was used by far more of our participants than any other illegal drug, as Table 4.1 shows. As we saw in Chapter 3, most participants had tried a variety of drugs over their lifecourse, and many had enjoyed an experimental phase when, for a time, a wider range of substances were used. However, as Plant (1975: 183) also found of his non-institutionalised drug users, after a period spent using an assortment of drugs, most of the participants had come to settle on cannabis as their drug of choice, and their days of consuming other illegal

Table 4.1 Types of illegal drugs currently used by participants

Type of illegal drug	*Number of participants declaring current use*
Cannabis	29
Cocaine / crack cocaine	6
Amphetamine	3
Ecstasy	3
Magic mushrooms	2
Heroin	2
LSD	1
Ketamine	1
DMT	1
Tranquilisers	1
Unspecified other drug	2

substances were firmly in the past. Winston's (58, academic, cannabis user) experience was typical:

> I reckon the last time I took anything that wasn't marijuana . . . would've been either cocaine or LSD . . . and that must be 19 . . . 80 . . . about 83. . . . That's a long time ago isn't it!

Despite the clear dominance of cannabis as the drug of choice amongst our sample, a number of participants expressed concerns about what they perceived as an increase in the strength of the cannabis strains generally available on the UK market today. These strains tend to be referred to collectively (and problematically) as 'skunk'.[1] Indeed, the Crime Survey for England and Wales found that older users are more likely to use cannabis resin, typically less potent, than younger users: 36 per cent of older (40 to 59 year old) users reported using resin in 2013–14 compared with 27 per cent of younger (16 to 39 year old) users (Home Office 2015a: 29), although the overwhelming majority of our participants avoided resin due to worries about poor quality and adulteration. Nevertheless, some participants reminisced fondly about what they remembered as the milder effects of the cannabis they used during their younger days:

> This is real old fogey stuff probably, but certainly [I] didn't like the rise of skunk, the stuff that was coming through, and you know . . . that felt,

1 On the problematic nature of the term 'skunk', see Potter and Chatwin (2012). As Stevens put it, 'skunk is used carelessly to describe any form of cannabis that has high potency' (2007: 14), including in official government reports (Home Office 2015a: 29), and the calculated use of the term has played a role in the 'othering' of today's supposed 'skunk' users (Stevens 2007: 16).

> you know, again very strange, that seemed like this isn't the real stuff that I used to have. This is not nice, this seemed different, different sort of effect. [I] experience it at dinner parties of course now, plenty of dinner parties over the last 20 or 30 years, where again marijuana would be smoked either before or after or during courses, but with the arrival of skunk suddenly friends who'd been smoking for a long time suddenly falling on the floor and staying there for an hour or two. You'd think "what is going on here?" you know. Like I say it's quite an interesting tale of the changing nature of consumption you know. *Winston, 58, academic, cannabis user.*
>
> When I used to smoke cannabis, or bush, or grass in the '70s, it was mellow, you used to never get yourself to a certain level, [just] nice and mellow and chilled out. *Matthew, 52, self-employed civil engineer, cannabis and occasional cocaine user.*

Despite these misgivings about the perceived increase in the potency of much of the product available today, the continued dominance of cannabis as our participants' drug of choice is wholly unsurprising. Cannabis remains comparatively affordable and easy to access, and its effects are relatively benign and easily managed. All these factors make it ideally suited to long-term, sustained use. Indeed, as we saw in the previous chapter, cannabis had been a consistent companion over many years for the bulk of the participants, and several of them were keen to outline the extent of their attachment to it. As Oscar (40, volunteer, cannabis user) put it, with his partner laughing in the background as she listened in to his telephone interview, 'well, apart from my partner it is my soulmate, cannabis'.

For the eight participants who used cannabis alongside other illegal drugs, it was cannabis that tended to be the most frequently used drug by some distance. Cannabis served as the mainstay of a drug repertoire, and other substances were used sparingly and often only on special occasions or when the participants were looking to 'treat' themselves to something out of the ordinary:

> I took my finals on speed actually. But since then, virtually all dope, occasionally, and it is very occasionally, a bit of coke, but that's very, very rare. *Ollie, 52, company owner, cannabis and occasional cocaine user.*
>
> Yeah, [I'm] really only doing cannabis, bush, grass, that sort of stuff. I haven't had any hard drugs in, oh, let me see, last Christmas I think it is. Normally, I'm a bit embarrassed about it, I will do a line of cocaine at Christmas, but that is it and I won't buy it! Somebody else will buy and say, "you wanna line?" It's like Christmas, like the spirit of Christmas, I mean you must know what it's like, but that'll be it, you know what I mean, it'll be like one line and that'll be it. It's like a treat to myself. *Matthew, 52, self-employed civil engineer and cannabis and occasional cocaine user.*

As we have already seen, Pat (51, unemployed, polydrug user) and Xavier (55, researcher, polydrug user) were notable in that they enjoyed a widely varied drug repertoire. They used an extensive range of substances including amphetamine and other stimulants, crack cocaine, ecstasy and heroin. Xavier, as we saw in Chapter 3, also indulged in a wide range of 'legal highs'. Nevertheless, both Pat and Xavier were also regular cannabis users, prolifically so in Xavier's case.

Only one participant, Ned (53, unemployed, amphetamine user), did not use cannabis at all. As we saw in Chapter 3, this was in part simply because Ned found that he enjoyed the effects of amphetamine to a greater extent than any other drug, and as a result he now used amphetamine alone: 'I did try other little bits and bobs, but as far as I was concerned it just didn't do for me what amphetamines do and that's it, and if it isn't amphetamines I don't want it'. The method of ingestion was also an issue for him: 'I don't even smoke, so I don't use cannabis, I don't like that'. Furthermore, as we will see, Ned was unique in still associating with a subculture, and his continued involvement in the northern soul scene also contributed to his enduring fondness for amphetamine.

Source of drugs

Our participants held relatively cautious attitudes when it came to sourcing their illegal drugs. This was the point at which their 'hidden' status was potentially most vulnerable, and as a result the bulk of the participants were keen to avoid engagement with the 'black market' and 'drug dealers' wherever possible. Although many of the participants' fears related to a somewhat stereotypical view of the 'drug dealer' that has been thoroughly debunked (for example, Coomber 2006), they far preferred to access illegal drugs within what Coomber and Turnbull (2007) have called 'arenas of transaction' that were largely separate from the wider commercial drug market. So-called 'social supply', where drugs are transacted between friends and acquaintances in a manner that is not commercially motivated (Potter 2009), was for the overwhelming majority of participants the favoured means of obtaining illegal drugs. Only when they were unable to attain drugs 'socially' did participants reluctantly turn to the commercial market, although some were not prepared to do so under any circumstances.[2]

There are clear precedents for these findings. The middle-class adult Canadian users in Hathaway's study, for example, shared the desire to avoid 'impersonal transactions with professional drug dealers' wherever possible (1997a: 118). In addition, the 2014–15 run of the Crime Survey for England and Wales showed that 42 per cent of adults sourced their last illegal drugs from 'a friend,

2 Coomber and Moyle (2014) have outlined a rationale for extending the concept of 'social supply' to one of 'minimally commercial supply'. They suggest that this better accommodates the actual circumstances of most supply transactions, where profit is not the motivation for the sale but some small gain may be realised, albeit not at a level that can meaningfully contribute to an improved lifestyle for the seller (2014: 163).

neighbour or colleague', a further 5 per cent from 'an acquaintance' and 3 per cent from 'a family member'. Eleven per cent sourced drugs from a 'known dealer', whilst only 9 per cent did so from 'a dealer not known personally' to them. Of the 21 per cent who did not answer, it would be reasonable to assume that a good proportion of them also sourced their drugs from family or friends and that their reluctance to answer was because they did not wish to incriminate their suppliers (Home Office 2015c). There is also some evidence that the appeal of 'social supply' is slightly greater for older users than it is for their younger counterparts. For example, according to the 2013–14 Crime Survey for England and Wales, 62 per cent of 45–59 year olds sourced their drugs from a family member or 'someone else well known' to them compared to 59 per cent of 16–24 year olds. Meanwhile, only 5 per cent of 45–59 year olds used 'a dealer not known to [them] personally', compared to 8 per cent of 16–24 year olds and 9 per cent of 30–34 year olds (Home Office 2014c). The same survey suggested that this cautious approach extends to the location where drugs are obtained. For instance, 62 per cent of 45–59 year olds obtained their last drugs either at their or someone else's home, compared to 49 per cent of 16–24 year olds and 43 per cent of 25–29 year olds. The younger cohorts were more likely to obtain their drugs outside of the private home environment, such as in bars, pubs, clubs or outdoors (Home Office 2014c).

Around 25 of the 30 participants in our sample were able to access illegal drugs through social supply channels all or at least some of the time. A small number of these participants were adamant that if they were unable to acquire their drugs in this way, then they would not consider going to the commercial market. This included Oscar (40, volunteer, cannabis user) and Liam (45, unemployed, cannabis user), who suggested, 'I've had bad experiences with drug dealers so it is better for me to be one step removed and get my friends to do it for me'.

Of those who were able to access supplies through social channels, most secured their drugs from friends or relatives in arrangements that had been enjoyed for a number of years:

> [I get it] from friends, it's always been either through friends, or indeed, you know, occasionally getting to someone slightly higher up through a friend, who's their friend. Never random, never random, never ever bought any off somebody I didn't know. . . . Sometimes long term friends who are back where I used to live for nearly 30 years . . . , you know, they bring some down if I ever needed any. It's always been that, it's always been that. *Winston, 58, academic, cannabis user.*

Five participants grew their own supplies of cannabis. This included Tom (41, horticulturalist, cannabis user), who grew various strains for different situations, and Adam (47, unemployed due to disability, cannabis user), who grew a small amount for his own use but also used the services of a commercial dealer on occasion. Oscar (40, volunteer, cannabis user) had started to grow his own supplies specifically in order to avoid having to make contact with commercial dealers (Decorte 2010, Potter 2010a, Potter et al. 2015):

> I make my own so I don't have to associate with dealers. . . . Yeah, that's the sole reason, yeah. It's not, I don't, it was never going to make money, it was just so I don't have to associate with [dealers]. I've never sold any of it in the whole time I've done it. I smoked every single bit, much to the annoyance of friends!

Similarly, Vince (42, academic, cannabis user) was also extremely reluctant to engage with commercial markets, and he disliked the strains that tended to be easily available commercially and had misgivings regarding their quality (Decorte 2010). For these reasons he used nothing but his own home-grown cannabis, as he explained:

> You know I grow it myself. I don't buy it from anywhere else, because I'm not particularly interested in engaging with any of that, those scenes, if you like. And also I don't like the products, that's the other thing, you know, a lot of the things that people sell are not all that good or they're kind of these super sort of hybrids and all that, which I don't like. So I kind of pretty much control the whole thing. [I] don't have any off those extra contacts, other than friends I guess, sometimes, who might want to grow some or who I might give some to, that kind of thing. [Home grown is] my entire source. . . . That would have started when I started up again in 1996. I had grown some a long time ago when I first started as a teenager, so I kind of knew what to do. So I had actually done it when I was about 16 or something, 17. So after a very long gap, I sort of came back to that. And partly, it's the gardening thing, I am a bit of a gardener, so for me it's quite, the activity itself is almost as enjoyable as the end product actually. You know, sort of the planting and the growing and all the rest of it. . . . I've always quite enjoyed the process of growing it. It's actually quite a difficult thing to do, to do it properly. So that's kind of an interesting challenge. So [I don't think I'll] stop doing it, even if I stopped taking it myself, because again it's something that's quite a nice gift or something to give away. So even if I didn't do it, I may still do it and just give it to friends and that kind of thing, possibly.

The enjoyment that Vince found in the actual process of cultivation has been noted in previous research as providing motivation for home growing (Hakkarainen and Perala 2011, Potter et al. 2015). However, he also was careful to exercise caution when inviting people into his home in view of the potential legal consequences of having his growing operation discovered:

> Having it and consuming it really doesn't bother me very much. It's just a fact that I think growing is considered to be more of a serious crime and

> I could get into more trouble for doing it. And that, you know, that could affect me, my professional standing, even my job possibly. . . . Occasionally it concerns me, and I have to be careful for instance if there are visitors at the house, workmen, that kind of thing, you've got some plants around, you've got to put them away somewhere where they can't see them. I think in this day and age, I don't think most people are bothered, but you're never quite sure, so you have to be a bit careful. So occasionally, yeah, occasionally it does concern me.

Indeed, a few participants suggested that they had decided against growing their own supplies as they were concerned about the potential legal sanctions that they might face. This included Yannis (47, regional manager, cannabis user):

> The problem with that for me is that I am aware of what I do for recreational use is illegal, however a small amount of cannabis in the UK for recreational use and personal use is in most cases dealt with by a caution or a warning, generally a slap on the wrist. When we start cultivating cannabis we are now taking the penalties for that crime to a whole new level and whilst I'm in favour clearly of cannabis being used for medicinal and recreational [purposes], I'm concerned about losing my liberty because the cultivation of cannabis is a more serious offence than just possession of a small amount for personal use.

Nathan (47, unemployed customs officer due to disability, cannabis user) and his friends, who were also keen to avoid what he called the 'black market', had come to an arrangement where they would 'club together' to buy seeds and one of their number would take the responsibility of growing them for the rest of the group. For the next cycle, another individual would become the grower, and so on. This represented something of an informal version, on a very small scale, of the 'cannabis social clubs' that are increasingly prominent across Europe (Arana and Montanes Sanchez 2011). Nathan was motivated in part to grow his own cannabis in order to satisfy his need for what he described as 'medical' cannabis of a particular type and quality (Hakkarainen et al. 2015). As we will see later in this chapter, he was not alone in this desire for 'medical' cannabis.

None of the participants in this study who grew their own cannabis did so for financial reasons, and no profit was sought or made by any of them (Weisheit 1991, Potter 2010b, Potter et al. 2015). Our home growers cultivated purely for their own use and the use of their friends. Occasionally, as in the case of Vince (42, academic, cannabis user), home growers would also use part of their harvest to give as gifts. It is well documented that the decentralised, small-scale cultivation of cannabis along these lines is becoming increasingly prevalent in the UK as well as in many other nation states (Decorte and Potter 2015, Potter et al. 2015). The undertaking of such cultivation is sometimes seen in explicitly political terms by those involved (Potter 2010b), although, with the exception of Tom (41, horticulturalist, cannabis user), this was not the case for our home growers.

Of course, growing one's own supply was only feasible for the cannabis users among our sample. For those who used other illegal drugs, engagement with the commercial market was often unavoidable. This was borne out by Xavier (55, researcher, polydrug user). Not only was he the most prolific user in the sample with the widest repertoire of illegal drugs, but he also had the widest range of sources. This included a variety of commercial dealers (some known to him, some not so) as well as friends and home growers. His approach was to use 'different dealers for different drugs'. On occasion Xavier would engage commercial dealers not known personally to him who delivered illegal drugs directly to his home:

> They're just kind of making money scallies who just deliver to the door. You know I don't know who they are, you just pick the number up off someone, they'll deliver to anyone, they don't give a shit who you are.

A number of participants provided accounts of encounters with commercial dealers that carried a greater degree of risk than their normal arrangements and compared unfavourably to more social forms of supply. Winston (58, academic, cannabis user), who as we have seen usually sourced drugs from his friends, was forced into the commercial market upon moving to his current location for work purposes and finding himself cut off from his regular supply network:

> It's funny, when I first moved here, a friend, I'd only just got to know, he said "oh I can introduce you to the guy that gets me the stuff you know", so I said [hesitantly] "well", and he said "oh, he's fine, he's cool". We went round and it was very strange, . . . it's the one time for a long time I'd gone round to someone I don't know, you know, and I did it once and I thought well I'm not doing that again, I'd rather not have it. Partly because it was clearly a place where a lot of people did go round to get this stuff, and if a student saw me, you know. . . . So, that's the only, a rare occasion when, possibly now it would be a friend that got it for me, possibly from that person, but I just thought that's too big a risk, it's not worth it, you know, it's not worth it.

The risks of engaging with commercial markets could be mitigated somewhat by the use of a regular supplier with whom a degree of trust had been built. Indeed, for Lenny (53, mechanic, cannabis user) the loss of his trusted supplier would have potentially significant consequences: 'I don't know, I suppose if he couldn't, and I couldn't get any, I would just fucking knock it on the head I suppose'.

The reality for most of the participants was that they utilised a variety of sources. Social supply was favoured, but when participants were unable to source product in this way they often then turned to alternative commercial sources. Eric (40, consultant for relocation firm, cannabis user), for example, engaged with a range of suppliers. Wherever possible, he obtained his drugs from one of a small number of social suppliers who were 'local sources that I trust'. Two of these people were friends of a similar age. However, when circumstances demanded, Eric could also turn to a couple of younger suppliers, one of whom was more of a commercial dealer who ran his operation as 'very much a business'. Similarly, Uri (47, care worker, cannabis user) enjoyed access to cannabis grown by his friends and relatives, but when he was unable to obtain supplies in this way he secured supplies from a trusted commercial dealer whom he had used for around a decade. Malcolm (44, student, cannabis user) had comparable arrangements:

> I've got a mate who lives a few miles away, he grows. And I usually get it off him if I can get it off him, because I can buy in bulk off him, but otherwise I just have to go to a local lad I know. . . . I can't remember the last time I couldn't get it. It's very easy to get.

As Nathan (47, unemployed customs officer due to disability, cannabis user) put it, if product was not immediately to hand, 'I have to go to the black market, that's my last option, is going to the black market for these commercial grows'. In Nathan's case this involved engaging the services of two commercial dealers that he trusted. In Derek's (50, gardener, cannabis occasional mushroom user) words, 'you have to be careful, that's part of the reason I don't try and get cannabis from random strangers, [but] someone who I know and trust'.

Thus, whilst Xavier's (55, researcher, polydrug user) claim that 'the older generation like me are much more cautious' was difficult to apply to himself, it certainly appeared to be true for the rest of the participants. As we have seen, they generally favoured social means of supply and only engaged with commercial markets and dealers when they could not access illegal drugs through some kind of social supply channel. Accessing illegal drugs through commercial markets was not only more risky to the participants' 'hidden status', but it also saw them lose control of the kind of product they were obtaining (Decorte 2010) and face the prospect of being 'ripped off', and it sullied the notion of illegal drug use as part of a transcendent communal experience that was especially important to those who had been influenced by, for example, hippie and acid house subcultures in their younger days. As a result, the participants tended to proceed with trepidation and caution when they were forced to source illegal drugs through more commercial means. For those participants who were in a position to obtain their illegal drugs solely from friends, grow their own cannabis, or adopt novel arrangements such as Nathan's (47, unemployed customs officer due to disability, cannabis user) growing club, these mechanisms acted as bulwarks against what they perceived as the growing intrusion of the commercial market and its often ruthless operators. Yet even when such methods were impractical or unavailable to the participants, the notion of social supply seemed to provide a measuring rod of sorts against which they assessed every act of sourcing illegal drugs. In such circumstances the ideal of social supply, despite being unattainable, helped to shape the participants' responses to the illegal drug transactions that they were able to engage in. Commercial transactions, even when completed safely and resulting in the acquisition of illegal drugs of the desired quality at what was considered a fair price, were always compared unfavourably to instances of social supply.

Frequency and consistency of consumption

There is good evidence that a fair proportion of those older adults who use illegal drugs do so with considerable frequency and consistency. This is particularly the case for those who use cannabis. According to the Crime Survey for England and Wales, 49 per cent of cannabis users aged 40–59 were 'frequent' users of the drug who used it more than once a month on average during the last year. Older cocaine and ecstasy users (aged 40–59) tended to indulge much less frequently, with 92 per cent of cocaine users and 100 per cent of ecstasy users taking each drug once a month or less (Home Office 2015a: 30). However, given that cannabis is by far the most popular illegal drug among older adults, it would seem that age is no real barrier to the continued regular use of such substances. Indeed, Notley found that the 'archetypal' adult non-problematic users in her study saw drug use as an 'integral part of life' (2005: 283).

The participants in our study also tended to be relatively frequent and consistent users. The majority of participants (18) used illegal drugs every day:

> I don't think it's any different today as what it was then, only that I do have a little bit every day now just to keep myself kicking on if you like, which if I'm sat there doing nothing all day, then I get very bored so I'll just do that. *Ned, 53, unemployed, amphetamine user.*
>
> It's been steady for the last nearly 20 years, 18 years, no, yeah call it 20 years and that would be relatively continuous usage. [I] tend to smoke just tobacco in the morning and then depending on my needs and demands for the day, then I might become intoxicated with marijuana in the afternoon, if I'm doing something pleasant like gardening. Or, especially if I've got a meeting, or interfacing with others, then I tend to stay straight until after that. So that would be [the] general pattern and . . . in terms of doses per day that would be 6 to 12 joints per day. *Tom, 41, horticulturalist, cannabis user.*
>
> Currently I smoke marijuana recreationally virtually every day. I'm smoking a spliff as we speak [laughs]! I am one of these people that do not see it as a problem at all. . . . Rather than when you come home from work, having a glass of wine or beer, I'd much rather have a couple of spliffs and

> relax into the night. . . . I don't think I've been not with a spliff for such a long time, it's part and parcel of my everyday life now. *Eric, 40, consultant for relocation firm, cannabis user.*

Pat's and Xavier's use was also daily, but theirs was markedly heavier than the rest of the participants and encompassed a much wider variety of substances. Xavier (55, researcher, polydrug user) was a prodigious user of a wide variety of substances, although this had not prevented him from building a successful and continuing career as a researcher. He described how his current use had 'kind of exploded a bit'. He was using 'every day, pretty much as soon as I wake up. Sometimes have a coffee first'. Meanwhile Pat (51, unemployed, polydrug user) injected heroin and speed every day, and her drug use contributed to the slightly chaotic lifestyle that she led. Whilst it would be difficult to argue that her drug use was out of control, of all the participants she was the one who had experienced the greatest struggles in incorporating her drug use sustainably into her life, a battle that was still on-going. Nevertheless, although a straightforward case could be made that her use was 'problematic', for example according to the definition provided by Anthony and Petronis (1995), her ability to sustain drug use over the long term whilst engaging in other more conventional pursuits would make such a diagnosis troublesome.[3] Furthermore, as per one of the criteria for inclusion in the study, she remained free from involvement in the 'capture systems' of the criminal justice system and treatment services (Parker, Aldridge and Eggington 2001), and to this extent at least her drug use could be considered to fall within the scope of the 'normal' (Hammersley 2005, 2011).[4]

The remaining participants indulged with varying frequency and regularity. Some would use every week, but mainly at weekends or when they were not working. Others used two or three times a month. Others were more occasional users but generally would use once every month or two.

> I've up until quite recently, you know, up until about two years ago I'd be a real regular, have a smoke every day really. . . . We very occasionally have it now, which is very occasional, say about, average about once a month. *Winston, 58, academic, cannabis user.*

3 Anthony and Petronis suggest that individuals can be considered as having a 'drug problem' if they self-report one or more of the following: feelings of dependency, withdrawal sickness, perceived tolerance to drug effects, failed efforts to reduce use, social problems attributed to drug use, other health problems attributed to drug use, and daily use for two weeks or more (1995: 11). Indeed, on this final measure alone, the majority of our participants would qualify as 'problem users'.

4 Coincidentally, in the study of cocaine users that led Murphy et al. to develop the notion of 'career use patterns', there was also one outlying respondent who did not fit into any of the four categories of use that were developed. Instead this respondent engaged in continued heavy use: 'she is the one respondent who bears some resemblance to the tragic figure of a compulsive cocaine abuser depicted in the popular media' (Murphy, Reinarman and Waldorf 1989: 434).

> Once again, like, somebody has a glass of wine, you know, when they go out, I might have the odd joint and a line of coke. I don't really see, to me I don't really see the difference because I don't think that for me as a person that it affects me to that extent. You know what I mean? I mean a lot of people go out every night and they're drinking loads and loads and loads of alcohol, you know, smoking lots and lots of cigarettes. I might occasionally have a joint and a line of coke. To me it's just the same. *Quinn, 51, market trader, cannabis and occasional cocaine user.*

Meanwhile, other participants had very little pattern to their use:

> There's breaks all the time really. . . . But then there can be quite concentrated periods, I mean I might go, I might go three months and smoke every day and then I might, you know, not smoke anything for a month, you know, so it's just how it is. . . . There's no real underlying pattern to it. *Ollie, 52, company owner, cannabis and occasional cocaine user.*
>
> Oh it's occasional. I mean occasional to steady. . . . If nothing special's on, because sometimes I get really busy with things, or run out for a while, and let it rest for a week or two. *Uri, 47, care worker, cannabis user.*
>
> Just, if I'm not doing anything else, if I'm not, I mean, doing anything in particular, I mean I'll have a smoke, which would be like where I'm going out like tonight, I'll have a smoke. *Lenny, 53, mechanic, cannubis user.*

These more occasional users tended to increase their use at certain times. Several participants mentioned that they would indulge more heavily and regularly around special occasions. The Christmas period in particular tended to be a period of more intense usage, as we saw earlier with Matthew (52, self-employed civil engineer, cannabis and occasional cocaine user), who explained how he would supplement his regular cannabis use with cocaine during the festive season. Quinn (51, market trader, cannabis and occasional cocaine user) also noted how use patterns could become more intense around celebrations such as birthdays, the new year and the like:

> So it's not something that I particularly do regularly, special occasions, birthdays, or a wedding [laughs]. Yeah. Not like at one time where it used to be, oh, every weekend, it'd be like all looking forward like we're going to have this and have that you know, great. Just if it so happens, like I say, maybe at Christmas, maybe at new year, or something like that. Or a special occasion, you know, something just to sort of keep you going.

Several participants had come to associate illegal drug use with going on holiday or enjoying a sabbatical of some kind from work. Such breaks tended to be a time of heavier use and occasionally involved some deviation from participants' customary substances and patterns of consumption. Vince (42, academic, cannabis user), for example, who recalled in Chapter 3 how he had been a daily user of cannabis during his thirties, had seen his intake reduce dramatically in the wake of his return to full-time employment. Now he had come to regard illegal drug use almost exclusively as something to be indulged in when savouring time off work:

> I again had very short periods, you know, maybe when I was on holiday or, you know, had some time off work, when I did it some more. So, I suppose I connect it with holidays now [laughs]. A kind of holiday activity. It's a holiday activity, but the activity itself is also a holiday, if that makes sense.

The change in the frequency and consistency of Vince's use reminds us that the drug careers of our participants tended to be contingent upon the other factors in their lives, as Chapter 3 discussed. Indeed, for some participants, their present circumstances had curtailed the extent of their drug use quite significantly. For example, Ian (46, unemployed, cannabis user), as we saw in Chapter 3, was left frustrated that at the moment he was only able to use cannabis 'once in a blue moon' as he was out of work and could not afford to buy it. Shukla (2006) and Hathaway (1997a) also found that regular, steady employment could facilitate 'normal' drug use as it provided the income with which to buy drugs and as it also tied individuals into something of a structured routine which assisted in the management and control of that use. For those like Ian in occupations characterised by uncertainty, attempting to cope with health issues that made work difficult, or facing periods of inactivity and tight finances every so often, there was often little consistency in their pattern of use over the medium or long term. It seems that as the social landscape in general, and working life in particular, becomes increasingly marked by uncertainty and precariousness, drug careers are increasingly subject to fluctuations. As Chapter 3 demonstrated, the next transition or turning point in a lifecourse always represented a potential threat to established patterns of use. One's current frequency and consistency of consumption could never be taken for granted.

Set and setting

All of the participants made attempts to manage both 'set' (the attitude and preparedness of the persons taking the drugs, including their knowledge of drug effects, and their thoughts, feelings and expectations of the experience) and 'setting' (the physical and social environment within which the drug use occurs) (Zinberg 1984). Notley's suggestion that 'for some drug users at least, the pattern of use in later life may become one of more considered, controlled use of a restricted range of substances, in certain settings only, as opposed to complete abstention' (2005: 288) was certainly supported by the experiences of our participants. By carefully controlling set and setting, they aimed to ensure that their drug use achieved its desired ends whilst simultaneously reducing the likelihood of negative consequences. Their wealth of experience with illegal drugs ensured that they tended to be extremely successful in this.

Set

Critical to the 'set' of all participants was the high degree of knowledge that they exhibited about the effects and risks associated with particular drugs. As one would expect of those with lengthy drug careers, they knew precisely what to expect from their preferred drugs. Indeed, that the majority of participants had settled on cannabis as their drug of choice was in large part down the fact that their considerable experience suggested that it provided the kind of high they were seeking whilst being relatively easy to use in a controlled and sustainable manner. As Lenny (53, mechanic, cannabis user) put it, 'I mean I've smoked for a few years and you tend to get to know, you know what sort of feelings or anything else you get'.

Participants who used a variety of drugs often demonstrated an incredibly finely calibrated sense of the effects of particular drugs upon them, and a concomitant awareness of which drugs they favoured given certain situations and moods. These participants shared a confidence, borne of knowledge and experience, in using specific illegal drugs to promote a desired outcome. As with those in Notley's sample, 'poly drug use in adulthood was understood as being something which assisted the individual in controlling a drug using experience, as opposed to rendering that experience risky and out of control' (2005: 288). This was particularly true of Xavier (55, researcher, polydrug user), whose consumption was greater than all of the other participants both in terms of its volume and in the range of drugs he used, and whose knowledge of the effects of his chosen substances was considerable. Nevertheless in his targeted and well-rehearsed use of certain drugs to achieve precise results, he remained emblematic of the rest of the sample:

> I choose the drugs I need to produce the mood I need to do the things that I need to do that day. So if I wake up in a low mood I'll use a stimulant and if I wake up in a hyperactive mood I'll use something that's more calming and sedating and if I hate the world and everything seems crazy I'll take a psychedelic, go to another world [chuckles].

Some participants had resolved to use drugs only when they were in an appropriate frame of mind, in a similar fashion to the 'controlled' heroin users studied by Warburton, Turnbull and Hough (2005). This was perhaps at its most pronounced in the approach of Quinn (51, market trader, cannabis and occasional cocaine user) who was very aware of her levels of tolerance and how drug use could exaggerate existing moods:

> I'm very sensitive and if I had a joint or if I had something [else] it would accentuate my original feelings and make them worse. So my sadness

> would become even worse. That's why I would only take drugs when I actually felt alright, not when I was actually feeling down. And I think what a lot of people do is they take drugs when they're actually down to make them feel better, but in actual fact it makes them feel worse in the long run.

The participants were unanimous that it was not desirable to get completely 'out of it' or 'wasted'. Inevitably this had happened on occasions, especially in the participants' younger days, but only very rarely indeed over more recent years when the tendency to restraint had become somewhat more prominent. This mindset dictated both the manner in which the participants used illegal drugs and the amount that they consumed:

> Again, I used to use pipes to avoid tobacco, but that was just too heavy a hit actually. I want to be able to have a joint and be able to cook dinner and watch telly and things like that. I don't want to like get stoned and stare out the window. That's pretty excessive I think. So it's always been a mild form. *Uri, 47, care worker, cannabis user.*
>
> I'm a functional marijuana smoker. . . . I want to get up and do something after . . . and that's part of the relishing of the state of mind. *Tom, 41, horticulturalist, cannabis user.*

Indeed, one reason why the participants had managed to sustain such lengthy drug careers was because of their on-going utilisation of a panoply of control mechanisms, the adoption of which is well documented in previous research (Blackwell 1983, Shewan, Dalgarno and Reith 2000, Coggans et al. 2004, Warburton, Turnbull and Hough 2005, Shukla 2006, Moore and Measham 2008). The restraint highlighted by Uri and Tom could be seen in this light, as could the participants' intimate knowledge of the effects of their drug of choice and the fact that most of them had settled upon a single favoured substance that they were able to easily incorporate into their lives. In addition, participants were careful to look out for physical and mental signs of failing health and well-being:

> Whenever I took anything, as soon as I started to feel not very good or I'd feel run down or I'd look at myself in the mirror and my skin would look a bit, you know, like dry or I'd look tired, I'd stop taking things for a while. So I always had this self-preservation, "OK that's enough, stop". *Quinn, 51, market trader, cannabis and occasional cocaine user.*

Others had witnessed friends or acquaintances lose control, and this vindicated and further encouraged their relative restraint and cautious approach to drugs:

> I lost three friends who died of heroin overdose. And [I] put [one of] them in the ground, . . . and there was about 28, 30 women that stood

> around crying and he could have went out with any one of them and that's what broke my heart about it all. And that's what stopped me from going on to the harder stuff. *Matthew, 52, self-employed civil engineer, cannabis and occasional cocaine user.*

More generally, most of the interviewees steadfastly adopted a life philosophy of moderation:

> I always used to say, it doesn't matter what you do, if you do too much of anything, as in . . . drinking, or say sex is the same, if you have too much of anything, it's not good for you. It doesn't matter what it is. I mean drugs, drink, food, you name it and isn't good for you if you get too much of it, and that's the same as drugs isn't it? So I mean, well, I think I'm sensible. *Lenny, 53, mechanic, cannabis user.*
>
> I always knew it was something that I liked. I just knew there were costs and [it was] something that had to be managed and so I left it alone for a long time. *Vince, 42, academic, cannabis user.*

As we will see, although a number of participants were conscious that their long-term use of drugs may have future implications for their health, the overwhelming majority reported no current significant health problems that were attributable to their drug use, and most were relatively happy with their physical and mental well-being. This suggested that their control and restraint had largely achieved its aims. Even those participants whose use was relatively heavy or who occasionally enjoyed binges had still for the most part been able to avoid serious drug-related problems and, as we have seen, were able to sustain careers, family lives and the other trappings of a 'normal' and conventional existence (Murphy, Reinarman and Waldorf 1989: 432).

Another important aspect of the 'set' of a number of the participants was the feeling that there was something alluring about partaking in an illegal activity. This was the case even though their current use was discreet and carefully hidden, as we will see. As Brian (52, company owner, cannabis user) suggested, 'I suppose it's a bit risky isn't it, I mean that gives it a little bit of spice I suppose'. Similarly, Vince (42, academic, cannabis user), who as we have already seen was fastidious in keeping his growing operation as clandestine as possible, also saw the appeal of engaging in the illicit:

> I like growing it. I mean, again there's the risk of the illegality of it and the risk of being prosecuted is quite dangerous, it may be a bit of a silly thing to be doing, in some respects. So maybe that's part of the intensity of the experience, is taking some risk there.

Uri (47, care worker, cannabis user) also felt that there was a comradeship between cannabis smokers, based largely upon their shared interest in an illegal activity that necessitated caution and discretion in order to avoid coming to the attention of the authorities. For him, this heightened the experience of using cannabis somewhat:

> There's sort of a comradeship among smokers as well, it exists and it kind of binds friendship bonds. I would say it goes with it, I guess partly because it's an illegal activity. So in a sense, you're looking after each other and [you] stay together and use coded words when you're talking about it in public. But having this kind of comradeship and illegal activity, you feel a bit on the side of [pauses], er, conspiratorial, yeah, you feel conspiratorial.

Setting

In terms of 'setting', there was a very clear sense that as the participants had grown older they had become increasingly likely to consume drugs in private, most often at one's own home or at the home of a friend. This represented one of the biggest changes from the participants' younger days when, as Chapter 3 showed, illegal drugs were routinely used in public settings such as on an evening out or in a nightclub. Such a finding chimes with Foster's (1990) suggestion that the 'delinquency' of youth often continues into middle and old age, but it becomes less visible and more discreet.

In this regard our participants represented the wider situation reasonably faithfully. As the 2013–14 run of the Crime Survey for England and Wales showed, the majority of illegal drugs are consumed in the home environment, and this is especially the case for older users. Fifty-nine per cent of 45–59 year olds who used illegal drugs consumed them in their own home on the last occasion that they indulged. A further 20 per cent consumed them at somebody else's home. Only 7 per cent consumed their drugs at a 'club, party or rave', 4 per cent in a bar or pub, and just 3 per cent in an outdoor area such as a park. Although most drug use occurred in the home environment regardless of age, younger users were much more likely to consume drugs outside of the home than older users. For example, in the 16–24 age cohort, 21 per cent of those who used illegal drugs did so in the home on the last occasion of their use, whilst 38 per cent used in somebody else's home. However, 18 per cent used in a 'club, party or rave', and 9 per cent used in an outdoor area. Meanwhile 15 per cent of 25–29 and 30–34 year old users consumed illegal drugs in a bar or pub on the last occasion that they had used (Home Office 2014c). The figures suggest that as one grows older, there is an increasing likelihood that illegal drug use will take place within the private home environment; by the age of 45 almost eight in ten experiences of drug use will be in the home, compared to less than six in ten for those aged 16–24 and 25–29.

As one might expect of an activity that predominantly occurred in the home, the overwhelming majority of our participants' drug use took place either alone, with one's partner, or with a very small group of close family and friends (Shukla 2006). Indeed, many participants seemed to have few, if any, remaining connections with other users, which contributed to the ineffectiveness of the snowball sampling employed in the research (see Chapter 2). It has been suggested that using illegal drugs in this way can assist with their integration into a 'meaningful' life (Frank, Christensen and Dahl 2013). This is because using alone enables one to largely conceal illegal drug use, and so it offers protection against the potential marginalisation and stigmatisation that can result in the event that one is 'outed'. Of course, ensuring that use remains concealed also minimises the chances of receiving legal sanction of some kind (Capel et al. 1972). As Ian (46, unemployed, cannabis user) said:

> I've actually never ever been caught smoking it or otherwise, because I'm not stupid enough to go outside and smoke it and when I do smoke it indoors I close all my windows because it's a built up area and you don't know, someone might say something, you know. I don't smoke at parties or anything like that. No one wants to get nicked [laughs].

Thus, the control that our participants maintained over this aspect of the 'setting' of their drug use had likely contributed to the sustained nature of their drug careers as well as their ability to uphold other more conventional roles and mitigate the potentially negative impacts of their use. Again, this was a marked shift from the participants' younger days, when it was commonplace for drugs to be taken with relatively large groups of friends who often regarded themselves as being but a small part of a wider subcultural milieu.

That drug consumption took place predominantly in the home and was now largely a solitary activity, or one engaged in at most with a very small number of other people, was one of the most repeated motifs of the interviews, alluded to time and again by the participants:

> Now, . . . I basically smoke on my own. *Simon, 61, researcher, cannabis user.*
>
> Most joints I probably have by myself actually. Come home from work, late at night, sometimes before I go out for a date. *Uri, 47, care worker, cannabis user.*
>
> Most of the time with myself, yes, because my partner she works in a pub in the evenings so I don't see her sort of three or four nights a week. . . . I do a lot of driving you see, I do sometimes about five or six hours driving as well as doing a full day's work, so when you come in I'm knackered. I just want to put some music on and have a spliff and a glass of wine and that's my evening, that's great. *Brian, 52, company owner, cannabis user.*
>
> I now feel a bit more like a . . . bloody old Victorian man, you know, [it's the] equivalent of having a cigar you know [laughs], your cigar at night, at the end of the day you know. And you're all nicely chilled, late night joint now and watch the football, you know, quite boring. [I] don't get out much. It's a quite domesticated use of it now you know. Never, ever think about having a joint and then going out somewhere. It is, you

know, it's the end of the day [sighs], food's been done, everything's been done, just sitting on the couch now, a couple of hours before going to bed, you know. *Winston, 58, academic, cannabis user.*

I still smoke with friends when friends are around, yeah, but obviously with life changing as you get older I tend to sort of like smoke on my own normally. *Eric, 40, consultant for relocation firm, cannabis user.*

My wife joins me. She's of similar age and obviously of similar sort of background and upbringing. So, with my wife. . . . If I was in the house bored I could roll a joint and watch the TV in the same way as I could open a beer and lay on the settee. So you know it's not an absolutely entirely socially driven thing, but that's the basis of it, you know. *Ollie, 52, company owner, cannabis and occasional cocaine user.*

I do most of my drug use here [at home] or at houses of friends who do drugs too. Yeah, yeah, I don't go to clubs or parties anymore. . . . Probably about half of it on my own and about half of it with friends, yeah. Just because there's no friends around sometimes when I want to do it. Don't particularly want to do it on my own but, I like drugs and sometimes I'm on my own. *Xavier, 55, researcher, polydrug user.*

Just with my wife, and if we've got visitors that we know are okay about it then yeah, with them maybe, but we have friends who we know don't particularly care for it so when they are round here we just don't bother, wait until they are gone or whatever. . . . At home, well maybe in our back garden but, away from the home or garden absolutely not, I wouldn't dare. . . . It's very pleasant, we sit on the settee, she messes around with her laptop, I watch the television. It's pleasant, it's companionable, it's sociable. She doesn't smoke anything like as much as I do, every three to four joints I'll have, she'll have one. I share it with her because it would be extremely selfish to do otherwise. *Keith, 63, retired civil servant, cannabis user.*

Despite this, there were a handful of participants who still enjoyed consuming illegal drugs away from the home as parts of nights out and the like, although where this was the case a great deal of caution was generally exercised. This attitude was exemplified by Brian (52, company owner, cannabis user), who occasionally used cannabis outside of the home: 'But you know you just have to be discreet. I mean I smoke it in my house, I do smoke it outside, I wouldn't think anything of smoking it down the pub, in the garden, but discreetly'. Lenny (53, mechanic, cannabis user) preferred to use on nights out and actually tried to avoid smoking cannabis in his home. However, he remained reluctant to carry anything more than a single joint when he was going out, often relying instead on friends who were more willing to carry with them. As we have already seen, Ned (53, unemployed, amphetamine user) used amphetamine as part of his continued involvement in the northern soul scene. As well as taking amphetamine at home on most days, he also used when he was out at northern soul events: 'I take some every day and then I have some on weekends when I go out . . . with different people, sort of my age, that go to soul all night discotheques'. Others, particularly those who used cocaine such as Quinn (51, market trader, cannabis and occasional cocaine user), would sporadically use illegal drugs as part of nights out with friends.

Set and setting, transitions and the demise of the subcultural form

The shift in the 'setting' of illegal drug consumption began to make sense when viewed as an accompaniment to the transitions that the participants had experienced over their lifecourse. For many of the participants, as they assumed greater responsibilities in other areas of life it was to a degree inevitable that their leisure became increasingly domesticated. Our participants had to work, to look after children, and so on. Their drug-taking associates tended to be in a similar position. Thus, it was little wonder that their opportunities for regular communal leisure had become restricted; that their illegal drug use now tended to take place quietly, privately and in isolation; and that 'users tended to develop relationships with the drug that were ultimately self-contained, genuinely personal' (Hathaway 1997a: 122). Although the steady accretion of responsibilities in other aspects of life was not a uniform trend, for those participants that it did apply to it was also likely to have influenced their 'set' as well as 'setting' and progressively reinforced their desire to use moderately and retain control.

However, it is also possible to see the changes to the 'setting' of the participants' drug use as being symptomatic of broader shifts associated with late modernity, some of which were noted in Chapter 3. For example, it has been suggested that, for young and old alike, leisure time has increasingly become centred on the private home rather than public space (Haywood et al. 1995: 154). The notion of the wider retreat into individualism (Bauman 2001) also clearly resonates here. Moreover, one is reminded of the debate surrounding the emergence of the supposed 'post-subcultural' era (Bennett 2011), in which some commentators have suggested that the subcultural form itself, at least as traditionally conceived, appears increasingly anachronistic in late modern conditions (Redhead 1990, Muggleton 2000). This, as Bennett has argued, has occurred as a result of social identities becoming 'more reflexive, fluid and fragmented due to an increasing flow of cultural commodities, images and texts through which more individualised identity projects and notions of self could be fashioned' (2011: 493). The result is that 'individualism has surpassed an emphasis on collectivity as a means by which social actors seek out desirable visual images, and construct sociocultural identities, for themselves' (2011: 495). Indeed, among our sample, as we have already seen, only Ned (53, unemployed, amphetamine user) still considered himself to be involved in a subculture, and those erstwhile members of long-decayed or fragmented subcultures now used illegal drugs almost exclusively in domestic settings. Two possibilities emerge here. On the one hand it might be that the shunning of subcultural involvement among the participants was an entirely predictable outcome of their growing older. It might simply be that as they aged, the participants had felt the horizons of once-expansive leisure lives narrow in response to transitions which resulted in the assumption of greater responsibilities elsewhere in life. On the other hand, it is possible that the participants' retreat from subcultural involvement hinted that the very form of the subcultures of their youth was no longer viable. Today's increasingly atomised and individualised social world might lack the stability and normative consensus required to foster anything other than extremely fleeting, ephemeral collectivities. Seen in this light, the participants might well be considered harbingers of the post-subcultural age.[5]

In sum, it was clear that the participants controlled 'set' and 'setting' very closely in order to ensure that each drug experience was a satisfying one. This process was aided by their years of experience, and there were very few variables left to chance. Our participants thus provided good evidence for the argument made by Dalgarno and Shewan that when '"set" and "setting" are correct, the "drug" itself becomes largely irrelevant and can be used with a higher degree of safety, with the effects being as intended for and expected by the user' (2005: 264). The extent to which shifts in the 'setting' of drug use were an inevitable result of growing older, or signalled a more fundamental transformation in the nature of the subject and the rise of individualism, remains an open question.

Reasons for use

Previous research has suggested that there are often straightforward reasons for 'normal' drug use. People tend to indulge simply because they enjoy the effects of their chosen substance (Sullum 2003, Coggans et al. 2004, Warburton, Turnbull and Hough 2005, Dalgarno 2006, Han, Gfroerer and Colliver 2009). Our participants confirmed this and generally held sanguine and uncomplicated attitudes towards their drug use. All of the participants used illegal drugs at least in part because, quite simply, they enjoyed doing so. Without exception they spoke warmly of the pleasant effects of their drug use. This attitude was succinctly expressed by Colin (41, internet entrepreneur, cannabis and occasional other drug user) when he was asked why he used illegal drugs: 'The same reason I'd eat chocolate. I like it', he explained. Most other participants agreed with this sentiment:

> Why? I think it's quite enjoyable to be perfectly honest. Yeah, nothing more than that really. *Ollie, 52, company owner, cannabis and occasional cocaine user.*
>
> I think I like the effects. I don't know if I can describe it! *Vince, 42, academic, cannabis user.*

5 Sandberg (2013) has argued that the contemporary subculture of cannabis use is best understood as a collection of rituals, stories and symbols rather than as a 'group of people' as the traditional view of subcultures would have it. He suggests that cannabis use still signals opposition and cultural difference despite its increasing abundance.

> Because I like them [drugs]. That's it basically, because I like them. *Jane, 47, delivery driver, cannabis, cocaine, and occasional ecstasy user.*
>
> Well, life is just better. Why put salt on the food, why put ketchup on the food? You know why, why when you wake up [to the] alarm, do you just go back down into that warm comfortable bed and you don't want to leave it? That's what cannabis is to me [laughs]. *Liam, 45, unemployed, cannabis user.*

However, as well as this general sense of enjoyment and pleasure, participants sought to achieve a number of very specific results through their use of illegal substances. It was clear that rather than using drugs unthinkingly and without direction, the participants' use was highly targeted and focussed on the pursuit of well-defined ends. Indeed, this desire to realise particular outcomes was a critical feature of each participant's 'set', and to a large degree dictated their substance of choice and the manner in which they used it.

Relaxation

More than anything else, our participants used illegal drugs to facilitate relaxation and stress relief. Of course, this was not a surprise in a sample dominated by cannabis users. The point that drug use was directed at this purpose was made time and again by a number of participants:

> You have a little small one, it like, it takes the pressure off and it relaxes me. . . . I use it [cannabis] simply and solely as a stress relief. *Matthew, 52, self-employed civil engineer, cannabis and occasional cocaine user.*
>
> Relaxation. I think that's what it is. *Uri, 47, care worker, cannabis user.*
>
> You know, I like my weed, I find, I suppose for me, you know there's loads of advantages of taking weed, for me personally, it keeps me mellow, it keeps me chilled, . . . and I like being mellow. *Jane, 47, delivery driver, cannabis, cocaine, and occasional ecstasy user.*
>
> I enjoy it. You know I enjoy it. . . . The reason I do it is because it's the simplest way for me to relax and switch off at the end of the day. I think we're under enough pressure culturally and you know, and the way we live our lives nowadays is at a hundred miles an hour and you know, most people have got no way of relaxing apart from coming in and busting a bottle of wine or whatever they do, meditation or, whatever their thing is. For me it's always been cannabis, it's the easiest and simplest way to relax. And it's fun, you know. *Brian, 52, company owner, cannabis user.*

Energy and alertness

Relaxation was not the only common end, however. For instance, those who used drugs other than cannabis often had very different objectives. Quinn (51, market trader, cannabis and occasional cocaine user), for instance, noted how cocaine lent her a feeling of vigour that was important to her on a night out. She suggested that she 'can't do clubbing without a couple lines of cocaine, you know what I mean. So it's very much like that now'. Meanwhile, Ned's (53, unemployed, amphetamine user) use of drugs was aimed at attaining a feeling of energy and alertness, particularly but not exclusively when he was attending northern soul events. This was reflected in the fact that his drug of choice was amphetamine, and, as we saw earlier, he was the only participant who did not use cannabis whatsoever:

> It makes me wide awake, it makes me do things, it, it helps me with the confidence I suppose, and [it's a] genuine way to stay awake when we go out all night. . . . I know that if ever I sit down in a chair and feel a bit tired and not wanting to do anything I can have a bit of that and I'm off, off I go again. . . . Oh no, it's not relaxing! . . . I hate being relaxed [laughs]. I don't like being, well, I don't mind sitting down, I can sit down and watch telly or sit down with somebody and it'll be alright but when I'm at it, I want to get up and get at it.

Enhancement

A number of participants used illegal drugs as 'enhancers' that could heighten the pleasure derived from other activities. Goode (1970) made a similar finding in his classic study of recreational marijuana users. Members of his sample consumed the drug for pleasure whilst engaged in pursuits such as eating, having sex, listening to music, socialising and watching movies and television. This was also commonplace among our own participants. Tom (41, horticulturalist, cannabis user), for example, suggested that 'it's almost as if it's an enhancer, that whatever you're doing, well if you're doing pleasant things then it'll enhance [them]'. Similarly, Vince (42, academic, cannabis user) discussed how his cannabis use increased the 'intensity' of experiences, even relatively mundane ones, and thus helped to alleviate boredom.

In Tom's (41, horticulturalist, cannabis user) case, his cannabis use was particularly important in enhancing his appreciation of art and music. This was also true of Winston (58, academic, cannabis user):

> I mean I like the effect, . . . making me sort of gently high, I guess, gently high, still able to really enjoy music a lot. Music's a big, big, big part of my life, watching movies and reading you know, that combination of things really, playing with the dog [chuckles].

Meanwhile, Brian (52, company owner, cannabis user) enjoyed the heightened inquisitiveness that his cannabis use encouraged. He felt that cannabis 'opens a door for me, it unlocks part of your mind that allows you to be inquisitive and converse, explore'.

Illegal drug use as a coping mechanism

As well as facilitating relaxation, engendering a feeling of alertness and energy and enhancing other activities, several participants suggested that their illegal drug use helped them to cope with maladies of various kinds. We have already seen that cannabis was often used for stress relief, and many participants also pointed out how their drug use was a useful tool that assisted in their attempts to live with difficulties such as depression, angst, loneliness and physical pain:

> I tried heroin . . . but a lot of times heroin was for the [physical] pain, because I was in that much pain. . . . Because it's just that escape, isn't it, from normal life, from my pain. I mean this, this thing I've got [rheumatoid arthritis], it's something I've had to accept in everyday life, and I keep thinking that eventually I'm going to end up in a wheelchair. *Pat, 51, unemployed, polydrug user.*
>
> It does help me, I've got a bit of a problem with my neck, it helps a little bit with that sort of side of things as well. But I mean, it does help, but how much I don't know really. *Lenny, 53, mechanic, cannabis user.*
>
> I'd say [drug use is] self-medicating, in terms of alleviating depression or coping with stress or accepting one of these conditions in life you can't do anything about. *Tom, 41, horticulturalist, cannabis user.*
>
> I find it very relaxing and as I say it stops me hurting, it stops my back aching and my neck aching, and that's important. *Keith, 63, retired civil servant, cannabis user.*

Other participants had more well-defined medical issues that they used illegal drugs to cope with. For instance, Xavier (55, researcher, polydrug user), as well as using drugs extensively for pleasure, also used them to control his mood and his bipolar disorder:

> I'm bipolar and I can't control my mood swings, and with drugs I can. If my mood swings in a way I don't want it to, I'll swing it back with some chemical or plant, you know, I'll be in control of my moods, not my fucked up brain. You know I had to live half my life in a kind of half-crazed state because I couldn't work out what was wrong and I've seen psychiatrists and I've been diagnosed and they've given me their horrible medicines that turn you into a cabbage and they don't work anything like as well as the illegal drugs and the legal highs do. These have a much, much better effect at self-medicating my mood states than any other.

The 'medical' use of cannabis

Indeed, in line with what is becoming an increasingly prevalent trend (Dahl and Asmussen Frank 2011, Chatwin and Porteous 2013, Hakkarainen et al. 2015), eight participants described their use of cannabis as being primarily for medical reasons. This included Adam (47, unemployed due to disability, cannabis user), who stated that he used cannabis 'purely to relieve, alleviate and reduce the effects of my essential tremor'. As we saw in Chapter 3, Fran (41, retired due to disability, cannabis user), who retired on medical grounds over a decade ago with various complaints, had turned to cannabis as she became increasingly unhappy with the heavy pain-relief medication she had been prescribed:

> I have two or three joints in the evening, my son goes to bed at about 11 o'clock because he works full time, so when he goes to bed at 11 I'll have two or three joints, and it feels, to me it feels like a maintenance dose, it feels like that, that takes me through the day, you know. I don't know whether it's psychological or whatever, but I feel like my body is numb, I'm not feeling as much pain. . . . It just gives me a couple of hours of relief from the life that I live really, you know. I choose to use it [as] part of my pain management.

Nathan (47, unemployed customs officer due to disability, cannabis user), dealing with the after effects of the serious spinal injury noted in Chapter 3 that had forced his early retirement, described how he used different strains of cannabis depending on the severity of his pain:

> I've got two types of cannabis that I smoke. I've got one that just usually allows you to sustain pain, and keep it on a lull but still allows you to be fully active, and then I've got one that's high in CBD, which allows me to, if the pain is really bad, I'll take some of that, . . . get to relax more, ease the muscles off and I can maybe get a sleep for an hour or two while I spasm. I end up with multiple spasms, and the cannabis subsides the spasms, takes them right down, so it works well.

Nathan, like Fran, considered cannabis to be a superior alternative to his prescription medication (which in his case was primarily morphine), as, although it was not quite as effective in terms of relieving his pain, it did not have the same debilitating side effects:

> I feel healthier when I'm using it [cannabis]. I'm on morphine and I've been doing self-detox. . . . It was just getting too much. I'm not feeling like me anymore, I'm feeling like I'm a little zombie walking around in a shell, so I've had to detox from it [morphine]. Because of the detox I've been replacing it with my cannabis and with my [cannabis] oil and it's helping. It's helping, it's not giving me the pain relief that the morphine was but it's getting me very, very close to it. So healthwise, if anything it helps me, because I'm not taking pharmaceutical.

Like Fran and Nathan, Oscar (40, volunteer, cannabis user) also favoured cannabis rather than the various prescription medications he had tried. He was suffering from insomnia and depression and had mental health issues relating to being abused in childhood. Cannabis had assisted him with these issues in a way that his prescription medications had been unable to:

> The worst part of my drugs experience has been with antidepressants that were prescribed to me by a doctor. [They] made me fat [laughs], they gave me anxiety issues, they gave me depression, they gave me suicidal thoughts. So yeah, the only thing that kept all that in check was getting a spliff. . . . [It] relieves stress, anxiety, it stops. Up until last year when I was trying the doctor's antidepressants and all that, I'd be lucky if I had more than four hours' sleep, continual sleep in years and years. So I can smoke a joint and I can pretty much do it. . . . I can pretty much do it for eight, ten, twelve hours sometimes, you know what I mean, I can't describe that feeling to you. . . . Okay, there has been some medication tablets that have knocked me out but I've woken up and I feel like a zombie, white foam coming out of the side of my mouth, . . . and there's none of that with cannabis. Just smoke that, have a nice sleep.

Grace (48, carer for child, cannabis user) suffered from complex regional pain syndrome, and her cannabis use had significantly assisted her attempts to cope with the condition by relieving the pain associated with it and, as with Oscar, helping her to a better night's sleep:

> I don't actually use that much, surprisingly. I'm very sensitive to most things so I only have to smoke maybe a gram a day, which . . . by medical standards is not much at all. Yeah and I use several different strains, different types of cannabis at different times, one throughout the day and then one just before I go to bed at night-time. Because I need a really small amount of that to just kick in because when I lie down and relax my foot just throbs for England and it just feels like it's going to burst, and the strain that I smoke at night time just takes the edge off that enough for me to go to sleep and get some sleep.

Every participant who considered their cannabis use to be for medical reasons acknowledged that they also used the substance for enjoyment and recreation. Often there was no distinction between instances of medical and non-medical use, and each time the participant took the drug it was simultaneously serving its medical purpose and engendering pleasure. Indeed, without exception 'medical users' spoke warmly of the effects of drug use on their social and leisure lives. This included Ian (46, unemployed, cannabis user), who was suffering from depression in addition to the osteoarthritis that we noted in Chapter 3:

> Well, I've got to say I do like the actual high it gives you, the recreational side, but it's also a very good painkiller and it also does help with my

> depression. . . . I'm not going to lie, I did start smoking it mainly for recreational use. . . . One of the reasons when I found out how good it was for pain was when I broke my arm, and when I smoked it the pain just went. You know, so that's why I still carry on smoking it, to deal with my osteoarthritis.

Furthermore, as in Ian's case, every 'medical user' of cannabis had originally used illegal drugs non-medically, and most of them had done so over the long term. For some, there had been a specific incident which led to them seeing their use in a different light, as we have seen in the case of Nathan (47, unemployed customs officer due to disability, cannabis user). His accident saw him repurpose his use and gear it towards pain relief, although he still cheerily accepted that he used for both medical and non-medical reasons. However, for other participants it was sometimes not quite so clear why they had gradually come to perceive of their use as being primarily for medical reasons. As a result of this it was often difficult to say where the line between medical use and non-medical use was. As Ian (46, unemployed, cannabis user) put it:

> For me it's been positive, because you know, the things it actually helps me with is amazing, it's nothing like prescription drugs. I mean I know there are other ways you can take it [cannabis] . . . that would make it more effective for pain, but if I smoke it, you get the recreational side as well [laughs].

Sullum (2003) has suggested that due to the stigma associated with illegal drug use and the pressure from various sources to abstain, many of those who do partake feel anxious about their use and attempt to provide justifications for it. During our interviews, it was often difficult to avoid the impression that participants' categorisation of their illegal drug use as being for medical purposes was a mechanism that allowed them to validate and legitimise that use both to themselves and to the interviewer. This was certainly not the case for all participants who saw their use in this light, but for some, by defining their use as 'medical', they were able to effectively differentiate it from more hedonistic, destructive styles of consumption and thus lend it something of an air of respectability.[6]

6 According to Sullum, this can result in an unhealthy hierarchy of use types. As he puts it, 'seeking a medical or religious exemption from drug prohibition amounts to asserting that *my* use of this substance is important, that it deserves respect in a way that more frivolous uses do not. . . . The urge to offer such excuses is based on the sense that drug use is morally suspect without an elaborate and serious sounding defence. . . . Wine drinkers generally do not feel compelled to proclaim that their beverage was endorsed by God, that it relieves anxiety or reduces their risk of heart disease. They simply say, "I like a nice glass of wine"' (2003: 267–8).

Other reasons

It was clear that all of the participants directed their illegal drug use at very particular ends and they saw their substances of choice as an efficient and effective way to achieve those ends. However, the participants were not merely cold, calculating and rational utility maximisers who used drugs solely on the basis of some crude cost-benefit analysis. To give this impression would be misleading, for the participants in fact tended to look upon drugs with an often touching and heartfelt warmth and affection. After all, the participants' life histories were intrinsically bound up with illegal drug use, and, as well as being a relatively consistent companion, drugs had often played an integral role in some significant life experiences.

Given this, it was unsurprising that a number of participants offered some rather more abstract reasons for their use of illegal drugs. Often these reasons lay in the background and could be obscured by the more immediate purpose of a drug-taking episode. Nevertheless, they provided powerful motivation for continued illegal drug use beyond the specific and desired result of each single instance of drug taking. For example, for a handful of participants, drug use remained a central part of a politically engaged lifestyle. This was the case for Tom (41, horticulturalist, cannabis user), who regarded the simple fact of his drug use as being a continuing statement against what he perceived to be unjust drugs laws. Meanwhile, for some participants, illegal drug use played an important spiritual role. Again, Tom was among this group. He discussed how his drug career had afforded him

> access to the timeless experience of being human, rather than just the experience of seeing the latest film or playing the latest game, so accepting modern culture exists and it is dominant but that human culture is actually much more extensive and timeless than that.

Similarly, Malcolm (44, student, cannabis user) felt that his use of cannabis 'keeps me spiritually connected, I think it keeps you rooted in the moment'. He saw his cannabis use as a means to help him avoid the materialism of modern Western society whilst remaining content with life:

> You know, I'm not materialistic. I think materialism, it's like trying to satisfy hunger by stapling sandwiches on the outside of your body, you know, it doesn't work, and [using drugs] just works for me. It keeps me happy and content I suppose, which at the end of the day is what all of us want isn't it? I suppose if anything it's that.

Xavier (55, researcher, polydrug user), who described himself as a 'psychonaut' (Newcombe 2008), used illegal drugs to help him cope with what he saw as the lack of spiritual meaning in life. He expressed this in particularly stark terms:

> [I use drugs] because they give my life meaning, because there's no spiritual meaning in life. I'm an atheist, there's no god. I've used drugs to find this out, there's no god.

Winston (58, academic, cannabis user) felt that his use of illegal drugs had constituted an important plank of his social identity for several decades. Indeed, he recalled a period during his long career as an academic when drug use was also an important part of his professional identity too:

> You know, probably since I was 20 you know, it's been for nearly 40 years, it's just been what you do, you know, it's been part and parcel of being a sort of, quotes, you know, "bohemian middle class", you know [chuckles]. . . . It's funny isn't it, as I say for a long time certainly it was part and parcel of being a "cool academic". If anything it might, it might've gone against you if you didn't, you know, [chuckles] if you were straight you were in a bit of a bad way really. So, you know, I knew some people and we looked down on some people who were seen as straight. It's a horrible arrogant sort of reversal isn't it?

However, it is important not to overstate this. Winston and Xavier were outliers in this respect, and most participants did not tend to see drugs as bestowing meaning to their lives or as being integral to their sense of self in this way (see also Shukla 2006: 176), nor did they regard their use as forming a part of their 'master status' (Hughes 1945, Lloyd 2010). In fact, even for those who did offer a more abstract reason for their illegal drug use (and not every participant did so), on a day-to-day basis their use tended to operate as more of a rather mundane coping mechanism that assisted in their efforts to manage the stresses and anxieties of life, and did so in an agreeably efficient and pleasurable manner. The initial thrill that many of the participants had felt as they were discovering drugs had long since passed, and their current use tended not to be characterised by the celebratory 'joyous outburst' of the teenage years that Roger (44, manager in a small firm, cannabis user) described in Chapter 3. Nevertheless the affection for illegal drugs lingered on. As Tom (41, horticulturalist, cannabis user) put it when reflecting upon his relationship with cannabis, 'I'll call it a crutch but maybe it is partly a partner in some sense, obviously not a human partner, but a companion in life'.

Legal alternatives

Interestingly, the use of illegal drugs among our participants was directed at purposes that could have been realised to a great degree through legally permissible means. Our participants might well have chosen to go to the cinema for enjoyment, drink alcohol for relaxation, smoke tobacco for stimulation, take prescription medication for pain, or meditate for spiritual reasons, and indeed sometimes they did. Yet illegal drugs were turned to time and again despite their illegality, the effort required in sourcing them and the expense involved in acquiring them. This was partly down to the fact that the participants often had more complex, abstract reasons for using illegal drugs as discussed above, but also simply because illegal drugs were considered by the participants to be a more effective means of obtaining their desired results than the legal alternatives.

Indeed, many participants were keen to compare their illegal drug use to the use of tobacco and, to an even greater extent, alcohol. Unequivocally, the participants saw illegal drugs as a superior alternative to drink. For example, as Matt (52, self-employed civil engineer, cannabis and occasional cocaine user) pointed out, choosing a cannabis joint over beer meant that 'I don't have to get up and go to the toilet, I don't wake up with a hangover in the morning, . . . you haven't got a splitting headache, you haven't got a mouth like a bloody, somebody's back door'. Colin (41, internet entrepreneur, cannabis and occasional other drug user) was particularly strident regarding this:

> On occasions when I've had far too much to drink and I've been obnoxious as a result of that, that's the only drug I can think of where I can say I've had a negative. Only alcohol. The only drug that ever turned me into something which I would regret because I know that's not me. . . . Alcohol is the only drug that has ever caused me to do things that I regret.

There was a decidedly liberal tone to the participants' opinions here. They felt that it was simply a matter of personal taste as to which substances individuals preferred when relaxing or socialising and distinctions between substances that were legal and those which were not were rather artificial in this sense. Indeed, most were stridently opposed to the illegal status of their drugs of choice, as we will see in Chapter 5. The essential sameness of individuals using substances for pleasure, be they legal or illegal, was commented upon by several participants:

> Somebody has a glass of wine, you know, when they go out. I might have the odd joint and a line of coke. I don't really see, to me I don't really see the difference. You know what I mean? I mean a lot of people go out every night and they're drinking loads and loads and loads of alcohol, you know, smoking lots and lots of cigarettes. I might occasionally have a joint and a line of coke. To me it's just the same. *Quinn, 51, market trader, cannabis and occasional cocaine user.*
>
> Maybe it's no different to, you know, wine or spirits. I mean yeah, I think it's probably as simple as that, you know, it's just personal taste and I don't think it's any more complicated than that. *Ollie, 52, company owner, cannabis and occasional cocaine user.*
>
> Because I think life is tough and I think we all need a little reprieve one way or another and I think we all do it in one way or another, whatever way that may be, and that's just my personal choice, that's just what I prefer. *Malcolm, 44, student, cannabis user.*

A 'normal' choice in a liminal world

In sum, our participants used illegal drugs for a variety of reasons. They tended to have a very clear idea of what they wanted from their illegal drugs, and their use was specifically targeted at those purposes. As we have seen, this included the promotion of enjoyment, relaxation and stress relief. Some used in order to feel energetic and alert, whilst for others drug use was an enhancer that made other activities more pleasurable. A number of participants also used illegal drugs for specific medical reasons. However, the decision to use illegal drugs was not merely a cold, calculated one; many commented upon the close nature of their relationship with their substances of choice, and often political and spiritual concerns provided the backdrop to use. Indeed, most participants saw their use as serving multiple ends and felt it a better option than the legal alternatives such as alcohol. All of this is not particularly surprising, and much of it has been noted before; Hathaway, for example, found that cannabis was 'rather routinely used as a practical tool with a variety of potential uses' (1997b: 230). As Eric (40, consultant for relocation firm, cannabis user) put it, 'it's given me the enjoyment of learning, definitely, it certainly made me more worldly, it definitely chilled me out no end, yeah, all positives really in my head'. Tom (41, horticulturalist, cannabis user) agreed, suggesting that cannabis was 'multipurpose in the sense of it'll enhance the highs, the natural highs, and help with coping with the lows'.

Seen in this light, the illegal drug use of our participants begins to look like a rather unremarkable activity in a social world shorn of the more stringent normative codes that characterised the immediate post-war years. As discussed above, for our participants, unlike in some previous research, illegal drug use generally did not seem to bestow identity, provide their 'master status' or contribute to their sense of self. Moreover, it did not represent an attempt at risky, boundary challenging 'edgework' (Lyng 1990, Reith 2005). It did not appear to be a celebratory aspect of their continual reinvention in the postmodern consumer bazaar. It did not foment any sense of emancipation. Instead, it was a routine and even rather workaday mechanism that provided some kind of limited relief from the stresses and anxieties of life. As Liam (45, unemployed, cannabis user) put it, 'when I have a negative outlook on life weed is very important because that makes things very bearable, it makes things a lot more congenial'. Thus, for our participants, illegal drug use was best seen as a 'peripheral but "normal"' (Pearson 2001: 173) part of the struggle to cope with what were often distinctly late modern pressures. It was 'peripheral' in the sense that it was always a contingent feature of existence as we saw in Chapter 3, and it was 'normal' in the sense that it was a largely unproblematic aspect of life for people who were, in Cohen and Sas's phrase, 'mainstream citizens' (1994: 72).

The bulk of recent work on liminality 'has a predominantly negative connotation', but some studies of liminality in specific organisational contexts have argued that liminality 'does not have to be experienced in negative terms' (Robinson, Burke and Millings 2016: 166). Beech (2011), for example, has argued that liminality offers the chance for potentially positive practices of reflection, experimentation and recognition as liminars seek to reconstruct their identity. Robinson, Burke and Millings found individuals who were 'seemingly unfazed or even energized by their "liminal" status' in their study of the restructuring of probation in England and Wales (2016: 166). However, this did not reflect the experience of our participants, who, as Chapter 3 suggested, generally saw the uncertainty and tumult of their lifecourse as something to be endured rather than enjoyed. And it was precisely here where the irony of the illegal drug use of our participants lay. At the very same time as their drug use provided a bulwark against the pressures of living in a social world marked by permanent liminality, it was also subject, like everything else, to the vertiginous uncertainty of that world. Abrupt and unforeseen changes in circumstances could, as we saw time and again in Chapter 3, engender changes in the consumption patterns of our participants so that the benefits they currently enjoyed as a result of their illegal drug use might become more difficult to realise at any given moment. The enjoyment, pleasure, relaxation, stress relief and energy that drug use promoted, the manner in which it enhanced and heightened other activities, the assistance it offered when participants were feeling low or suffering from ill health, its contribution to their political and spiritual selves and the warm and enduring relationship that they enjoyed with their drug of choice could all be potentially lost at a stroke. As we will see in the following chapter, no participant had any plans to stop drug use. Yet because the current use patterns detailed in this chapter were contingent upon the participants' present circumstances, when those circumstances changed, as they surely would, then illegal drug use would once again need to be reconfigured. One could not say with any conviction which direction lifecourse trajectories would move in, and therefore one could never be sure that the relief currently offered by illegal drug use would endure.

The effects of illegal drug careers

The participants were, on the whole, remarkably relaxed about the impacts of their drug careers on their lives and tended to see their drug use in positive terms. Of course, it was not always easy for participants to provide an assessment of the long-term effects of drug use on other lifecourse trajectories, for as Zach (66, retired fitter, cannabis user) suggested, 'I don't know what my life would have been like without it'. This issue notwithstanding, this section will consider the participants' views on the effects of their drug careers on family life, working life and their health. It will end with an exploration of their feelings on the overall impacts of their lengthy drug careers.

Effects on family life

The participants generally considered that the effects of their drug careers on their families and relationships had been minimal. Only five participants felt that there had been some negative impact. This included Fran (41, retired due to disability, cannabis user), whose drug use made her son uncomfortable and Pat (51, unemployed, polydrug user), whose daughter had long struggled to come to terms with her mother's drug use. However, two-thirds of the participants said that there had been little or no effect. Nevertheless, even for those who were sanguine about the effects of their drug career on family life, it remained clear that the integration of illegal drug use into one's domestic life was often not straightforward. For example, as we saw in Chapter 3, some participants had experienced difficulties in the past with partners who were not as keen on illegal drug use as they were (see also Hathaway 1997a). That said, many participants felt that their drug use had been beneficial to their relationships with partners, children and friends, helping them, for instance, to be more sociable (Zach, 66, retired fitter, cannabis user) or to be a more patient and forgiving parent (Nathan, 47, unemployed customs officer due to disability, cannabis user).

Effects on working life

Similarly, just under two-thirds of the participants felt that their working lives had not been particularly affected one way or another by their illegal drug use. Most were keen to stress that they did not mix their drug use with work and were always careful to ensure that their performance was not hindered by it (Shukla 2006). Uri (47, care worker, cannabis user), for example, stated, 'I never mix it with work. . . . I know probably it'd affect my efficiency and all the rest'. Quinn (51, market trader, cannabis and occasional cocaine user) shared a similar outlook: 'I always kept work together. I never, never didn't go to work. . . . I might have been a bit spaced out going to work, but I would always rigidly keep work together. I would never have a day off'. Indeed, refraining from using illegal drugs when in particular contexts, such as when at work, was one of the methods by which the cannabis users in Frank, Christensen and Dahl's (2013) study maintained a 'meaningful' life. As Sullum suggests, 'the same social and economic forces that encourage moderation in drinking – the need to earn a living, a sense of obligation to family and friends, the desire to see oneself and be perceived by others as responsible and productive – would encourage moderation in the use of other drugs' (2003: 272). This was certainly also the case for our participants.

A handful of participants suggested that their illegal drug use had actually been beneficial to them in their working lives (Hathaway 1997b), making them more focussed (Grace, 48, carer for child, cannabis user), better at problem solving (Yannis, 47, regional manager, cannabis user) and more creative (Adam, 47, unemployed due to disability, cannabis user). Brian (52, company owner, cannabis user) also felt his drug use had contributed to his creativity and made the point with an allusion to one of his favourite bands: 'The Beatles right, the Beatles were writing 'Love Me Do', and then they took acid and they wrote *Sgt. Pepper*. Now, there's got to be a link! [laughs] There has to be a link!' The use of illegal drugs for stress relief and relaxation, which as we have seen was very common among our participants, also had knock on effects in the working lives of some, as Vince (42, academic, cannabis user) described:

> I think [drugs have had] mainly a positive effect, quite therapeutic, and I very much doubt if I would have stayed in the job I'm in now as long if

> I hadn't used that as a crutch, as something that I go back to occasionally or that I can always take refuge in occasionally, to escape the kind of stress that I experience in my job. So, I've come very close to packing it in a lot of times and I suspect that using it and using it in a therapeutic way has actually helped me to, in the longer term, survive work.

On the other hand, participants continuously faced the possibility that they would somehow become embroiled with the authorities regarding their illegal drug use, and they were very aware that this could have potentially serious impacts upon their working life. The care that participants took to ensure their use remained 'hidden' was, in part, designed to ensure that this did not happen. As Uri (47, care worker, cannabis user) suggested:

> You had to be really careful . . . you don't want a record and it affects things like job prospects. I do care about work now and it was the one thing I was worried about and might have got me out of a job.

For a handful of participants there had been occasions when their efforts at keeping their drug use hidden had failed and the very fact of their drug use (rather than any real or perceived negative effects) had resulted in serious consequences in their working lives. Most notably, Nathan (47, unemployed customs officer due to disability, cannabis user) had been suspended from a previous job after a neighbour tipped off the police about his modest home-grow operation: 'I'd been growing it for several years and it hadn't been a problem, just one of my neighbours happened to know. I got too friendly and [got] found out'. Although no plants were recovered, Nathan's equipment for growing and the remnants of previous batches were enough to earn him a police caution and a suspension from work.

Despite Nathan's difficulties, it was clear that in general the participants did not feel that their drug use had negatively impacted upon their working lives. If anything they were keener to point out the benefits that drug use had brought, as we have seen. Ollie (52, company owner, cannabis and occasional cocaine user), discussing the impacts of his drug career on his working life and family life, perhaps best summed up the general attitude of the participants in this regard:

> If the implication is has it adversely affected it, then I would say no I don't think it has. I mean I've got 80 people work for me here, you know. I've been reasonably successful in business, been married 27 years, got two kids who are pretty normal, you know. I can't really see that it could have affected me particularly adversely at all.

Effects on health

The perceived effects of illegal drug use on health were more ambiguous. Those who did not see their use as being for medical purposes tended to be more conscious of the potentially deleterious effects of lengthy drug careers on their general well-being. Vince (42, academic, cannabis user), for example, felt:

> I can't believe that smoking anything is going to be very good for you, you know, for your lungs and your respiratory system. So that's another thing which makes me feel more careful about what I do, you know, and I've considered other ways of taking it if I'm going to take it at all. So yeah, it's hard to know where it's going to go from here, you know, if my asthma does get worse, then I'll really have to maybe make a sacrifice then.

Malcolm (44, student, cannabis user) voiced similar concerns:

> More than anything it's my lungs. Yeah. I've been smoking organic baccy, I started smoking organic baccy about five years ago because my lungs were so bad, my lungs were gurgling, I could hear myself at night, you know, and I started smoking this organic baccy about five years ago. . . . I mean my lungs are better now than they were five years ago, because for 20-odd years I smoked normal tobacco, with resin, resin soapbar. It's got tar in it, it's got plastic in it, it's got curry powder in it, you know, so I did that for twenty years and I've done more damage then than I've probably done in the last five years, because now I smoke organic baccy. But yeah my lungs, you know when I was a kid I just used to be running everywhere, now I couldn't get to the end of the street [laughs].

For some participants such as Winston (58, academic, cannabis user), health-related concerns had already motivated them to begin to reduce the frequency of their use, and the amount that they consumed when they did use. As Winston put it, 'if [it's] not made me stop, it's put the brakes on it dramatically'.

Others, however, were far less concerned. Tom (41, horticulturalist, cannabis user) felt that his drug intake had only had a 'very minor' impact on his health, as 'by remaining physically active outdoors I think I'm compensating for the bad effect of tobacco smoking'. Yannis (47, regional manager, cannabis user) was also extremely relaxed about the potential health implications of his drug use:

> I just feel healthy and fit, not as healthy and fit as I did at 20 but I'm sure there's not many at my age that could say that. I don't have any difficulties with doing anything physical. I feel wonderfully healthy.

Similarly Brian (52, company owner, cannabis user), despite admitting that he was unsure as to the actual health impacts of his drug use, showed little concern:

> I don't know. I haven't got a clue. I mean I might drop down tomorrow as far as I know. I haven't been ill for years, I still go up ladders high, I

> can still run without getting out of breath. I had asthma quite bad when I was younger but smoking cannabis alleviates the asthma, and now I feel it's almost gone, I hardly use my pumps any more. So no, not that I know, I mean I'm a bit overweight but that's because I eat too much and I like my beer too much but apart from that not really no, I don't think.

Some of the cannabis users in the sample, especially those who considered their use as being for primarily medical purposes, had ceased smoking and were now using a vapouriser to ingest the drug instead. Liam (45, unemployed, cannabis user), who did not consider himself a medical user but had made the switch, felt that doing so had brought noticeable health benefits:

> Once I saw the light and got the vapouriser I don't think it [using cannabis] has any ill effect on my health, insomuch as anything really has. . . . Mental health most definitely, most definitely a positive effect on my mental health. Just knowing that I have it there, I know I have that release just waiting for me to go back to. Five minutes to warm up the vaporiser than five minutes to warm up the weed once it's in there, then I've got vapour coming through. About four and a half minutes to fill the bag, and then I'm there [laughs].

Those who characterised their use of illegal drugs as being for primarily medical reasons had a very different take on the health impacts of their use. As we have already seen, these participants were extremely keen to stress the health benefits that their drug use had engendered. Adam (47, unemployed due to disability, cannabis user), for example, was eager to tell of the relief that cannabis offered him:

> I've got essential tremor, which is a non-fatal version of Parkinson's disease. Right, I've had deep brain stimulation, I've got a neural stimulator in, in the last five years . . . Apparently I was born with this illness and they didn't find out about it until five years ago, so you know it was a bit awkward. So I've been going through my whole life with symptoms of Parkinson's disease, you know, shaking, memory problems, walking problems, you know, so taking drugs was sort of like a nice release from it, you know, I didn't have to worry about it. . . . Throughout all the time of all these other drugs I tried I've been smoking cannabis. I've been smoking cannabis since I was 17, for 30 years. Constantly. Because it helps my neurological condition.

As we have seen, the use of prescription medications had proved problematic for a number of participants. This included Xavier (55, researcher, polydrug user), who had experienced difficulties with prescription antidepressants and suggested that illegal drugs had provided him with a more agreeable alternative:

> I'd probably be dead now if it wasn't for drug use because of the terrible, terrible dark depression I've had to go through in my life. Yeah, it was only

> drugs that brought me out of them, all the stuff the doctor gave me did nothing, so it might have knackered my [physical] health a bit but hey, I wouldn't be here at all if it wasn't for drugs.

Fran (41, retired due to disability, cannabis user), as we saw earlier, felt that her cannabis use had contributed significantly to colossal improvements in her general quality of life:

> I took antidepressants for 20 years, and I lived in pretty much a dark cloud for much of that time. When I stopped taking medication, I mean just the act of stopping taking medication . . . just stopping taking the medication helped massively. What I smoke now, I feel that it helps me deal with the pain, the pain that I live with, the physical pain that I live with and I also don't have the depression anymore.

Fran also used cannabis as part of a battery of techniques, including meditation, which helped her to combat her long-standing and debilitating anxiety. Whilst she remained uncertain as to which of these techniques was most valuable and the extent to which any single one would be effective in isolation from the others, she was convinced that her drug use had a massively positive effect on her health and indeed on her life in general.

Nathan (47, unemployed customs officer due to disability, cannabis user) made a similar point. In addition to assisting him with health issues resulting directly from his spinal injury, Nathan's long-term cannabis use, he felt, had also contributed to the general good health he had enjoyed throughout his life. Again, this was clearly very difficult to measure, but Nathan was in little doubt as to cannabis's more general benefits, and if nothing else it provided him with the peace of mind and sense of contentment that is often so vital to a healthy life. As he put it, 'I enjoy how it makes me feel. I've enjoyed the health benefits of it, growing older with no colds, no flu, no headaches, never taken a day off work. [It's] got to be down to something'.

Effects on life in general

If the participants were somewhat equivocal as to the impact that illegal drug use had on their health, with some showing concern at the potential effects of a lifetime of use, and others being enthusiastic champions of the medical use of illegal substances, there was a clearer consensus regarding the impacts of drug use on their lives in general, with the overwhelming majority of participants seeing their drug careers in extremely positive terms.

That said, this feeling was not quite universal. There were eight participants who suggested that the impacts of illegal drug use on their lives had been somewhat ambiguous, although they did tend towards the positive. Derek (50, gardener, cannabis and occasional mushroom user), for example, had seen the direction of his life take a turn after discovering illegal drugs and becoming involved in a different milieu. Although he was happy and relaxed about his subsequent direction, he did wonder what may have been if he had remained more career focussed:

> Yeah, I think it's affected my life a lot. I think my life would be very different had I not come across it. I think initially I had a kind of big shift in perspective, a change of consciousness even. . . . I started doing lots of things that I'd never thought about before and that was quite a lot of political kinds of activism, things like that, social activism, that I started doing around the same time with the same people that I smoked [with]. At the college I was at . . . there was a group that were trying to get the college to divest South African investments, shares and things, and that was led by some kind of refugee students from South Africa who smoked. And smoking with them I really kind of picked up on their, on their passion for, you know, this cause of [the] anti-apartheid movement. And campus occupations and things like that which seemed to be, you know I got into that, into that sort of thing as a result of smoking, and that meant that I then probably became a lot less career oriented. Maybe if I hadn't tried it I'd have gone into, I mean not that I haven't worked in technical jobs since then, but I would have been maybe more motivated to make money, rather than trying to help social causes I suppose.

Pat (51, unemployed, polydrug user) was perhaps the most downbeat of all when asked about the general impact of illegal drug use on her life. As we have already discussed, Pat's life was arguably the most chaotic of all the participants, and she had suffered from debilitating health issues, including depression, for many years. Her attitude to drugs was extremely ambivalent. On the one hand she 'wouldn't recommend it [drug use] to nobody, actually', but she still enjoyed using a wide variety of drugs and felt that her life may have ended up in a worse state if she had not sustained a lengthy drug career: 'Honestly and truthfully, I don't know where I would have been now if I hadn't have took them. Where would I be, I don't know, I just don't know'.

For a handful of participants, there had at certain times during their drug careers been a sense of unease at breaking the law. This, rather than any effects of drug use in and of itself, had sometimes had a negative impact on the participants, for it had encouraged a nagging and persistent anxiety. This was perhaps best expressed by Fran (41, retired due to disability, cannabis user):

> It makes you feel like a criminal, you know. I'm constantly concerned. I hate, I absolutely hate having to go out to pick up drugs basically, because it's illegal at the end of the day, and it makes me feel like a criminal, it makes me feel like I'm doing something so wrong. And I'm also constantly concerned I'm going to get pulled by the police. I'd be terrified to get pulled by the police, I'm a generally law abiding person apart from that I buy illegal drugs you know.

Harry (40, NHS support worker, cannabis user) shared these sentiments to the extent that the bulk of his use was reserved for his regular trips to Amsterdam, so reluctant was he to break the law at home:

> I don't want to break the law. I mean I have, don't get me wrong. Sometimes somebody gives you a bit of weed but I consciously don't do it all the time. . . . At the end of the day if it was legal, if they legalised it today, then definitely I would probably start [to use more regularly at home].

For Jane (47, delivery driver, cannabis, cocaine, and occasional ecstasy user), the feelings of unease that she associated with partaking in an illegal activity had increased in intensity as she had grown older and experienced major transitions and turning points such as becoming a parent:

> Funnily enough as I get older, obviously I'm getting a lot older, and it's the legalities of it now. I start to think, you know, god, if I was busted you know, what would happen? Maybe that's because I'm a mum as well, I'm a parent, but you know, yeah as I get older and that, it does [concern me], you know.

Yet these participants were in the minority. Most participants, whilst they often vehemently opposed the illegal status of their substances of choice (as we will see in the next chapter), were relatively unconcerned about becoming tangled up in the machinery of the legal system. They were generally happy to go about their drug use as they pleased without giving too much thought to its illegality, although of course they did tend to take precautions to ensure they remained hidden from the authorities.

> I don't think about, I don't think about it at all. Not that I go out and do anything else illegal, but there you are. *Zach, 66, retired fitter, cannabis user.*

Overall, despite the reservations that were expressed by some participants, the clear majority (over two-thirds of the sample) were overwhelmingly positive about their lengthy personal histories with illegal drugs. Their upbeat take on their drug careers to date and their continued enthusiasm for drug use was palpable:

> I don't think that looking back over the years it has caused me any negatives. I think it makes me calmer, a more rounded individual. *Yannis, 47, regional manager, cannabis user.*
>
> It hasn't really had any effect on the major choices I've made my life, no not at all. . . . It has made me into a more sociable sort of fellow really, I think so. . . . You know I find it's helped me get through life. *Zach, 66, retired fitter, cannabis user.*
>
> Yeah, I mean for me it's always been positive. I've never allowed any of the drugs to interfere with my working life. . . . It hasn't affected me

> negatively at all. I still get up at five, six in the morning, I work hard, I earn good money, I maintain good relationships, I've got a great relationship with my ex-wife, my children hang out with me. *Brian, 52, company owner, cannabis user.*
>
> [Drugs have] also given me insights into the nature of reality and into things beyond reality that most ordinary people will never experience in this non-spiritual capitalist brick cage that we live in called the modern world. *Xavier, 55, researcher, polydrug user.*

Indeed, for all of the participants, even those who held some reservations about the overall impacts of drug use, there was a distinct sense that their illegal drug careers had added something positive, however intangible, to their lifecourse. And, for most of the participants, there were no regrets at all:

> But the thing about the whole thing is I don't regret any of it. I don't regret doing a single thing. *Malcolm, 44, student, cannabis user.*

Summary

This chapter has highlighted a number of clear tendencies in the current drug-use patterns of the participants in the study. Together they can be taken as some modest evidential building blocks for what Hammersley (2011: 414) calls a 'theory of normal drug use' for this particular cohort. Cannabis was overwhelmingly the favoured drug among the participants, although other drugs were used by some. With one or two exceptions, those who did still enjoy a varied repertoire most frequently used a single drug of choice (usually cannabis), and other drugs were generally reserved for special occasions. Participants obtained drugs from a variety of sources, but there was a clear preference for 'social supply' channels, which would be used whenever possible. Many of the participants used drugs every day, but for some their use was more occasional than in the past. Some participants saw their use increase around holidays. There was for many a recognition of the contingency of their current use patterns and an awareness that they may not be able to continue with them indefinitely if their circumstances were to change. All the participants made attempts to control set and setting. They demonstrated a high level of knowledge about the effects of their chosen drugs, and were generally minded towards moderation. Some basic control mechanisms had been adopted across the sample. In terms of setting, participants tended to consume drugs at home, either alone or with a small number of family members or close confidants. This was suggestive of broader processes of individualisation associated with late modernity. The participants generally used illegal drugs simply because they enjoyed the effects; most appreciated the stress relieving and relaxing properties of their drug of choice. A smaller but still substantial group of cannabis users had redefined their use as taking place for primarily medical reasons, but all in this group still found their use pleasurable. In general participants felt that the impact of illegal drugs on their lives had been positive and had not hindered their family lives, relationships or working lives. There was less consensus on the issue of health, with some participants showing concern over the potential effects of long-term drug use, whilst others were positively evangelical about the impacts of their cannabis use on a range of physical and mental maladies.

In sum, it was clear that our participants enjoyed a happy and relatively uncomplicated relationship with illegal drugs. They indulged simply because they found their drugs of choice to be pleasurable and beneficial in a number of ways, and they were generally relaxed about any potential deleterious effects of their use. It was also plain that sustained drug use in and of itself had proven to be no barrier to an otherwise 'conventional' life involving family, employment and so on. In addition, illegal drug use offered participants some relief from the unsettling and unpredictable nature of day-to-day existence in a social world increasingly marked by insecurity. The irony was that the participants' illegal drug use, being so dependent upon other aspects of their lives as we saw in Chapter 3, was itself also subject to uncertainty; it was as provisional as the liminal world that it offered some small respite from. The future, which we turn to in the next chapter, was fundamentally unknowable.

5 Future

Prospects for hidden illegal drug use among older adults

This final chapter will assess the prospects for the future of 'normal', hidden illegal drug use among older adults. It will begin by looking at the future intentions of the participants in this research study with regard to their illegal drug use. Then it will consider the issue of illegality, exploring the participants' views on the fact that their drug use is a proscribed activity and reflecting upon the implications of such 'normal' drug use for the legalisation debate. Next, we tentatively move beyond the confines of our own data and reflect upon the question of normalisation. We will speculate that there is considerable potential for illegal drug use among older adults to become progressively normalised as younger, more drug-involved cohorts grow older, but also as the disruptive forces of late modernity render the idea of a 'mainstream', non-deviant culture increasingly problematic. Following this, we consider the limits of this rather modest study and the potential way forward for research with a similar focus. Finally, we will end the book with a summary of the main arguments that we have put forward and offer some brief concluding thoughts.

Future intentions

Previous research suggests that adults who are using illegal drugs 'normally' generally see no reason to stop their use and have no intentions to do so provided that their circumstances do not significantly change (Warburton, Turnbull and Hough 2005). This was supported by the participants in this study. As we saw in Chapter 4, they tended to view their drug careers in a very positive light and felt them to be relatively unproblematic. Given this, it was unsurprising that not a single participant had any plans to stop using illegal drugs. Time and again, the participants were extremely clear about this:

> With all the difficulties with it being illegal, with it being difficult to source, with the quality and availability being erratic and with all those things making it difficult, I still think they're all enough of a price to pay for something that we enjoy doing. And you know, much the same way that some people enjoy a glass of wine, some people a walk up a mountain, or a cup of coffee, or whatever it is that floats your boat, and that is one of the things

> that floats my boat, makes me happy. I can combine it with a number of other things in my life without having any real negatives. I really can't think of a reason why I would try and stop. *Yannis, 47, regional manager, cannabis user.*
>
> I really have got no reason to stop. *Zach, 66, retired fitter, cannabis user.*
>
> I could say that I've virtually stopped now, but stopping forever and ever, I don't see it as a problem. Probably not. *Simon, 61, researcher, cannabis user.*
>
> I'm sure it's possible but I don't plan on stopping. I do plan on cutting down, but only just! *Uri, 47, care worker, cannabis user.*
>
> I've never thought about stopping as such. It's never occurred to me I might stop, I mean, you know, I might not have any for ages, but I wouldn't think I'd stopped. *Roger, 44, manager in a small firm, cannabis user.*
>
> I mean why would I stop smoking? Why would I stop smoking? No, I can't think of a good reason, no. *Brian, 52, company owner, cannabis user.*
>
> I will do this hopefully until the day I die. *Jane, 47, delivery driver, cannabis, cocaine, and occasional ecstasy user.*
>
> Even if I was dying of cancer and they told me I needed to stop I would still go down with one. I would still go down with one. *Nathan, 47, unemployed customs officer due to disability, cannabis user.*

Those participants who considered their use of cannabis to be primarily for medical reasons not only had no plans to stop but also often felt that they had little choice but to carry on using the drug in the absence of better alternatives. Grace (48, carer for child, cannabis user), for example, who as we saw in Chapter 4 suffered from complex regional pain syndrome, stated, 'I don't see it [stopping] as being an option because when I have to travel and I don't have access to medical cannabis, I start to go into flare up with it, [after] about three or four days, so for me, no, it's not really an option'.

Whilst the participants had no desire to give up their illegal drug use, many of them did suggest that if their circumstances were to change in certain ways, then they may well stop at some point in the future. The participants' continued well-being was especially important to them, and many felt that if their drug use began to detrimentally affect their health, then they would be reluctantly forced to consider giving up.

> I reckon I'll still occasionally have it when I feel like having it, but as I say I increasingly worry about, every time I do smoke it you know, coughing's not good. . . . Yeah I'd quite happily, if I was healthy and 90 I'd think it's bloody great to have a good fat joint, and do sculpting and do stuff with time on my hands, you know. . . . I don't see the downside of it, unless it felt like it was affecting your ability to intellectually function. You know, so it'd be health, health or paranoia I think. You know, health and feeling it's somehow [affecting] physical health and mental health, they'd be the two, that's the bottom line isn't it? *Winston, 58, academic, cannabis user.*

> [I would stop] only for health reasons. And that would either be for physical health or for mental health. But I don't envisage mental health problems, because I know the parameters I feel you should or shouldn't do, or what I should and shouldn't do and what I can and can't do. So that's kind of about managing it, so yeah, I think really only for medical health reasons. That would be the only reason that I would maybe want to stop taking it. *Vince, 42, academic, cannabis user.*

If health issues would not necessarily force the participants to stop their use entirely, then they would at least make them consider changing their patterns of consumption and reducing the amount that they used. Xavier (55, researcher, polydrug user), for example, was beginning to seriously think about cutting down on his amount of smoking and had discussed the matter with his son:

> If my breathing gets so bad that I can't get up those stairs [chuckles] then, yeah, I'd probably stop smoking. I'd take just snorting, swallowing, injecting. There's always the rectal route, never tried that. . . . Yeah, you know, I mean I've switched to these electronic cigarettes like I said . . . that's a compromise, so yeah the only thing I'm likely to do is to stop smoking drugs. My son's mainly on my case about it. He said, "look dad, I know you're 55 and you still take more drugs than the average bloody 25 year old, but can you stop the smoking you know, give up the weed and the smokable herbs". So we're having a discussion about that at the moment and I said I am prepared to consider giving up smoking drugs but I won't stop swallowing, sniffing, injecting and otherwise imbibing. . . . If they could give me some new lungs it wouldn't be a problem, but they can't. I did ask!

Derek (50, gardener, cannabis and occasional mushroom user) was also pondering a plan to reduce his pattern of use and the overall amount of his consumption in light of health concerns.

> I've got no plan to quit, but . . . I'm coming round more to the point of view that I should sort of abstain for a while. You know regularly, you know, maybe a month without it every year or something. . . . So I'm not, I don't see giving it up entirely but I would quite like to change my pattern of use and have regular breaks from it.

As we saw in Chapter 4, some of the participants who were regular users of cannabis had already stopped or significantly reduced their smoking of the drug and were instead using vaporising machines. Such a switch was particularly common amongst those who considered themselves to be primarily medical users. This switch was not the only one that was being considered, however:

> Ultimately I enjoy it too much. . . . Even if there was an ultimate health risk, [if] someone said to me "right, okay, you've got lung cancer", I'd

> probably fine tune how to make the batter and then start making cookies. So maybe the delivery method will change but not the actual substance. *Eric, 40, consultant for relocation firm, cannabis user.*

In addition to worries about their health, many of the participants also felt that changes in their other circumstances might affect their continued use of illegal drugs. In discussing this, the participants demonstrated a keen awareness of the liminal nature of their current situations and the likelihood of future transitions and turning points. It seemed that a lifecourse marked by shifts and swings in circumstance had made all participants conscious of the fact that their present conditions could not be taken for granted and that their status as illegal drug users was always necessarily provisional. A good example of this was provided by those who suggested that a change in their family circumstances or the meeting of a new partner might threaten their continued use:

> [If I had children] I probably still wouldn't give it up, but I would then become very, very limited when I would do it I think. And, as I said, I have a friend, who I've known since I was a teenager, who stills smokes occasionally and he's got kids now and he does less and less. But occasionally he grabs the opportunity but it has to be very, very carefully managed and he has very little time. *Vince, 42, academic, cannabis user.*
>
> Yeah I mean, it just depends. I mean, certainly if I got married and I was with somebody and not going out to these [events] then I suppose I would do [stop], but I have no reason not to. *Ned, 53, unemployed, amphetamine user.*
>
> Well actually, a funny thing happened to me over Christmas, yeah. I met a girl and I was sure, we didn't talk about this, but I was sure she wouldn't like me smoking. She probably knows I smoke cigarettes but probably didn't know I smoke cannabis. And it was getting serious, nothing came of it anyway, but the question had come to me: "If she didn't like someone smoking would I give up for her?" . . . Because a lot of my girlfriends were smokers already. . . . But for this one I did think long and hard about it. I was prepared. I thought if she didn't want me to smoke full stop, I wouldn't. I'd negotiate some kind of weekend! *Uri, 47, care worker, cannabis user.*

For one or two participants, there was a sense of unease at being a drug-using grandparent, and this shift in their family dynamic had started to impact upon their use. Lander (2015) detected a similar attitude among her sample of older drug-using women, one of whom felt that 'it's not acceptable as a grandmother'. For Lander, this comment captured the 'institutionalized expectations that exist about what constitutes correct and incorrect behaviour for older women, and thus also the expectations that exist in relation to this group of women. The expression illustrates how the self-biographies are produced in relation to discursive conceptions about how our lives should be lived'

(2015: 275).[1] Our participants dealt with the schism between what was expected of them as grandparents and their continued illegal drug use by ensuring that their use was always well concealed from their grandchildren and did not affect their ability to spend time with them and partake actively in their lives. Winston (58, academic, cannabis user) was among those in this situation. He discussed his adoption of an alternative persona, 'granddad', which was carefully isolated from his drug-using self. As he put it, 'obviously, . . . as "granddad" now, he doesn't ever really [use drugs]. That's strictly, very strictly separated now'.

For other participants, a change in their work or occupation would be likely to force a reconsideration of the way that illegal drug use was integrated into their lives. Again, this suggested the participants were all too aware of the somewhat flimsy nature of their present arrangements and drug use patterns:

> I don't plan on stopping. . . . [But] I could, yeah, change of environment, change of work. Yeah, if I had to worry about work, different types of work. *Uri, 47, care worker, cannabis user.*
>
> I don't see myself stopping it but as I'm about to start full-time college and start working as well, I would imagine that my usage of it will probably become part-time. [But] I don't see myself ever stopping cannabis no, no. That would be like stopping breathing [laughs]. *Oscar, 40, volunteer, cannabis user.*

Supply issues were another worry for some participants to the extent that they had been compelled to consider a future without illegal drugs. For example, in addition to having some concerns about the health impacts of his drug use, Malcolm (44, student, cannabis user) had also become increasingly troubled by the expense of his product and felt that things were approaching a tipping point, with high prices being charged for what he considered to be a generally 'crap' product. Keith (63, retired civil servant, cannabis use) also had concerns about the supply of his product and suggested that if his source, a home grower, was unable to continue supplying him with product, then he may be forced to give up:

> If he stops for any particular reason there's a certain extent to which I can grow myself but that's not going to supply [me] routinely. I'm certainly not going to try and get back into the general market because it's too risky. . . . You know, as I say if the supply runs out, that's it, it runs out. So that's as far as I've got thinking about that. . . . If it was entirely up to me, oh glory be, I'd carry on! [Laughs.]

1 The strength of institutionalised expectations about what constitutes appropriate conduct for older women may have been a factor in the reluctance of some to participate in this study (see Chapter 2).

For many of the participants, retirement loomed on the horizon, and some, of course, had already retired. As these participants considered this significant transition, they faced the belated prospect of a potentially more settled and enduring phase of the lifecourse. As Grenier puts it, older people's experiences 'may be more permanent and ongoing' than the liminal would seem to allow (2012: 130). Once in retirement, on the face of it there seems to be little prospect of one's social status being repeatedly transformed, and individuals may well feel a step removed from the transience that marks much of contemporary social life, not least because by definition they are not directly exposed to the uncertainties of the late modern labour market. Yet despite this, among our participants there was no real sense that retirement would bring a definitive end to the liminal life and usher in a new period of stability and predictability. This was chiefly due to the omnipresent threat of ill health (Levy and Anderson 2005: 254). For those who currently considered themselves to be healthy, there was a subtle but pervasive fear of the possibility that future health problems might puncture any stability that retirement engendered. These participants seemed to be constantly on guard and prepared for illness and affliction, and conscious of the fact that their onset might mean the end of their drug careers. Meanwhile, for those already living with chronic health problems, their sense of liminality was exaggerated as they continually grappled with the effects of their conditions and sought to postpone any deterioration that might force their drug use to cease. Retirement promised no end to this. In fact, those who saw their illegal drug use in medical terms perhaps had the keenest sense that the future of their drug careers might not necessarily be straightforward. Among this group, it was often illegal drug use itself that allowed life to continue in some relative degree of comfort. As a result, the prospect of further health issues (or indeed transitions in other aspects of life) that might stymie their drug use was faced with a sense of foreboding. Again, the risk of such issues occurring was not reduced by retirement. Indeed, those 'medical users' who had already stopped working due to ill health felt no more secure in their ability to continue drug use indefinitely than any other participant.[2] Ultimately, as they considered their retirement, be it imminent or already underway, most of the participants repeatedly slipped into a so-called 'illness narrative' (Kleinman 1988) whereby maladies threatened to become the defining quality of their lifecourse. The perpetual threat of ill health meant that the provisional nature of a drug career could never be escaped, even, it seemed, once the vicissitudes of working life had been left behind.

Overall, it was clear that despite none of the participants having any desire to give up illegal drugs in the future, their experiences of transitions and turning points, and the ways in which they had already been forced to

2 This group consisted of Adam (47, unemployed due to disability, cannabis user), Fran (41, retired due to disability, cannabis user) and Nathan (47, unemployed customs officer due to disability, cannabis user).

reconfigure their drug use at various points, meant that they were very aware of the contingencies upon which their continued use was dependent. Be it the potential for health problems, changing family or relationship dynamics, or changing working lives, when discussing their future intentions, the participants' awareness of the conditional and ever-provisional nature of their illegal drug use was writ large. Our participants were cognisant, albeit sometimes subconsciously, of their status as liminars (Beech 2011), forever in between the transitions and turning points that mark the unstable lifecourse trajectories of late modernity. Tom (41, horticulturalist, cannabis user), when discussing some of the students who attended his courses on allotment keeping, captured this rather astutely:

> Another student about the same age as me, I asked my students to fill in their CV, educational qualifications and jobs, and he'd done ever such a lot of things. He'd retrained, re-qualified, tried this, tried that, tried the other thing and not found a settled pattern. But that is part of my learning as I've got older, that it's not all as simple as you think it's going to be when you're young and that actually, chaos and the chaotic things that happen, that occur to us often completely without our control, are part of life.

Notwithstanding this, the fact that our participants had no desire whatsoever to give up their illegal drug use and generally envisaged continuing their drug careers for as long as possible starkly demonstrated the redundancy of the maturation hypothesis. Our participants were people who had remained steadfast drug users despite all the transitions and turning points that they had lived through, and they were determined that this would continue to be the case. They had most certainly not 'matured out' of their use, nor did this look likely to happen at this relatively late stage of the lifecourse. Yet as the participants contemplated their futures, they remained aware that their drug use would remain forever contingent upon circumstances. Their on-going fears regarding their health suggested that even retirement seemed to offer only partial respite from an unsettlingly liminal existence, even though one of the main sources of that liminality, the unstable nature of employment and the fickle quality of the labour market, would be no longer an issue. Just as we saw in Chapter 4, our participants' illegal drug careers provided a welcome release from the pressures and uncertainties of life whilst at the very same time being subject to them. There was little to suggest that this was likely to change. As Liam (45, unemployed, cannabis user) put it, 'it's the imperfect world isn't it?'

The legalisation debate

In the previous chapter, we saw hints that the illegal nature of the participants' drug use had caused some of them a considerable degree of anxiety and worry. A number of participants were quick to point out that they were otherwise law-abiding individuals and that engaging in illegal drug use sometimes made them feel distinctly uncomfortable. Participants took care to avoid unnecessary contact with the authorities, and this shaped their patterns of use to a substantial extent. For example, it contributed towards the dominance of the home as the favoured setting for drug use, and compelled the home growers amongst the sample to take special precautions to keep their activities concealed. Indeed some had decided against home growing solely because of the legal implications they could face should they be caught.

Yet despite this, in general the participants remained extremely relaxed about the illegal status of their drug use. For some, as we saw in Chapter 4, there was even a certain allure about partaking in an illegal activity; Brian (52, company owner, cannabis user), for example, felt that it added 'spice' to his use of cannabis. However, for the most part, the illegality of their activities was not something that the participants considered on a day-to-day basis, and little energy was wasted in worrying about it, notwithstanding the exceptions noted above and in Chapter 4. Indeed, whilst some participants were extremely well informed regarding the illegality of their drug use, others had little idea where they stood in relation to the law:

> I'm completely confused to be honest. I've no idea what would happen if I was to be found in possession. I mean I would never have more than a quarter of an ounce of dope in the house at any one time. . . . And now I have to say I haven't the slightest clue whether or not that would constitute a criminal offence or not, I just, I don't know, I really don't know. I can understand if I've got 200 ecstasy tablets in the house, then that might well constitute a criminal offence, but you know I wouldn't have that. And if my kids, who don't live with me anymore, had that amount in the house, I would actively discourage them not to have that amount in the house, you know. I don't really understand where the law is on this issue now. *Ollie, 52, company owner, cannabis and occasional cocaine user.*

On the rare occasions when participants had come into contact with the authorities in spite of their best efforts, in general they had emerged unscathed from the experience, with the notable exception of Nathan (47, unemployed customs officer due to disability, cannabis user) who as we saw in Chapter 4 had been suspended from his previous job and cautioned by the police when they discovered his home-grow equipment after intervention from a neighbour. More common was the experience of, for example, Liam (45, unemployed, cannabis user), who had enjoyed what he described as 'positive, very benign' interactions with the police when they had called at his shared house on several occasions in respect of other matters. Once, when the police called looking for a housemate, Liam had his joints out on the table and the smell of cannabis smoke was thick in the air, but the police turned a blind eye. On another occasion, two officers were conducting house-to-house inquiries regarding an assault in the area: 'they saw me with my weed and they were like "don't worry about that stuff" [laughs]'. This had helped to make him 'somewhat blasé' about the potential legal consequences of his use.

Experiences such as Liam's offer support to the notion that, to a certain extent, some illegal drug use has become a form of 'tolerable deviance', technically illegal behaviour that is seldom officially challenged (Hathaway 1997a: 104).[3] Indeed, Winston (58, academic, cannabis user) felt that the legal consequences of illegal drug use had been much more serious in the past than they were today, and his own concern over getting caught had diminished over time, although as he acknowledged, this was as much related to his status as a middle-class professional as it was a result of changing attitudes:

> Well it's de facto decriminalised to a large extent. . . . It's not a big deal. No, very different compared, of course, with the '70s when we were scared to shit of getting done. I had friends who were busted, you know, for stuff, you know, quarter of an ounce and ending up banged up in cells for a long time, couple got sent down for, you know, minor, minor dealing for other friends. So very different from the '70s when we were petrified of getting caught in possession. . . . Massively so, yeah. It's partly about being, of course, in a much, all the stuff we know about the protection that more affluent members of society have, you know. When you're a very affluent person in a very good home and you're smoking dope at very nice dinner parties, where you're eating the best food, great wine, nothing scary at all about it, you know. But as I say when we more saw ourselves as the front line troops, you know, of the, you know, sort of "the movement", very different, yeah, yeah.

Despite the generally relaxed attitude of the participants about their own drug use and its illegality, there was a definite sense of incredulity at the fact that they were partaking in a criminal activity simply by being in possession of controlled substances. This sentiment was raised time and again:

> I don't think it should, I don't [see] any reason whatsoever, I can't understand for the life of me why, why it's illegal. I just don't comprehend that. If I'm going out and doing something to upset anybody or hurt anybody I could understand it. *Ned, 53, unemployed, amphetamine user.*
>
> I've never really thought about it as being illegal. . . . I just find the whole thing quite juvenile the way this society approaches the whole issue. You know I just find it bizarre, I really do, I really do. *Ollie, 52, company owner, cannabis and occasional cocaine user.*
>
> I mean, you know, it's just crazy that something, something that is natural to this planet [cannabis] is illegal. It's like how can something that grows

3 Hathaway's claim was based on the situation in Canada regarding cannabis use.

naturally on the planet be illegal? It's been used by cultures for millennia, in different guises. *Brian, 52, company owner, cannabis user.*

I think the law sucks. I think the law was put in place for little men to control the majority to be quite honest with you. . . . Why is a cabbage that you can grow in the garden legal, when a herb you can grow in your garden isn't legal? *Nathan, 47, unemployed customs officer due to disability, cannabis user.*

At times, as in the case of Colin (41, internet entrepreneur, cannabis and occasional other drug user), this incredulity shaded off into outright anger:

> How dare the government tell me I can't use cannabis, how dare they! These are people that, they moralise about it, then they're selling arms and torture equipment to some of the most despotic regimes in the world. You know, they have no right to moralise because they are some of the most immoral people in the country.

Unsurprisingly, the overwhelming majority of the participants felt strongly that the law should be changed. A handful of them had been or still were actively involved in campaigning for the legalisation of at least some substances. This included Uri (47, care worker, cannabis user), who was involved in campaigning despite considering himself uninterested in politics, as well as Grace (48, carer for child, cannabis user), Ian (46, unemployed, cannabis user) and Nathan (47, unemployed customs officer due to disability, cannabis user). Tom (41, horticulturalist, cannabis user) saw his use as being motivated in part by a desire to live his life as something of a 'statement' about what he saw as the 'injustice' inherent in the very existence of drug laws. Others were similarly trenchant:

> I'm a harm reductionist. I think drugs should be legal and you should teach people how to use them as safely as possible. . . . You know, mountain climbing is more dangerous that drug taking. I wouldn't climb a mountain. I think people are stupid for doing it. But I wouldn't ban them from doing it. *Xavier, 55, researcher, polydrug user.*
>
> What I'd like to see is it decriminalised and legalised for recreational and medical use in this country. . . . I'd like to see it, I really would. . . . Just people who want to be left alone and have a quiet smoke, not hurting anyone. *Adam, 47, unemployed due to disability, cannabis user.*

In Chapter 1, we noted that the 'war on drugs' is increasingly perceived to be failing on a number of levels and that those who are in favour of some kind of liberalisation of the drug laws have won some notable successes in certain countries. We also saw that although the UK government is still of a prohibitionist mindset, even it has acknowledged the ineffectiveness of harsh penalties for personal possession and some of the limits of a criminal-justice-led approach (Home Office 2014a). Of course, the on-going debate over the legalisation of currently illegal substances is an enormous and seemingly endlessly nuanced one, and it is the site of clashes between an assortment of often-entrenched positions. We cannot hope to do it justice here. However, on the basis of what we have found, it is possible to make a number of brief observations.

First, in keeping with the 'utilitarian format' (Bean 2010: 8) that characterises much of the legalisation debate where the increase or decrease of harms tends to be the focal concern, we would suggest that our participants' drug careers demonstrated that the careful long-term use of illegal drugs does not necessarily lead to speedy physical and mental deterioration or to broader criminal inclinations. Our participants had integrated illegal drug use into their lives without suffering serious negative consequences. For them, illegal drug use was a normal part of otherwise largely 'conventional' and law-abiding lives. Our participants were not the junkies of popular imagination but ordinary people who held down jobs, ran businesses and were bringing up or had brought up children. Their experiences suggest that, used sensibly, illegal drugs *in and of themselves* do not inevitably cause serious harm to an individual.

Indeed, one might be tempted to go further and tentatively contend that the bulk of the harm that our participants had suffered over the duration of their lifecourses was inflicted not by their consumption of illegal drugs but by the liminality of late modern existence. Our participants' lifecourses had coincided with the emergence and consolidation of a brutally competitive, asocial and atomising social world, shot through with a vertiginous uncertainty and instability. Their illegal drug use was for the most part simply an attempt to find some kind of temporary respite from that world. Whilst commentators can argue that 'we need to see drug use for what it is – a profoundly harmful domain of human experience that threatens society in a multitude of ways' (Mckeganey 2011: 45) – the drug careers of our participants would seem to suggest that we should look at the issue in precisely the opposite direction. Although we would clearly not claim that their experience was universally shared, for our participants it seemed that it was society itself that harmed, whilst illegal drugs, so often maligned, were able to provide some welcome albeit momentary relief.

Given this, one might wonder why the state deems illegal numerous substances that can be used routinely and sustainably over the long term, resulting in generally positive impacts upon the user and leading to no discernible harm to either themselves or others. Of course, it would be ridiculous to deny that some patterns of illegal drug use can be harmful and damaging, but the same is patently also true of alcohol and tobacco, as our participants repeatedly stressed. Indeed, the potential for harm of various kinds to be caused by alcohol and tobacco would seem to be far greater than many of the substances that are listed in the Misuse of Drugs Act 1971, and as such the government's classifications seem rather arbitrary (Nutt et al. 2007, Nutt, King and Phillips 2010), a situation that is likely to be compounded by the impending enactment of the Psychoactive Substances Bill. Viewed in this light, the prohibition of certain substances can plausibly be considered an example of a sectional 'censure' (Sumner 1976, 1990) that gives concrete form to the ideologies and interests of those in a position to decisively shape the law, rather than being based upon sound scientific evidence on the likelihood of harm, or indeed some other rational principle.

And yet stubbornly large numbers of people continue to use illegal drugs despite their prohibition, including our participants. The law is being habitually flouted for leisure, for pleasure and increasingly for medical reasons, despite the threat of stiff penalties. One is reminded of Tom (41, horticulturalist, cannabis user), who as we have seen felt that the simple fact of his continued drug use constituted something of a statement against prohibition. This is a long, slow riot (Curtis 1985, Wacquant 1994, 2008, Young 2007: 181) of sorts against government policy. If normalisation processes begin to occur among older cohorts, as we will suggest is perfectly possible in the next section, then the perversity of prohibition in the face of the widespread use and acceptance of illegal drugs will be brought into even sharper relief. One might assume that there is a point when a generally benign activity becomes so prevalent and tolerated that its continued prohibition becomes unsustainably incongruous and untenable. Yet, as Blackman (2004) has pointed out, increasing rates of drug use have on occasion been used by the UK government as a justification for harsher anti-drugs policies, despite this seeming to be counterintuitive; an equally rational response would be to relax the prohibition of an activity that large numbers of people engage in regularly without negative outcomes. But, if our predictions for the future of illegal drug use among older adults are correct, then we might soon find that the limits of the law are being pushed up against, and those with an interest in ending the 'censuring' of their use will perhaps sense that the tangibility of change is growing. The dam could be about to burst.

For the participants in this study and the doubtless many others who use illegal drugs in a similar fashion to them, there would appear to be few appropriate policy responses available short of allowing them to continue their drug careers free from the threat of interference by the state, provided that they continue to use illegal drugs sensibly and responsibly. Criminalisation and all that it entails, such as the possibility of the loss of work and the threat to future employability (Boeri 2002: 288), would be a completely disproportionate and unnecessary response to the kind of drug use that our participants engaged in. Meanwhile, other policy approaches such as harm minimisation would seem to have little relevance for our participants as they had suffered few, if any, negative consequences as a result of their use. As Duff has trenchantly argued, 'it should not be surprising that a policy that concerns itself almost exclusively with the harms associated with illicit drug use should find it so difficult to address the concerns of more than a small minority of drug users' (2004: 388). Duff continues:

> In focusing solely on the nature of risks and harms, and the means of their prevention, drug policy effectively misunderstands the culture and the context of illicit drug use. This is not for a moment to suggest that the emphasis on harm minimisation is misguided, indeed, it is vital; it is only

> to argue that a focus on harms must be wedded to an appreciation of pleasure and the ways in which harms, risks and pleasures are entwined in any experience of illicit drug use. To understand and accommodate these complex interactions is to provide a conceptual framework adequate to the task of designing and implementing good policy.
>
> (2004: 392)

Because our participants had generally been able to avoid legal sanction over the course of their drug careers, it might be suggested that there is little need to change the law; after all, our participants demonstrated that it is perfectly possible to avoid becoming entangled in legal machinery if one uses drugs carefully and discreetly. One is also reminded of the tolerance displayed by the police that, for example, Liam (45, unemployed, cannabis user) experienced in his interactions with them. However, this would be to deny the chance, however slim, that users such as our participants might *potentially* be criminalised or that the attitudes of the authorities might harden. It also raises the question as to why individuals should be forced to conceal their engagement in a largely benign pursuit. And it would be to ignore the anxiety, described in Chapter 4, that participants such as Fran (41, retired due to disability, cannabis user), Harry (40, NHS support worker, cannabis user) and Jane (47, delivery driver, cannabis, cocaine, and occasional ecstasy user) felt as a result of their partaking in an activity deemed illegal.

In the end, the simple, brute absurdity of the current legal situation is made all the more stark when one has been in the company of the participants in our study. They were ordinary people, using illegal drugs quietly and privately in order to help them deal with the everyday stresses and strains of what is often an unsettlingly liminal lifecourse. In our view, the evidence provided by their lengthy careers with illegal drugs adds considerable weight to the arguments of those who would like the direction of drug policy to be significantly rethought. Of course, this would not be a straightforward task, for even if there was a will to do so, 'it would be extremely difficult, but not impossible, for the UK to unravel its international obligations' (Bean 2010: 12), most notably its status as a party to the UN Single Convention on Narcotic Drugs of 1961 and the Convention on Psychotropic Substances of 1971, which find their domestic expression in the Misuse of Drugs Act. But, as Jock Young wrote a long time ago, one way or another policy makers must 'learn to live with psychotropic drug use' (1971: 222), for, despite prohibition, it is not going to simply go away. The older adults in our study had been able to make this accommodation. For whatever reason, it seems that those in the corridors of power still have not.

Towards normalisation?

The normalisation thesis suggests that illegal drug use is becoming a normal and routine part of the lives of young people in the United Kingdom. Its roots lie in the North West Longitudinal Study, which began in 1991, and it has been developed and refined over a number of works (see especially Measham, Newcombe and Parker 1994, Parker, Measham and Aldridge 1995, Measham, Parker and Aldridge 1998, Parker, Aldridge and Measham 1998, Measham, Aldridge and Parker 2001, Williams and Parker 2001, Parker, Williams and Aldridge 2002, Parker 2005, Measham and Shiner 2009, Aldridge, Measham and Williams 2011). In their defining statement of normalisation, *Illegal Leisure*, Parker, Aldridge and Measham measured the phenomenon across six 'key features' (1998: 153): drug availability, levels of drug trying, levels of current drug use, being 'drug wise' regardless of individual experiences with drugs, future intentions, and the 'cultural accommodation' of drugs and drug use in wider society. The thesis proposes that drugs are becoming 'normal' even for those who do not use them; rather as somebody who does not drink alcohol in the UK would likely be aware of it and its cultural impact, so drug abstainers will encounter drugs and their influence in the everyday ebb and flow of their lives. Drugs are thus becoming normalised in a cultural sense. As Manning suggests, normalisation is essentially 'the argument that recreational drug use is now so familiar to those aged below 35 years that it should be regarded as "normal", rather than as an activity confined to minority subcultures' (2007: 49). Similarly, for Parker and his collaborators, the notion of normalisation 'cannot be reduced to the intuitive phrase "it's normal for young people to take drugs"; that is both to oversimplify and overstate the case'. Instead, normalisation suggests that recreational drug use has moved from the 'margins towards the centre of youth culture where it joins many other accommodated "deviant" activities such as excessive drinking, casual sexual encounters and daily cigarette smoking' (Parker, Aldridge and Measham 1998: 152).

Despite the normalisation thesis arguably becoming something of an academic and popular orthodoxy, there have been a number of criticisms mounted against it. Most famously, Shiner and Newburn (1996, 1997, 1999) contended that the extent of illicit drug use and the rate of its increase, as well as claims about its normative context, were exaggerated. Blackman argued that the thesis is 'too expansive, over simplistic, reliant on the distinction between recreational and dependent drug use and exaggerated' (2007: 54), and it has been suggested that the thesis obscures the continuity that exists in patterns of drug use over time and between cohorts (Shiner 2009). Critics have also claimed that there are weaknesses in the methodological underpinnings of Parker et al.'s original work (Shiner and Newburn 1997, 1999, Ramsey and Partridge 1999, Blackman 2007). In addition, as Blackman (2004, 2007) has noted, the idea of normalisation has been used politically to justify increasingly prohibitive and punitive responses to drug use (see also Huggins 2007). This is contrary to the hopes of those who developed the idea, who anticipated that their data could potentially lend weight to arguments in favour of decriminalisation and harm reduction (Aldridge, Measham and Williams 2011: 225).

A number of refinements to the normalisation thesis have been suggested. For instance, originally the thesis had been limited to 'primarily cannabis but also nitrites, amphetamines and equivocally LSD and ecstasy' (Parker, Aldridge and Measham 1998: 152). However, the decline in the use of LSD and the rise in the use of cocaine has led to an acknowledgement that 'the characteristics of normalisation – how it manifests itself – will change' (Aldridge, Measham and Williams 2011: 223). Aldridge, Measham and Williams have also suggested that it is wise to conceive of normalisation as a process rather than in 'all-or-nothing' terms (Aldridge, Measham and Williams 2011: 219). Perhaps more fundamentally, the sense that the original thesis overplayed agency at the expense of social and structural factors has been addressed (Aldridge, Measham and Williams 2011: 223–5), for example in the work of Shildrick (2002). Her concept of 'differentiated normalisation' allows for the fact that different drugs and different types of use may be normalised for different groups of people, for instance in the clubbing world (Duff 2003). In a similar vein, Measham and Shiner (2009), despite their previous differences, have both come to see drug use among the young as an example of 'structured action' or 'situated choice'. Duff et al. have suggested that there is a 'need for a new wave of normalization research and theorising, more cognisant of local cultures and contexts of illicit drug use, and more sensitive to the social and structural determinants of this use' (2012: 272). In this light, Pennay and Moore's (2010) notion of the 'micro-politics' of normalisation and the idea that normalisation processes work differently dependent upon local contexts and settings is especially important.

Those who developed the normalisation thesis have remained consistently committed to its central ideas. Parker has maintained that 'the process of the normalisation of "sensible" recreational drug use continues', and that this is particularly the case for cannabis, where 'the process is sufficiently advanced to allow the claim that recreational cannabis use is largely normalised' (2005: 212). The idea of normalisation has also served as a useful 'corrective to the stigmatised understanding of young people who consume drugs on a recreational, non-problematic basis, who are neither deviant nor criminal' (Blackman 2007: 57). Ultimately, whatever its weaknesses, the notion of normalisation undoubtedly helped to capture the sense that, during the 1990s:

> Drug taking became more prevalent; defied traditional class and gender boundaries; and became "accommodated" to an extent even by abstainers, thus moving from the periphery to the mainstream of youthful behaviour. . . . The insight of normalisation has therefore been to recognise that at least some drug taking, and at least some drug takers, are no longer viewed as exclusively or even typically deviant.
>
> (Aldridge 2008: 198)

The focus of those involved in the debate on normalisation has been on young people. However, as Erickson and Hathaway (2010) have suggested, there is a need to analyse normalisation processes among older adults as well as among younger users. Whilst we did not explicitly set out to test the normalisation thesis with regard to older people, our feeling was that there was very little evidence that illegal drug use amongst older adults had become 'culturally accommodated' (Parker, Aldridge and Measham 1998: 157) in any meaningful sense at all. Most obviously, rates of drug use among older adults remain relatively low despite the small increases seen over recent years (see Chapter 1). In addition to this, the efforts that many of our participants made in order to keep their drug use private and discreet suggested that they remained suspicious that others would not share their relaxed attitudes towards drug use (see Chapter 4). Furthermore, the medical justifications that some participants gave for their use were likely designed to mark it off as being acceptable (Sullum 2003; see Chapter 4), a tactic that would presumably be unnecessary in a social world where drug use by older adults was normalised. Finally, the great difficulties we encountered in simply trying to get hidden older users to take part in the study (see Chapter 2) signalled, among other things, that older users remain cautious in disclosing their relationship with illegal drugs in the face of potential disapproval. Taken together, this does not suggest a social environment where the illegal drug use of older adults is becoming increasingly acceptable. And, even if an embryonic form of normalisation was found to be occurring among this cohort, as Hathaway, Comeau and Erickson (2011) have shown in relation to cannabis use in Canada, extra-legal forms of stigma can prove persistent and are often internalised by users. This can result in the reinforcement of established cultural requirements that emphasise, for example, self-control or, as Lander (2015) found, the notion that grandparents should not use illegal drugs.

However, we would speculate that over the coming years, rising numbers of older adults are likely to join the ranks of hidden illegal drug users. We saw in Chapter 1 the modest increases in use that have already occurred among older people, but something much more significant could be on the horizon. Perhaps counterintuitively, the best evidence for this is provided by the marked decline in rates of use among young people following a peak around the turn of the century. This has occurred as the teenagers of the 1990s, who used drugs more than their predecessors and their successors, have moved into higher age bands (Aldridge 2008, Home Office 2015a: 1–2). One possible future consequence of this cohort effect is that we might well see drug-use rates increase for older adults as this most drug-involved cohort enters middle age. Indeed, the North West Longitudinal Study's original 1991 sample was made up of 14 year olds (Parker, Aldridge and Measham 1998: 32). These people will be aged 40 by 2017. In this light, it would hardly be a surprise if we begin to see the rate of drug use among older adults climb steeply in the coming years. The potential for a parallel development in the US has also been noted (Han, Gfroerer and Colliver 2009). As Roger (44, manager in a small firm, cannabis user) rather hyperbolically put it:

> I'd be amazed if anybody under 40 hasn't tried illegal drugs, I mean in the entire country now. There must be very few. I'm of the sort of generation where everything started to change.

Not only is there clear potential for a substantial increase in the number of older adults using illegal drugs, but the tantalising prospect is raised that the process of normalisation may in effect repeat itself higher up the age range in the coming years. The teenagers of the 1990s grew up at a time when illegal drugs were relatively commonplace. Even those who did not use themselves came of age in a milieu where drugs were often seen as being a routine and ordinary part of life. The prospects for normalisation appear strong if such attitudes are retained as these erstwhile teenagers grow older. Thus, a change in the general attitudes of older adults towards illegal drugs might well accompany increased usage rates among that cohort. Such shifts, if they do occur, would amount to something of a perfect storm of normalisation among older adults.

Late modernity and normalisation

We would suggest that, just as we saw with regard to trajectories, transitions, and turning points in Chapter 3, the process of normalisation can be properly understood only in the light of broader historical contexts and social structures (Measham and Shiner 2009, Aldridge, Measham and Williams 2011: 223). As we also saw in Chapter 3, it has been argued by a number of scholars that a creeping erosion of the normative expectations associated with post-war industrial society has occurred. Relatively clear, shared conventions, often subconscious, that governed passages into adulthood, gender roles, working life and leisure are dissolving. For Bauman, the difference between the industrial world of modernity and post-industrial late modernity is 'seminal', for 'life organised around the producer's role tends to be normatively regulated', whereas life organised around consumption 'must do without norms' (2000: 76). If this is somewhat exaggerated, less contentious is Bauman's sense that as relatively stable employment becomes increasingly rare, 'work can no longer offer the secure axis around which to wrap and fix self-definitions, identities and life-projects. Neither can it be easily conceived of as the ethical foundation of society, or as the ethical axis of individual life' (2000: 139). In place of the solidarity of industrial workers in occupational communities who enjoyed a shared sense of fate, consumer society 'elevates the principle of individual competitiveness', has atomised the worker (Lash and Urry 1987: 227–8) and has led to a sense of ontological insecurity (Giddens 1990, 1991). Parker, Aldridge and Measham themselves see this rise of 'individualisation' as a central outcome of the neoliberal shake out of society. They argue that a young person's 'life course and who they journey with, what they do and where they go is less deeply etched by tradition or privilege, by gender or by social class or by growing up in a "community" be it steel town or coal mining village, than in the past' (1998: 25). Indeed, Giddens (1991) famously described how individuals, 'lifted out of the confines of tradition' (Everingham 2003: 246), must now create meaning and self-identity by themselves through the negotiation of a plethora of life choices. These choices are increasingly made in the context of a capitalist consumer marketplace; the 'soldier producers' of modernity are being replaced by the 'sensation gatherers' of late modernity (Bauman 1997: 146).

We would argue that these processes could have two major consequences for normalisation. First, it is perfectly possible that the strains and stresses of vertiginous life in late modernity will increasingly encourage individuals to take refuge in drug use. We saw hints of this in Chapter 3 and Chapter 4. In the former chapter we saw how a lifecourse consisting of abrupt and unpredictable transitions and turning points is likely to foster anxiety and insecurity, whilst in the latter it was particularly striking how most of our participants used illegal drugs for, among other things, stress relief and relaxation. Indeed, in the rapidly emerging consumerist 'society without limits' (Handelman 1994), it would seem that 'the most prized commodities . . . are those which appear to offer a temporary respite or escape from the sense of threat, the turmoil of constant change, the everyday striving and, indeed, the sense of defeat and despair that life in a competitive market society seems often to involve' (Taylor 1999: 82). So, late modern neoliberalism and its attendant liminality might well provide powerful motivation for beleaguered subjects to seek out the sense of release that illegal drugs can often provide. And of course, this applies to older adults just as it does to younger people.

Second, the erosion of widely held normative standards that scholars such as Bauman have discussed has increasingly made illegal drug use a choice that is not the almost exclusive preserve of those engaged in some kind of alternative lifestyle. For many years it was widely considered that drug taking was indeed a largely subcultural phenomenon (Becker 1953, Cloward and Ohlin 1960, Hebdige 1976), and as Chapter 3 showed many of our own participants had belonged to a subcultural group at some point in the past. Drug use, so the theory went, was generally confined to groups whose members tended to suffer from constrained opportunity and 'did not share the norms and values of their conforming counterparts' (Aldridge 2008: 192). Of course, these observations were always overstated to an extent. As early as 1970, Goode was able to conclude on the basis of his study of recreational marijuana smokers that 'marijuana use is the product of the same essentially normal values and beliefs of large groups of people that guide other kinds of everyday activities and choices' (1970: 310). And, in time, the idea that illegal drug use was essentially restricted to a number of fringe groups at the margins of society was exploded by a range of empirical observations, new theories of youth culture, the supposed emergence of the 'post-subcultural' era that we discussed in Chapter 4 and the normalisation thesis itself. As we have seen, by the time of their classic statement of normalisation, Parker, Aldridge and Measham were able to declare that there had been a 'spread of deviant activity and associated attitudes from the margins *towards* the centre of youth culture where it joins many other accommodated "deviant" activities' (1998: 152). If it is the case that the normative scripts that implored older adults not to use illegal drugs (Lander 2015) are losing their authority, then we might expect to see an increase in the numbers of older people who feel able to indulge. In simple terms, once widely held normative standards begin to dissolve, then illegal drug use will become a more plausible choice for a greater number of individuals.

The idea that the normative uncertainty of the late modern social world might allow illegal drug use to move towards the 'centre of culture' provides the basis for a potentially satisfying account of normalisation. However, we would suggest that it also offers the promise of a more thoroughgoing reconfiguration of the entire notion of normalisation itself. In a social world shorn of norms, the centre of culture that Parker, Aldridge and Measham talked of becomes increasingly difficult to identify, precisely because the shared practices and understandings that a centre of culture must be based upon are largely missing. To exaggerate, if there were no widely held normative standards at all, then, by definition, there could be no centre of culture and therefore no deviation. In such a situation, what was once considered to be deviant, exotic or dangerous behaviour might no longer be confined to marginal social capsules constituted by groups of threatening and incomprehensible 'others'. Instead, highly atomised individuals might face similarly isolated subjects across yawning chasms of misunderstanding, each being baffled by facets of the behaviour of the other in the absence of a shared normative code. As the idea of social deviance disappears 'into the vortex of the globalised, culturally diverse world' (Sumner 2012: 175), behaviour that is incomprehensible from one's own vantage point will increasingly become a perfectly normal and inescapable feature of the social landscape.[4] Indeed, according to Sumner, this process is well underway, and the entire notion of deviance, which was classically conceived as nonconformity to tacit but generally unquestioned consensus expectations (1990: 18), has already been rendered redundant as an 'appropriate way of seeing' (1994: 3). If Sumner is correct, then Parker, Aldridge and Measham's view that deviant activity has moved 'from the margins towards the centre' of culture is turned on its head: it is the very centre of culture itself that is disintegrating, and the distinction between behaviour which is accepted and that which is deviant is becoming largely meaningless. As Sumner himself puts it, 'deviation is now the norm, or the anti-norm, depending on which way you look at it' (Sumner 2004: 24).

In sum, we would suggest that normalisation has the potential to occur among older adults for a number of interconnected reasons. First, as the current generation of younger people grow older, the cohort effect means that we can expect to see increased rates of drug use occurring higher up the age scale. In addition, these individuals grew up in an era of relatively relaxed attitudes towards drugs during the period that gave rise to the normalisation thesis itself, and they may well carry these attitudes into older age with them. We would also speculate that the wide-ranging social changes wrought by late modernity, including the permanent liminality, uncertainty and anxiety discussed in Chapter 3, have the potential to make the refuge that illegal drugs can provide an increasingly attractive proposition for older adults. In addition, as late modern neoliberalism's

4 This is the 'world of censure' (Sumner 2012: 175), where the behaviour of others can still provoke disapproval, disgust and condemnation, but such reactions are far less likely to be rooted in any shared principles or normative consensus.

exhaustive shake out of society continues to 'erode what appears in retrospect as the regional stability of modernity' (Crook, Pakulski and Waters 1992: 220), there is a strong likelihood that normalisation will gather pace. As normative scripts that were once widely adhered to progressively disintegrate, the notion of deviation away from a well-defined 'centre' of culture will become increasingly outmoded. In this context there is clear potential for illegal drug use to increase as it ceases to be regarded as a deviant, outré activity. We have a sense that this is the real motor of normalisation. Thus, although it remains clear that illegal drug use among older adults has not yet become normalised in any meaningful way, it is certainly possible that we may be standing on the cusp of a sea change in older adults' rates of illegal drug use and their general attitudes towards drugs. An extensive reconstruction of the boundaries of acceptable conduct for older adults (as well as the rest of the 'sensation gathering' worker-consumers of late modernity) appears to be well underway. Our participants, and others like them, might well be the harbingers of a coming age of normalisation.

Limits of the study and the way forward

This study has a number of limitations worthy of mention, the most obvious of which is the small sample size. As we described in Chapter 2, we encountered great difficulties in getting older adults to speak to us regarding their illegal drug use, which was to be expected given that we were specifically seeking those whose drug use was 'hidden'. The findings from the final sample of 30 participants are clearly not generalisable, and as such the study is best regarded as an exploratory effort that has documented and offered some tentative understanding of the drug use of a hitherto largely ignored group.

As well as rendering the findings non-generalisable, the small sample size meant that work comparing the different subsets within the sample was not feasible. Although the sample contained individuals who were spread fairly widely across the social spectrum, from unemployed and relatively poorly paid manual workers to successful business owners and well-remunerated professionals such as academics, only five women were represented, and there was nobody from a minority ethnic background. As a result our analysis focussed upon those general trends that were evident throughout the sample, but the specificity of the experiences of, for instance, the long-term unemployed or the middle class user were not explored.

The decision to reduce the qualifying age of the study from 50 to 40, the resultant age range of the sample (40–66) and the length of time the study took to bring to fruition (see Chapter 2) also meant that the participants' birth dates spanned a 30-year period. There are likely to be considerable differences in the experiences of those who were born in the 1940s as compared to those born in the 1970s. Ultimately we decided that the opportunity to more easily construct a larger sample trumped this concern. Nevertheless, the fact that all of our participants had lived at least some part of their life in what might be called the post-war period, prior to the momentous social convulsions of the 1970s and 1980s, lent at least some element of cohesion to our sample.

Of course, there is no reason to suppose that those younger hidden users who were born after our participants will enjoy similarly structured drug careers as they journey through the lifecourse. The very different historical time and place (Elder 1985b, 1994) that we now live in make it possible that the 'particular set of experiences' (Levy and Anderson 2005: 256) of, for instance, current cohorts of teenagers will be markedly different from those of our participants. This brings to mind an issue that all work on the lifecourse must confront. As Levy and Anderson have argued:

> One of the potential dangers of examining human activities from a life course perspective lies in the temptation to commit what Riley (1973) refers to as the "life course fallacy". That is, it is tempting to assume that what is characteristic of one group of people at one historical time-point holds true for individuals who are like them in other times and places.
>
> (2005: 256)

To offer just one example, if the teenage illegal drug users of today are to experience an experimental period of use at some point, it seems unlikely that it will be framed quite so distinctly by a specific subcultural movement, even though this proved so important for many of our own participants.

Notwithstanding these limitations, it is clear that there are plentiful opportunities for further work in this area. One priority for such work might be to construct a bigger, more robust sample of hidden older illegal drug users, a task which will likely require greater resources than were at the disposal of this study. A research team containing members who are part of the population to be investigated would possibly assist in this regard. Of course, our own findings suggest that older 'normal' drug users are often not particularly well connected with other users and remain keen not to draw attention to themselves, so even some kind of 'insider' status would not necessarily offer a panacea for *all* the problems of sample building among this population. However, it would be likely to increase trust and encourage involvement among potential participants. It might also allow for some kind of nonintrusive observation of older illegal drug users. Pearson, who adopted just such an approach, rightly argued that

> more formal approaches such as life history interviews would have risked giving drug issues an artificial and undue prominence in an environment in which drug use was more likely to go unremarked, or to receive fleeting mention in a conversation before these fragmentary exchanges were interrupted by more important considerations – to welcome someone, to buy a round of drinks, to talk about sport, football, or horse racing.
>
> (2001: 73)

Future studies might also choose to focus solely on the hidden illegal drug use of those aged over 60, or perhaps even 70, to investigate whether post-retirement lives offer a more stable and predictable context for continued illegal drug use, or whether this is stifled by, among other things, health concerns. In this way a more complete picture of drug use across the entire lifecourse can potentially be constructed, although of course the problems of sample building are likely to be exacerbated among the very oldest hidden users, not least because they are fewer in number. A different line of inquiry might be to analyse the impact of factors such as class, gender and ethnicity upon drug careers, although this would require a larger sample and a more targeted recruitment procedure, as discussed above. One might also compare the use patterns and self-perceptions of those who characterise their use as being largely for pleasure and those who see it as being primarily for medical purposes. Such work might shed more light on how fluid, malleable drug careers are able to constantly adapt to changing circumstances. Studies comparing hidden older users in different regions or nation states might also result in a better understanding of those elements of drug careers and 'normal' use that are common across boundaries and those that are specific to particular locales.

Alternatively, as Measham, Williams and Aldridge (2011) have argued, lengthy drug careers might be best investigated through some kind of longitudinal research. Their own work on the North West Longitudinal Study is in this vein, as is the work on heroin addicts by Stimson, Oppenheimer and their colleagues (Oppenheimer, Stimson and Thorley 1979, Stimson and Oppenheimer 1982, Oppenheimer et al. 1994, Tobutt, Oppenheimer and Laranjeirna 1996). If studies such as the North West Longitudinal Study are continued once the participants reach their forties and beyond, a far clearer understanding of drug careers among particular cohorts and the way they relate to their socio-historical context could potentially be evolved. Furthermore, our predictions regarding the normalisation of illegal drug use among older adults would be best tested through some kind of longitudinal study. Of course, to realise this 'gold standard' of sustained, long-term investigation would be incredibly time consuming and expensive, as well as requiring considerable foresight and planning.

In short, there is an abundance of fertile territory for further work in this area. Our own study has merely provided a beginning, but it points to several potentially fruitful lines of inquiry. Of particular note is the evidence we have provided that transitions and turning points in other aspects of the lifecourse can have dramatic effects on 'normal' drug careers, and the sense that the liminal nature of the contemporary social world is the wellspring of instability and uncertainty that both motivates and encumbers illegal drug use. These can operate as 'sensitising concepts' (Blumer 1954) to inform future work as the task of understanding the illegal drug use of older adults begins in earnest.

Summary and concluding thoughts

In Chapter 1, we set the scene by considering the mounting evidence that illegal drug use by older adults (defined by us as those aged 40 and over) is becoming increasingly commonplace, albeit slowly and from a very low base. Indeed, some commentators have suggested that we may be on the cusp of a major increase (for example Colliver et al. 2006, Royal College of Psychiatrists 2011), and the phenomenon of the older user is increasingly part of the popular imagination. The maturation hypothesis (Winick 1962), the accuracy of which was always questionable, is finally being rendered obsolete. We also assessed the current state of knowledge regarding the so-called 'normal' (Hammersley 2005) illegal drug use of older adults. With the notable exception of a handful of studies in the UK (Pearson 2001, Notley 2005, Shewan and Dalgarno 2005) and North America (Boeri 2002, 2004, Anderson and Levy 2003, Osborne and Fogel 2008), the focus of most drugs research is on younger or more 'problematic' users. With this in mind, we studied a small group of hidden, older current users of illegal drugs in the UK in an attempt to begin to understand the role that drug use played in their lives and how they had sustained 'drug careers' over the duration of their lifecourses.

Chapter 2 outlined the methodological approach adopted by the study. This curiosity-driven, unfunded research project endured a rather lengthy and troubled gestation. In particular, the construction of the sample, attempted through a form of snowball sampling, was a somewhat arduous task as individuals accustomed to keeping their illegal drug use hidden proved understandably reluctant to talk to us. The adoption of a semi-structured variant on the 'life story' interview was examined, and the ethical implications of the work were considered. This was particularly important given the fact that participants were being asked to discuss their involvement in an illegal activity. Chapter 2 also introduced the 30 participants who took part in the study.

In Chapter 3 we looked at the history of the participants' illegal drug use over their lifecourses. Their first experiences of illegal drugs tended to be unplanned and spontaneous, and enjoyed with friends. Relatively regular illegal drug use soon followed for the bulk of the participants. Most also went through an experimental period where their use became heavier and encompassed a wider range of substances. This usually occurred fairly early in the drug career, and tended to take place within relatively bounded contexts such as during one's involvement with a subculture or whilst at university. Over time, drug careers ebbed and flowed, and patterns of use were frequently reconfigured in response to transitions and turning points in other aspects of the participants' lives. Work, family and other concerns always took priority over illegal drug use, and, when circumstances changed, a new way to integrate drug use into one's life had to be found. This was the defining feature of the participants' drug careers. As a result we suggested that those drug careers, and specifically the manner in which use patterns had repeatedly changed, could be best understood in the context of so-called 'permanent liminality' (Szakolczai 2000), where late modern lifecourses are increasingly characterised by a radical uncertainty, and where insecurity and 'broken narratives' have replaced the relatively settled normative paths that guided individuals during the comparatively stable years of post-war modernity.

The current use of the participants was detailed in Chapter 4. Cannabis was the most commonly used drug among the sample. Many used cannabis alone, and only one participant did not use it at all. For participants who used multiple drugs, cannabis tended to be their staple. Although a range of different sources were utilised, participants would source drugs through social supply channels wherever possible. Many participants remained daily users, but others had seen their use drop off slightly. All participants made efforts to control the set and setting of their drug use. They tended to use moderately and at home, either alone or with a small number of others. In general, illegal drugs were used by the participants because they enjoyed the effects; the stress relieving and relaxing properties of illegal drugs were particularly cherished. Some had come to see their use as being for primarily medical reasons. Participants tended to consider that the overall impact of their drug use had been positive, and they did not feel that it had unduly affected their working or family lives, for example. Some did have concerns about the health impacts of their drug use, although others were sanguine about this and actually felt that drug use had benefitted their health. Chapter 4 clearly suggested that the participants enjoyed a straightforwardly happy relationship with illegal drugs. There was also a definite sense that illegal drugs offered the participants a means of coping with the vertiginous instability engendered by liminal late modern life. Yet, as Chapter 3 showed, because illegal drug use itself was always contingent upon the present circumstances of the participants, it was indelibly marked by the same uncertainty as the rest of their lifecourses. Thus, the relief that illegal drugs provided could never be taken for granted.

Chapter 5 has focussed upon the future of 'normal' illegal drug use, both for our participants and more broadly among older adults in general. Our participants had no wish to stop using illegal drugs, although they were all too aware that changed circumstances might force them to do so. They appeared very conscious of the liminality of their current situation and foresaw that they would have to go through further transitions into unknowable futures that could well affect their continued drug use. Worries about the potential for failing health were especially prominent here. On the other hand, with one or two exceptions the participants were not particularly concerned that their drug use was illegal, and the threat of sanction did not unduly worry them. They had, of course, proved adept at remaining under the authorities' radar over many years, so this was unsurprising. Nevertheless, all opposed the illegal status of at least their drug of choice, and most were vehemently opposed to the war on drugs in general. Indeed, the very existence of long-term users such as our participants who appear to have suffered few, if any, ill effects as a result of their lengthy illegal drug careers highlights the absurdity of the law. Why is it that some of their favoured substances are prohibited whilst other potentially harmful ones remain perfectly legal? We went on to speculate that, if predictions about a coming increase in the number of older users are correct, we might well begin to see a process of normalisation occur among older adults that mirrors the supposed normalisation of drug use among younger people. This process is likely to be encouraged by the ageing of those younger cohorts, users or otherwise, who see illegal drug use as an unremarkable feature of life, and may also derive strength from the increasing atomisation of society and the concomitant erosion of normative certainties. In such a changing context, the very notion of deviance away from consensus expectations, of which illegal drug use has long been seen as a classic example, has become increasingly anachronistic, and the normalisation of what were once seen as fringe activities is likely to gather pace. We ended by considering some of the limits of the study, most notably the small sample size which prevents our findings from being generalisable. However, we would suggest that they may well provide a way of thinking about drug careers that can be of benefit to future research endeavours. Rich opportunities for further work in the area exist, with a focus on the very oldest users and the potential for longitudinal studies of some kind being among the most exciting.

A few general points are worth briefly recalling by way of closing this work, which, if nothing else, has at least documented the existence of older adults who have enjoyed lengthy illegal drug careers and continue to use to this day. We have shown that our participants have been able to use illegal drugs over extended periods of time in a sustainable manner whilst simultaneously enjoying otherwise quite routine lives. Beyond this, we would agree with Hammersley that there is a 'need to study and theorise "drug use" rather than "drug users" ' (2011: 414), and move away from the medicalisation and pathologisation of the latter. It was with this in mind that we have attempted to place the 'normal' illegal drug use of our participants into some kind of context. The manner in which factors external to drug use affected our participants' lengthy drug careers was one of the starkest findings of the study. As our participants underwent transitions in other aspects of their lives, they adapted their patterns of drug use to fit their changed circumstances. The abundance of such transitions was something that we linked to the vertiginous, liminal social world we currently inhabit. It seemed to us that drug careers were determined to a large extent by the vicissitudes of life in late modernity whilst at one and the same time providing some small relief from such an existence. Thus, it was only when seen in the context of late modern liminality that the shape of our participants' drug careers – their ebbs and their flows – began to make any kind of sense. We would hope that these ideas, despite the modest size and scope of the study that gave rise to them, can provide some kind of foundation for the research on older illegal drug users that is likely to follow as such individuals become greater in number and increasingly embedded in public consciousness over the coming years.

In the end, what was perhaps most remarkable about the drug use of our participants was how unremarkable it was. It was not a defining characteristic of their lives, nor did it prevent them from successfully engaging in other pursuits. These were people who happened to use illegal drugs simply because they had found them to be helpful in coping with life's troubles and capable of providing just a soupçon of pleasure and release. From businessperson to professional to manual worker, big city to market town to rural village, rambling country cottage to suburban semi to block of council flats, these older adults from various walks of life used illegal drugs just as others drink alcohol, smoke cigarettes, go to the football game or walk the dog. As Ned (53, unemployed, amphetamine user) put it, 'I mean it's just the same old story as any normal life I would think'.

References

Abbott, A. (1997). 'On the concept of turning point', in Mjoset, L. and Engelstad, F. (eds.), *Comparative social research (Vol. 16): Methodological issues in comparative social science*, p. 85–105. Greenwich, CT: JAI Press.

Abrams, R. and Alexopoulos, G. (1998). 'Geriatric addictions', in Frances, R. and Miller, S. (eds.), *Clinical textbook of addictive disorders (2nd edition)*, p. 374–96. New York: The Guilford Press.

Agar, M. (1973). *Ripping and running: A formal ethnography of urban heroin addicts.* New York: Seminar Press.

Agrawal, A. and Lynskey, M.T. (2009). 'Correlates of later-onset cannabis use in the National Epidemiological Survey on Alcohol and Related Conditions (NESARC)', *Drug and Alcohol Dependence*, 105: 71–5.

Aitken, S., DeSantis, J., Harford, T. and Fe Caces, M. (2000). 'Marijuana use among adults: A longitudinal study of current and former users', *Journal of Substance Abuse*, 12: 213–26.

Aldridge, J. (2008). 'Decline but no fall? New millennium trends in young people's use of illegal and illicit drugs in Britain', *Health Education*, 108(3): 189–206.

Aldridge, J., Measham, F. and Williams, L. (2011). *Illegal leisure revisited: Changing patterns of alcohol and drug use in adolescents and young adults.* Hove: Routledge.

Andalo, D. (2005). 'Anger over "harmless heroin" study', *The Guardian*, 3 February 2005, http://www.theguardian.com/society/2005/feb/03/drugsandalcohol.drugs

Anderson, T. and Levy, J. (2003). 'Marginality among older injectors in today's illicit drug culture: Assessing the impact of ageing', *Addiction*, 98(6): 761–70.

Anthony, J.C. and Petronis, K.R. (1995). 'Early onset drug use and risk of later drug problems', *Drugs and Alcohol Dependence*, 40: 9–15.

Arana, X. and Montanes Sanchez, V. (2011). 'Cannabis cultivation in Spain: The case of cannabis social clubs', in Decorte, T., Potter, G. and Bouchard, M. (eds.), *World wide weed: Global trends in cannabis cultivation and its control*, p. 163–77. Farnham: Ashgate.

Askew, R. (2013). *Negotiating the criminality and deviance associated with illicit substance use: A discourse analysis of interviews with adult recreational drug takers*, PhD thesis, Manchester: The University of Manchester.

Atkinson, R. (1991). 'Alcohol and drug abuse in the elderly', in Jacoby, R. and Oppenheimer, C. (eds.), *Psychiatry in the elderly*, p. 819–51. Oxford: Oxford University Press.

Atkinson, R. and Flint, J. (2001). 'Accessing hidden and hard-to-reach populations: Snowball research strategies', in Gilbert, N. (ed.), *Social research update no. 33*, p. 1–4. Guildford: Department of Sociology, University of Surrey.
Avico, U., Kaplan, C., Korczak, D. and Van Meter, K. (1988). *Cocaine epidemiology in three European Community cities: A pilot study using a snowball sampling methodology*. Brussels: European Communities Health Directorate.
Ayres, R., Eveson, L., Ingram, J. and Telfer, M. (2012). 'Treatment experience and needs of older drug users in Bristol, UK', *Journal of Substance Use*, 17(1): 19–31.
Ball, J. (1967). 'The reliability and validity of interview data obtained from 59 narcotic drug addicts', *The American Journal of Sociology*, 72(6): 650–4.
Ball, J. and Snarr, R. (1969). 'A test of the maturation hypothesis with respect to opiate addiction', *UN Bulletin on Narcotics*, 4(2): 9–13.
Baltes, P. (2003). 'On the incomplete architecture of human ontogeny: Selection, optimization, and compensation as foundation of development theory', in Staudinger, U.M. and Lindenberger, U. (eds.), *Understanding human development: Dialogues with lifespan psychology*, p. 17–43. Boston, MA: Kluwer.
Baltes, P.B. and Baltes, M.M. (1990). 'Psychological perspectives on successful aging: The model of selective optimization with compensation', in Baltes, P.B. and Baltes, M.M. (eds.), *Successful aging: Perspectives from the behavioral sciences*, p. 1–34. New York: Cambridge University Press.
Bauman, Z. (1997). *Postmodernity and its discontents*. Cambridge: Polity.
Bauman, Z. (2000). *Liquid modernity*. Cambridge: Polity.
Bauman, Z. (2001). *The individualized society*. Cambridge: Polity.
BBC News (2005). 'Heated debate over heroin report', 3 February 2005, http://news.bbc.co.uk/1/hi/scotland/4230985.stm
BBC News (2014). 'Norman Baker quits as Home Office minister', 4 November 2014, http://www.bbc.co.uk/news/uk-politics-29891132
Bean, P. (1974). *The social control of drugs*. London: Robertson.
Bean, P. (2010). *Legalising drugs: Debates and dilemmas*. Bristol: Policy Press.
Becker, H. (1955). 'Marihuana use and social control', *Social Problems*, 3(1): 35–44.
Becker, H.S. (1953). 'Becoming a marihuana user', *American Journal of Sociology*, 59(3): 235–42.
Becker, H.S. (1963). *Outsiders: Studies in the sociology of deviance*. New York: Macmillan.
Beech, N. (2011). 'Liminality and the practices of identity reconstruction', *Human Relations*, 64(2): 285–302.
Bell, C. (2004). 'Doing sociological research: The genre of "owning up"', *International Journal of Social Research Methodology*, 7(1): 29–33.
Bell, V. (2015). 'Theresa May's futile war on psychoactive drugs', *The Observer*, 13 December 2015, http://www.theguardian.com/science/2015/dec/13/vaughan-bell-legal-highs-psychoactive-drugs-bill
Bennett, A. (2011). 'The post–subcultural turn: Some reflections 10 years on', *Journal of Youth Studies*, 14(5): 493–506.
Berg, B. (2001). *Qualitative research methods for the social sciences (4th edition)*. Boston: Allyn and Bacon.
Berg, S. (1988). 'Snowball sampling', in Johnson, N.L. and Kotz, S. (eds.), *Encyclopaedia of statistical sciences (Vol. 8)*, p. 528–32. Chichester: John Wiley and Sons.
Bergman, S. and Amir, M. (1973). 'Crime and delinquency among the aged in Israel', *Geriatrics*, 28(1): 149–57.

Bertaux, D. (1990). 'Oral history approaches to an international social movement', in Øyen, E. (ed.), *Comparative methodology*, p. 158–70. London: Sage.

Beynon, C. (2009). 'Drug use and ageing: Older people do take drugs', *Age and Ageing*, 38(1): 8–10.

Beynon, C., Mcveigh, J. and Roe, B. (2007). 'Problematic drug use, ageing and older people: Trends in the age of drug users in northwest England', *Ageing and Society*, 27(6): 799–810.

Beynon, C., Stimson, G. and Lawson, E. (2010). 'Illegal drug use in the age of ageing', *British Journal of General Practice*, 60(576): 481–2.

Biernacki, P. and Waldorf, D. (1981). 'Snowball sampling: Problems and techniques of chain referral sampling', *Sociological Methods and Research*, 10(2): 141–63.

Black, P. and Joseph, L. (2014). 'Still dazed and confused: Midlife marijuana use by the baby boom generation', *Deviant Behavior*, 35(10): 822–41.

Blackman, S. (2004). *Chilling out: The cultural politics of substance consumption, youth and drug policy*. Maidenhead: Open University Press.

Blackman, S. (2007). '"See Emily Play": Youth culture, recreational drug use and normalisation', in Simpson, M., Shildrick, T. and MacDonald, R. (eds.), *Drugs in Britain: Supply, consumption and control*, p. 39–59. Basingstoke: Palgrave Macmillian.

Blackwell, J.S. (1983). 'Drifting, controlling and overcoming: Opiate users who avoid becoming chronically dependent', *Journal of Drug Issues*, 13(2): 219–35.

Blumer, H. (1954). 'What is wrong with social theory?', *American Sociological Review*, 19(1): 3–10.

Boeri, M.W. (2002). *"I'm an addict, but I ain't no junkie": An ethnographic analysis of the drug career of baby boomers*, PhD thesis, Atlanta: Georgia State University.

Boeri, M.W. (2004). '"Hell, I'm an addict, but I ain't no junkie": An ethnographic analysis of aging heroin users', *Human Organization*, 63(2): 236–45.

Boeri, M.W., Sterk, C.E., Bahora, M. and Elifison, K.W. (2008). 'Poly–drug use among ecstasy users: Separate, synergistic, and indiscriminate patterns', *Journal of Drug Issues*, 38(2): 517–41.

Boeri, M.W., Sterk, C.E. and Elifson, K.W. (2006). 'Baby boomer drug users: Career phases, social control and social learning theory', *Sociological Inquiry*, 76(2): 264–91.

Boeri, M.W., Sterk, C.E. and Elifson, K.W. (2008). 'Reconceptualizing early and late onset: A life course analysis of older heroin users', *The Gerontologist*, 48(5): 637–45.

Boeri, M.W. and Tyndall, B.D. (2012). 'A contextual comparison of risk behaviors among older adult drug users and harm reduction in suburban versus inner-city social environments', *Journal of Applied Social Science*, 6(1): 72–91.

Boeri, M.W., Whalen, T., Tyndall, B.D. and Ballard, E. (2011). 'Drug use trajectory patterns among older drug users', *Substance Abuse and Rehabilitation*, 2: 89–102.

Brannen, J. (2013). 'Life story talk: Some reflections on narrative in qualitative interviews', *Sociological Research Online*, 18(2). http://www.socresonline.org.uk/18/2/15.html

Browne, K. (2005). 'Snowball sampling: Using social networks to research nonheterosexual women', *International Journal of Social Research Methodology*, 8(1): 47–60.

Bulmer, M.I.A. (1975). 'Sociological models of the mining community', *The Sociological Review*, 23(1): 61–92.

Cain, L. (1964). 'The life course and social structure', in Faris, R. (ed.), *Handbook of modern sociology*, p. 272–309. Chicago: Rand McNally.

Capel, W., Goldsmith, B., Waddell, K. and Stewart, G. (1972). 'The aging narcotic addict: An increasing problem for the next decades', *Journal of Gerontology*, 27(1): 102–6.

Capel, W. and Peppers, L.G. (1978). 'The aging addict: A longitudinal study of known abusers', *Addictive Diseases*, 3(3): 389–403.

Carlsson, C. (2012). 'Using "turning points" to understand processes of change in offending: Notes from a Swedish study on life courses and crime', *British Journal of Criminology*, 52(1): 1–16.

Carnwath, T. and Smith, I. (2002). *Heroin century*. London: Routledge.

Carstensen, L.I. (1992). 'Social and emotional patterns in adulthood: Support for socioemotional selectivity theory', *Psychology and Aging*, 7(3): 331–8.

Cavendish, L. and Porter, M. (2013). 'The rise of midlife drug users', *The Times*, 2 December 2013. http://www.thetimes.co.uk/tto/health/article3935571.ece

Chatwin, C. and Porteous, D. (2013). 'Insiders? The experiences and perspectives of long-term, regular cannabis users', *Contemporary Drug Problems*, 40(2): 235–57.

Chen, K. and Kandel, D. (1995). 'The natural history of drug use from adolescence to the mid-thirties in a general population sample', *American Journal of Public Health*, 85(1): 41–7.

Chivete-Matthews, N. and Maggs, P. (2002). *Crime, policing and justice: The experience of older people*. Statistical Bulletin 08/02. London: Home Office.

Clausen, J.A. (1986). *The life course: A sociological perspective*. Englewood Cliffs, NJ: Prentice Hall.

Clausen, J.A. (1998). 'Life reviews and life stories', in Giele, J.Z. and Elder, G.H. (eds.), *Methods of lifecourse research: Qualitative and quantitative approaches*, p. 189–212. Thousand Oaks, CA: Sage.

Cloud, W. and Granfield, R. (2004). 'The social process of exiting addiction: A life course perspective', in Blomqvist, J., Koski-Jannes, A. and Ojesjo, L. (eds.), *Addiction and life course*, p. 185–202. Helsinki: Nordic Council on Alcohol and Drug Research.

Cloward, R.A. and Ohlin, L.E. (1960). *Delinquent boys: The culture of the gang*. New York: Free Press.

Coggans, N., Dalgarno, P., Johnson, L. and Shewan, D. (2004). 'Long-term heavy cannabis use: Implications for health education', *Drugs: Education, Prevention and Policy*, 11(4): 299–313.

Cohen, P. (1990). *Drugs as a social construct*, PhD thesis, Amsterdam: Universiteit Van Amsterdam.

Cohen, P. and Sas, A. (1994). 'Cocaine use in Amsterdam in non-deviant subcultures', *Addiction Research*, 2(1): 71–94.

Coleman, J.S. (1959). 'Relational analysis: The study of social organizations with survey methods', *Human Organization*, 17(4): 28–36.

Collin, M. (1997). *Altered state: The story of ecstasy culture and acid house*. London: Serpent's Tail.

Collinson, M. (1996). 'In search of the high life: Drugs, crime, masculinities and consumption', *British Journal of Criminology*, 36(3): 428–44.

Colliver, J.D., Compton, W.M., Gfroerer, J.C. and Condon, T. (2006). 'Projecting drug use among aging baby boomers in 2020', *Annals of Epidemiology*, 16: 257–65.

Coomber, R. (2006). *Pusher myths: Re-situating the drug dealer*. London: Free Association Books.

Coomber, R. and Moyle, L. (2014). 'Beyond drug dealing: Developing and extending the concept of "social supply" of illicit drugs to "minimally commercial supply"', *Drugs: Education, Prevention and Policy*, 21(2): 157–64.

Coomber, R. and Turnbull, P. (2007). 'Arenas of drug transactions: Adolescent cannabis transactions in England—social supply', *Journal of Drug Issues*, 37(4): 845–65.

Cramb, A. (2005). 'Heroin "safe" claim attacked', *The Telegraph*, 4 February 2005, http://www.telegraph.co.uk/news/uknews/1482744/Heroin-safe-claim-attacked.html

Crome, I. and Crome, P. (2005). '"At your age, what does it matter?" Myths and realities about older people who use substances', *Drugs: Education, Prevention and Policy*, 12(5): 343–7.

Crome, I., Wu, L.T., Rao, R. and Crome, P. (2015). *Substance use and older people*. Chichester: Wiley.

Crook, S., Pakulski, J. and Waters, M. (1992). *Postmodernization: Change in advanced society*. London: Sage.

Curtis, L.A. (1985). 'Introduction', in Curtis, L.A. (ed.), *American violence and public policy: An update of the National Commission on the Causes and Prevention of Violence*, p. 1–13. New Haven: Yale University Press.

Dahl, H.V. and Asmussen Frank, V. (2011). 'Medical marijuana: Exploring the concept in relation to small scale cannabis growers in Denmark', in Decorte, T., Potter, G. and Bouchard, M. (eds.), *World wide weed: Global trends in cannabis cultivation and its control*, p. 57–73. Farnham: Ashgate.

Daily Mail (2011). 'Old habits die hard: Rise in number of alcohol and drug addicts over 50 in the U.S.', 18 May 2011, http://www.dailymail.co.uk/news/article-1388364/Old-habits-die-hard-Rise-number-alcohol-drug-addicts-50-U-S.html#ixzz3QbKRJC7G

Daily Mail (2014). 'Comment: Clegg and a deadly gamble over drugs', 31 October 2014, http://www.dailymail.co.uk/debate/article-2815164/DAILY-MAIL-COMMENT-Clegg-deadly-gamble-drugs.html

Dalgarno, P. (2006). *Non-problematic drug use*, PhD thesis, Glasgow: Glasgow Caledonian University.

Dalgarno, P. and Shewan, D. (2005). 'Reducing the risks of drug use: The case for set and setting', *Addiction Research and Theory*, 13(3): 259–65.

Dannefer, D. and Settersten, R. (2010). 'The study of the life course: Implications for social gerontology', in Dannefer, D. and Phillipson, C. (eds.), *The Sage handbook of social gerontology*, p. 4–21. London: SAGE Publications.

Davies, J.B. (1992). *The myth of addiction*. Chur, Switzerland: Harwood.

Davies, J.B. (1997). *Drugspeak: The analysis of drug discourse*. Amsterdam: Harwood.

Decorte, T. (2010). 'The case for small scale domestic cannabis cultivation', *The International Journal of Drug Policy*, 21(4): 271–5.

Decorte, T. and Potter, G.R. (2015). 'The globalisation of cannabis cultivation: A growing challenge', *International Journal of Drug Policy*, 26(3): 221–5.

Department of Health (2001). *National service framework for older people*. London: Department of Health. Available at https://www.gov.uk/government/uploads/system/uploads/attachment_data/file/198033/National_Service_Framework_for_Older_People.pdf

De Vaus, D.A. (1990). *Surveys in social research (2nd edition).* London: Unwin Hyman.

DeWit, D., Offord, D. and Wong, M. (1997). 'Patterns of onset and cessation of drug use over the early part of the life course', *Health Education and Behavior*, 24(6): 746–58.

Dickinson, T. (2015). 'The war on drugs is burning out', *Rolling Stone*, 8 January 2015, http://www.rollingstone.com/politics/news/the-war-on-drugs-is-burning-out-20150108

Ditton, J. and Hammersley, R. (1996). *A very greedy drug: Cocaine in context.* Amsterdam: Harwood Academic.

Douglas, J. (1976). *Investigative social research: Individual and team research.* Beverly Hills, CA: Sage.

Drugscope (2014). *It's about time: Tackling substance misuse in older people.* Drugscope on behalf of the Recovery Partnership. http://www.drugwise.org.uk/wp-content/uploads/its-about-time-report.pdf

Duff, C. (2003). 'The importance of culture and context: Rethinking risk and risk management in young drug-using populations', *Health, Risk and Society*, 5: 285–300.

Duff, C. (2004). 'Drug use as a "practice of the self": Is there any place for an "ethics of moderation" in contemporary drug policy?', *International Journal of Drug Policy*, 15: 385–93.

Duff, C.J., Asbridge, M., Brochu, S., Cousineau, M., Hathaway, A.D., Marsh, D. and Erickson, P.G. (2012). 'A Canadian perspective on cannabis normalization among adults', *Addiction Research and Theory*, 20(4): 271–83.

Duff, C.J. and Erickson, P.G. (2014). 'Cannabis, risk and normalisation: Evidence from a Canadian study of socially integrated, adult cannabis users', *Health Risk and Society*, 16(3): 210–26.

Duncan, S. and Edwards, R. (1999). *Lone mothers, paid work and gendered moral rationalities.* Basingstoke: Macmillan.

Edmunds, J. and Turner, B. (2002). *Generations, culture and society.* Buckingham: Open University Press.

Eiser, J.R. (1982). 'Addiction as attribution: Cognitive processes in giving up smoking', in Eiser, J.R. (ed.), *Social psychology and behavioural medicine*, p. 281–99. Chichester: Wiley.

Eiser, J.R. and Gossop, M. (1979). '"Hooked" or "sick": Addicts' perceptions of their addictions', *Addictive Behaviors*, 4: 185–91.

Elder, G. (1974). *Children of the Great Depression.* Chicago: University of Chicago Press.

Elder, G. (1975). 'Age differentiation and the life course', *Annual Review of Sociology*, 1: 165–90.

Elder, G. (1985a). *Perspectives on the life course.* Ithaca: Cornell University Press.

Elder, G. (1985b). *Life course dynamics: Trajectories and transitions 1968–1980.* Ithaca: Cornell University Press.

Elder, G. (1994). 'Time, human agency, and social change: Perspectives on the life course', *Social Psychology Quarterly*, 57(1): 4–15.

Elder, G. (1998). 'The life course as developmental theory', *Child Development*, 69(1): 1–12.

Erickson, P.G. and Hathaway, A.D. (2010). 'Normalization and harm reduction: Research avenues and policy agendas', *International Journal of Drug Policy*, 21: 137–9.

European Monitoring Centre for Drugs and Drug Addiction (2004). *Statistical bulletin 2004*. Available at http://www.stats04.emcdda.europa.eu/html.cfm/index5220EN.html

European Monitoring Centre for Drugs and Drug Addiction (2008). *Substance use among older adults: A neglected problem*. Office for Official Publications of the European Communities. Available at http://www.emcdda.europa.eu/attachements.cfm/att_50566_EN_TDAD08001ENC_web.pdf

European Monitoring Centre for Drugs and Drug Addiction (2011). *Drug policy profiles: Portugal*. Luxembourg: Publications Office of the European Union. Available at http://www.emcdda.europa.eu/attachements.cfm/att_137215_EN_PolicyProfile_Portugal_WEB_Final.pdf

Everingham, C. (2003). 'Self-actualisation and the ageing process from an intergenerational lifecourse perspective', *Ageing and Society*, 23(2): 243–53.

Eysenbach, G. and Till, J.E. (2001). 'Ethical issues in qualitative research on internet communities', *British Medical Journal*, 323: 1103–5.

Eysenbach, G. and Wyatt, J. (2002). 'Using the internet for surveys and health research', *Journal of Medical Internet Research*, 4(2): e13.

Fagan, J. and Chin, K. (1991). 'Social processes of initiation into crack', *Journal of Drug Issues*, 21(2): 313–43.

Fahmy, V., Hatch, S.L., Hotopf, M. and Stewart, R. (2012). 'Prevalences of illicit drug use in people aged 50 years and over from two surveys', *Age and Ageing*, 41(4): 553–6.

Falkingham, J. (1987). 'Who are the baby boomers? A demographic profile', in Evandrou, M. (ed.), *Baby Boomers: Ageing in the 21st century*, p. 15–40. London: Age Concern.

Faugier, J. and Sargeant, M. (1997). 'Sampling hard to reach populations', *Journal of Advanced Nursing*, 26: 790–7.

Faupel, C. (1991). *Shooting dope: Career patterns of hard-core drug users*. Gainsville: University of Florida Press.

Finlayson, R. (1995). 'Misuse of prescription drugs', *The International Journal of the Addictions*, 30(13 & 14): 1871–901.

Fitzgerald, J. and Hamilton, M. (1996). 'The consequences of knowing: Ethical and legal liabilities in illicit drug research', *Social Science Medicine*, 43(11): 1591–600.

Fitzgerald, J. and Hamilton, M. (1997). 'Confidentiality, disseminated regulation and ethico-legal liabilities in research with hidden populations of illicit drug users', *Addiction*, 92(9): 1099–107.

Ford, M. (2011). 'Old habits die hard for ageing addicts', *The Guardian*, 26 January 2011, http://www.theguardian.com/society/2011/jan/26/older-drug-users-habits-die-hard

Foster, J. (1990). *Villains: Crime and community in the inner city*. London: Routledge.

Frank, V.A., Christensen, A.S. and Dahl, H.V. (2013). 'Cannabis use during a life course—integrating cannabis use into everyday life', *Drugs and Alcohol Today*, 13(1): 44–50.

Gambert, S. (1992). 'Substance abuse in the elderly', in Lowinson, J., Ruiz, P., Millman, R. and Langrod, J. (eds.), *Substance abuse: A comprehensive textbook (2nd edition)*, p. 843–51. Baltimore: Williams and Wilkins.

George, L. (1993). 'Sociological perspectives on life transitions', *Annual Review of Sociology*, 19: 353–73.

George, L. (1996). 'Missing links: The case for a social psychology of the life course', *The Gerontologist*, 36(2): 248–55.

Gfroerer, J., Penne, M., Pemberton, M. and Folsom, R. (2003). 'Substance abuse treatment among older adults in 2020: The impact of the aging baby-boom cohort', *Drug and Alcohol Dependence*, 69: 127–35.

Giddens, A. (1990). *The consequences of modernity*. Cambridge: Polity.

Giddens, A. (1991). *Modernity and self identity: Self and society in the late modern age*. Cambridge: Polity.

Giele, J.Z. and Elder, G.H. (eds.) (1998). *Methods of life course research: Qualitative and quantitative approaches*. Thousand Oaks: Sage.

Gilleard, C. and Higgs, P. (2002). 'The third age: Class, cohort and generation', *Ageing and Society*, 22: 369–82.

Glantz, M. and Backenheimer, M. (1988). 'Substance abuse among elderly women', *Clinical Gerontologist*, 8(1): 3–26.

Glaser, B.G. and Strauss, A.L. (1967). *The discovery of grounded theory—strategies for qualitative research*. London: Weidenfeld and Nicholson.

Goodchild, S. (2005). 'Meet the "silver sniffers": The pensionables snorting and smoking', *Independent on Sunday*, 23 January 2005, http://www.independent.co.uk/news/uk/crime/meet-the-silver-sniffers-the-pensionables-snorting-and-smoking-the-unmentionables-6154204.html

Goode, E. (1969). 'Marijuana and the politics of reality', *Journal of Health and Social Behaviour*, 10(2): 83–94.

Goode, E. (1970). *The marijuana smokers*. New York: Basic Books.

Goode, S. (2000). 'Researching a hard-to-access and vulnerable population: Some considerations on researching drug and alcohol-using mothers', *Sociological Research Online*, 5(1). http://www.socresonline.org.uk/5/1/goode.html

Goodman, L.A. (1961). 'Snowball sampling', *Annals of Mathematical Statistics*, 32: 148–70.

Goodman, L.A. (2011). 'Comment: On respondent-driven sampling and snowball sampling in hard-to-reach populations and snowball sampling not in hard-to-reach populations', *Sociological Methodology*, 41(1): 347–53.

Gossop, M. and Moos, R. (2008). 'Substance misuse among older adults: A neglected but treatable problem', *Addiction*, 103(3): 347–8.

Green, B. (1982). 'Structural antecedents of psychoactive drug use among the elderly', *Ageing and Society*, 2(1): 77–94.

Grenier, A. (2012). *Transitions and the lifecourse: Challenging the constructions of "growing old"*. Bristol: Policy Press.

Griffiths, P., Gossop, M., Powis, B. and Strang, J. (1993). 'Researching hidden populations of drug users by privileged access interviewers: Methodological and practical issues', *Addiction*, 88(12): 1617–26.

Groger, L., Mayberry, P. and Straker, J. (1999). 'What we didn't learn because of who would not talk to us', *Qualitative Health Research*, 9(6): 829–35.

Gubrium, J. and Holstein, J. (2009). *Analysing narrative reality*. London: Sage.

Hagestad, G.O. and Neugarten, B.L. (1985). 'Age and the life course', in Binstock, R.H. and Shanas, E. (eds.), *Handbook of aging and the social sciences (2nd edition)*, p. 36–61. New York: Van Nostrand Reinhold.

Hakkarainen, P., Frank, V.A., Barratt, M., Dahl, H., Decorte, T., Karjalainen, K., . . . and Werseet, B. (2015). 'Growing medicine: Small-scale cannabis cultivation for medical purposes in six different countries', *International Journal of Drug Policy*, 26(3): 250–6.

Hakkarainen, P. and Perala, J. (2011). 'With a little help from my friends: Justifications for small scale cannabis growers', in Decorte, T., Potter, G. and Bouchard, M. (eds.), *World wide weed: Global trends in cannabis cultivation and its control*, p. 75–90. Farnham: Ashgate.

Halberstam, J. (2005). *In a queer time and place: Transgender bodies, subcultural lives*. New York: New York University Press.

Hall, E. (1983). 'Substance abuse in the aging', in Bennett, G., Vourakis, C. and Woolf, D. (eds.), *Substance abuse: Pharmacological, developmental, and clinical perspectives*, p. 192–206. New York: John Wiley and Sons.

Hall, S., Winlow, S. and Ancrum, C. (2008). *Criminal identities and consumer culture: Crime, exclusion and the new culture of narcissism*. Cullompton: Willan.

Hammersley, M. (1989). *The dilemma of qualitative method: Herbert Blumer and the Chicago tradition*. London: Routledge.

Hammersley, R. (2005). 'Theorizing normal drug use (editorial)', *Addiction Research and Theory*, 13(3): 201–3.

Hammersley, R. (2011). 'Developing a sociology of normal substance use (invited editorial)', *International Journal of Drug Policy*, 22(6): 413–4.

Hammersley, R. and Dalgarno, P. (2013). *Trauma and recovery amongst people who have injected drugs within the past five years*. Glasgow: Scottish Drugs Forum.

Hammersley, R., Khan, F. and Ditton, J. (2002). *Ecstasy and the rise of the chemical generation*. London: Routledge.

Han, B., Gfroerer, J.C. and Colliver, J.D. (2009). *An examination of trends in illicit drug use among adults aged 50 to 59 in the United States*. Rockville, MD: Substance Abuse and Mental Health Services Administration, Office of Applied Studies.

Han, B., Gfroerer, J.C., Colliver, J.D. and Penne, M.A. (2009). 'Substance use disorder among older adults in the United States in 2020', *Addiction*, 104(1): 88–96.

Handelman, S. (1994). *Comrade criminal: The theft of the second Russian revolution*. London: Michael Joseph.

Hareven, T. and Masaoka, K. (1988). 'Turning points and transitions: Perceptions of the life course', *Journal of Family History*, 13(3): 271–89.

Hathaway, A.D. (1997a). 'Marijuana and tolerance: Revisiting Becker's sources of control', *Deviant Behavior*, 18(2): 103–24.

Hathaway, A.D. (1997b). 'Marijuana and lifestyle: Exploring tolerable deviance', *Deviant Behavior*, 18(3): 213–32.

Hathaway, A.D., Comeau, N.C. and Erickson, P.G. (2011). 'Cannabis normalization and stigma: Contemporary practices of moral regulation', *Criminology and Criminal Justice*, 11(5): 451–69.

Hathaway, A.D., Hyshka, E., Erickson, P.G., Asbridge, M., Brochu, S., Cousineau, M.M., . . . and Marsh, D. (2010). 'Whither RDS? An investigation of respondent driven sampling as a method of recruiting mainstream marijuana users', *Harm Reduction Journal*, 7(15): 15–26.

Haywood, L., Kew, F., Bramham, P., Spink, J., Capenerhurst, J. and Henry, I. (1995). *Understanding leisure (2nd edition)*. Cheltenham: Stanley Thornes.

Hebdige, D. (1976). 'The meaning of mod', in Hall, S. and Jefferson, T. (eds.), *Resistance through rituals: Youth subcultures in post-war Britain*, p. 71–9. London: Routledge.

Hebdige, D. (1979). *Subculture: The meaning of style*. London: Methuen.

Heckathorn, D.D. (1997). 'Respondent-driven sampling: A new approach to the study of hidden populations', *Social Problems*, 44(2): 174–99.

Heckathorn, D.D. (2002). 'Respondent-driven sampling II: Deriving valid population estimates from chain-referral samples of hidden populations', *Social Problems*, 49: 11–34.

Heckathorn, D.D. (2007). 'Extensions of respondent-driven sampling: Analyzing continuous variables and controlling for differential recruitment', *Sociological Methodology*, 37(1): 151–207.

Heckathorn, D.D. (2011). 'Comment: Snowball versus respondent-driven sampling', *Sociological Methodology*, 41(1): 355–66.

Hirsch, M., Conforti, R. and Graney, C.J. (2001). 'The use of marijuana for pleasure: A replication of Howard Becker's study of marijuana use', in Inciardi, J.A. and McElrath, K. (eds.), *The American drug scene: An anthology (3rd edition)*, p. 27–35. Los Angeles: Roxbury.

Hockey, J. and James, A. (2003). *Social identities across the life course*. Basingstoke: Palgrave Macmillan.

Holbrook, B. and Jackson, P. (1996). 'Shopping around: Focus group research in north London', *Area*, 28: 136–42.

Holstein, J. and Gubrium, J. (2000). *The self we live by: Narrative identity in a postmodern world*. Oxford: Oxford University Press.

Home Office (2014a). *Drugs: International comparators*. London: Home Office.

Home Office (2014b). *Drug misuse: Findings from the 2013/14 crime survey for England and Wales*. London: Home Office.

Home Office (2014c). *Accessibility of drugs: Drug misuse 2013 to 2014*. London: Home Office. Available at https://www.gov.uk/government/statistics/tables-for-drug-misuse-findings-from-the-2013-to-2014-csew

Home Office (2015a). *Drug misuse: Findings from the 2014/15 crime survey for England and Wales*. London: Home Office.

Home Office (2015b). *User guide to drug misuse statistics*. London: Home Office.

Home Office (2015c). *Drug misuse: Findings from the 2014/15 crime survey for England and Wales (appendix tables)*. London: Home Office.

Honigmann, J. (1982). 'Sampling in ethnographic fieldwork', in Burgess, R. (ed.), *Field research: A sourcebook and field manual*, p. 121–39. London: Unwin.

Hooton, C. (2014). 'These grandmas smoking weed for the first time are wonderful', *The Independent*, 20 November 2014, http://www.independent.co.uk/news/world/americas/these-grandmas-smoking-weed-for-the-first-time-are-wonderful-9871906.html#

Horvath, A. (2013). *Modernism and charisma*. Basingstoke: Palgrave Macmillan.

Horvath, A., Thomassen, B. and Wydra, H. (2015). 'Liminality and the search for boundaries', in Horvath, A., Thomassen, B. and Wydra, H. (eds.), *Breaking boundaries: Varieties of liminality*, p. 1–8. Oxford: Berghahn Books.

Hser, Y., Anglin, M.D., Grella, C., Longshore, D. and Prendergast, M.L. (1997). 'Drug treatment careers: A conceptual framework and existing research findings', *Journal of Substance Abuse Treatment*, 14: 543–58.

Hser, Y., Hamilton, A. and Niv, N. (2009). 'Understanding drug use over the life course: Past, present and future', *Journal of Drug Issues*, 39(1): 231–6.

Hser, Y., Huang, D., Chou, C. and Anglin, M.D. (2007). 'Trajectories of heroin addiction: Growth mixture modeling results based on a 33-year follow-up study', *Evaluation Review*, 31: 548–63.

Hser, Y., Longshore, D. and Anglin, M.D. (2007). 'The life course perspective on drug use: A conceptual framework for understanding drug use trajectories', *Evaluation Review*, 31(6): 515–47.

Huggins, R. (2007). 'Systematic "normalisaton"? Mapping and interpreting policy responses to illicit drug use', in Manning, P. (ed.), *Drugs and popular culture: Drugs, media and identity in contemporary society*, p. 260–77. Cullompton: Willan.

Hughes, E. (1945). 'Dilemmas and contradictions of status', *American Journal of Sociology*, 50: 353–9.

Israel, M. (2004). 'Strictly confidential? Integrity and the disclosure of criminological and socio-legal research', *British Journal of Criminology*, 44(5): 715–40.

Ives, R. and Ghelani, P. (2006). 'Polydrug use (the use of drugs in combination): A brief review', *Drugs: Education, Prevention and Policy*, 13(3): 225–32.

Jessup, M.A., Ross, T.B., Jones, A.L., Satre, D.D., Weisner, C.M., Chi, F.W. and Mertens, J.R. (2014). 'Significant life events and their impact on alcohol and drug use: A qualitative study', *Journal of Psychoactive Drugs*, 46(5): 450–9.

Johnson, B.D., Goldstein, P.J., Preble, E., Schmeidler, J., Liption, D.S. and Spunt, B. (1985). *Taking care of business: The economics of crime by heroin abusers*. Lexington, MA: Lexington Books.

Joseph, C. (1995). 'Alcohol and drug misuse in the nursing home', *The International Journal of the Addictions*, 30(13 & 14): 1953–84.

Judt, T. (2006). *Postwar: A history of Europe since 1945*. London: William Heinenann.

Kandel, D., Yamaguchi, K. and Chen, K. (1992). 'Stages of progression in drug involvement from adolescence to adulthood: Further evidence for the gateway theory', *Journal of Studies on Alcohol*, 53(5): 447–57.

Kaplan, C.D., Korf, D. and Sterk, C. (1987). 'Temporal and social contexts of heroin-using populations: An illustration of the snowball sampling technique', *Journal of Mental and Nervous Disorders*, 175(9): 566–74.

Kleinman, A. (1988). *The illness narratives: Suffering, healing and the human condition*. New York: Basic Books.

Kluger, J. and Ressner, J. (2006). 'Balding, wrinkled, and stoned', *Time*, 15 January 2006, http://content.time.com/time/magazine/article/0,9171,1149389,00.html

Kreuger, A. (2013). 'Shuffleboard? Oh, maybe let's get high instead', *The New York Times*, 22 March 2013, http://www.nytimes.com/2013/03/24/fashion/more-older-americans-use-marijuana.html?pagewanted=all&_r=0

LabourList (2015). 'Almost 200,000—Labour membership rises to highest point since 2005', 2 February 2015, http://labourlist.org/2015/02/almost-200000-labour-membership-rises-to-highest-point-since-2005/

Lander, I. (2015). 'Gender, aging and drug use: A post-structural approach to the life course', *British Journal of Criminology*, 55(2): 270–85.

Lang, F.R. and Carstensen, L.L. (1998). 'Social relationships and adaptation in late life', in Bellack, A.S. and Hersen, M. (eds.), *Comprehensive clinical psychology*, p. 55–72. Oxford: Pergamon.

Lash, S. and Urry, J. (1987). *The end of organised capitalism*. Cambridge: Polity.

Laub, J. and Sampson, R. (1998). 'Integrating quantitative and qualitative data', in Giele, J.Z. and Elder, G.H. (eds.), *Methods of life course research: Qualitative and quantitative approaches*, p. 213–29. Thousand Oaks, CA: Sage.

Laub, J. and Sampson, R. (2003). *Shared beginnings, divergent lives: Delinquent boys to age 70.* Cambridge, MA: Harvard University Press.

Lazar, K. (2010). 'As pot-smoking, pill-popping baby boomers age, new health problems may arise', *The Boston Globe*, 8 February 2010, http://www.boston.com/news/health/articles/2010/02/08/illicit_drug_use_among_baby_boomers_is_on_the_rise_as_are_long_term_health_concerns/

Lee, R. (1993). *Doing research on sensitive topics.* London: Sage.

Levy, J. and Anderson, T. (2005). 'The drug career of the older injector', *Addiction Research and Theory*, 13(3): 245–58.

Lister, S., Wall, D. and Bryan, J. (2004). *Evaluation of the leeds distraction burglary initiative.* Home Office Online Report 44/04. London: Home Office.

Little, M., Jordens, C.F., Paul, K., Montgomery, K. and Philipson, B. (1998). 'Liminality: A major category of the experience of cancer illness', *Social Science and Medicine*, 47(10): 1485–94.

Lloyd, C. (2010). *Sinning and sinned against: The stigmatisation of problem drug users.* London: UK Drug Policy Commission.

Lopez, W.D., Kreuger, P.M. and Walters, S.T. (2010). 'High-risk drug use and sexual behaviors among out-of-treatment drug users: An aging and life course perspective', *Addictive Behaviors*, 35(5): 432–7.

Lyng, S. (1990). 'Edgework: A social psychological analysis of voluntary risk taking', *American Journal of Sociology*, 95(4): 851–86.

Lynskey, M.Y., Day, C. and Hall, W. (2003). 'Alcohol and other drug use disorders among older aged people', *Drug and Alcohol Review*, 22(2): 125–33.

Maddux, J. and Desmond, D. (1975). 'Reliability and validity of information from chronic heroin users', *Journal of Psychiatric Research*, 12(2): 87–95.

Maddux, J. and Desmond, D. (1981). *Careers of opioid users.* New York: Praeger.

Magnani, R., Sabin, K., Saidel, T. and Heckathorn, D.D. (2005). 'Review of sampling hard to reach and hidden populations for HIV surveillance', *AIDS*, 19(Suppl. 2): S67–72.

Malksoo, M. (2015). 'The challenge of liminality for international relations theory', in Horvath, A., Thomassen, B. and Wydra, H. (eds.), *Breaking boundaries: Varieties of liminality*, p. 226–43. Oxford: Berghahn Books.

Manning, P. (ed.) (2007) *Drugs and popular culture: Drugs, media and identity in contemporary society.* Cullompton: Willan.

Marshall, C. and Rossman, G.B. (1999). *Designing qualitative research (3rd edition).* Beverley Hills: Sage.

Marshall, V. and Levy, J.A. (1990). 'Aging and dying', in Binstock, R.H. and George, L.K. (eds.), *Handbook of aging and the social sciences (3rd edition)*, p. 245–60. New York: Academic Press.

Mauro, P., Canham, S., Martins, S. and Spira, A. (2015). 'Substance-use coping and self-rated health among US middle-aged and older adults', *Addictive Behaviors*, 42: 96–100.

McAdams, D. (1993). *The stories we live by: Personal myths and the making of the self.* New York: William Morrow.

McCormack, M., Adams, A. and Anderson, E. (2012). 'Taking to the streets: The benefits of spontaneous methodological innovation in participant recruitment', *Qualitative Research*, 13(2): 228–41.

Mckeganey, N. (2011). *Controversies in drugs policy and practice.* Basingstoke: Palgrave MacMillan.

McKim, W.A. and Mishara, B.L. (1987). *Drugs and ageing*. Toronto: Butterworths.

McSweeney, T. and Turnbull, P. (2007). *Exploring user perceptions of occasional and controlled heroin use: A follow-up study*. York: Joseph Roundtree Foundation.

Measham, F., Aldridge, J. and Parker, H. (2001). *Dancing on drugs: Risk, health and hedonism*. London: Free Association Books.

Measham, F., Newcombe, R. and Parker, H. (1994). 'The normalization of recreational drug use amongst young people in north-west England', *The British Journal of Sociology*, 45(2): 287–312.

Measham, F., Parker, H. and Aldridge, J. (1998). 'The teenage transition: From adolescent recreational drug use to the young adult dance culture in Britain in the mid-1990s', *Journal of Drug Issues*, 28(1): 9–32.

Measham, F. and Shiner, M. (2009). 'The legacy of normalisation: The role of classical and contemporary criminological theory in understanding young people's drug use', *International Journal of Drug Policy*, 20(6): 502–8.

Measham, F., Williams, L. and Aldridge, J. (2011). 'Marriage, mortgages and motherhood: What longitudinal studies can tell us about gender, drugs "careers" and the normalisation of adult "recreational" drug use', *International Journal of Drug Policy*, 22(6): 420–7.

Metz, D. and Underwood, M. (2005). *Older richer fitter: Identifying the customer needs of Britain's ageing population*. London: Age Concern.

Midwinter, E. (1990). *The old order: Crime and older people*. London: Centre for Policy on Ageing.

Miller, N., Belkin, B. and Gold, M. (1991). 'Alcohol and drug dependence among the elderly: Epidemiology, diagnosis, and treatment', *Comprehensive Psychiatry*, 32(2): 153–65.

Mills, C.W. (1959). *The sociological imagination*. Oxford: Oxford University Press.

Mitchell, B.A. (2003). 'Life course theory', in Ponzetti Jr., J.J. (ed.), *International encyclopedia of marriage and family (2nd edition)*, p. 1051–5. New York: Macmillan.

Moore, K. and Measham, F. (2008). '"It's the most fun you can have for twenty quid": Motivations, consequences and meanings of British ketamine use', *Addiction Research and Theory*, 16(3): 231–44.

Morgan, D. (1998). *The focus group guidebook*. London: Sage.

Moxon, D. and Waters, J. (2010). '"I don't know just where I'm going": Older adult drug users, illegal leisure and broken narratives', *International Journal of Crime, Criminal Justice and Law*, 5(1 & 2): 81–98.

Muggleton, D. (2000). *Inside subculture: The postmodern meaning of style*. Oxford: Berg.

Murphy, S., Reinarman, C. and Waldorf, D. (1989). 'An 11-year follow-up of a network of cocaine users', *British Journal of Addiction*, 84(4): 427–36.

Neugarten, B. (1976). 'Adaptation and the life cycle', *The Counseling Psychologist*, 6(1): 16–20.

Newcombe, R. (2008). 'Ketamine case study: The phenomenology of a ketamine experience', *Addiction Research and Theory*, 16(3): 209–15.

Notley, C. (2005). 'Four groups of illicit substance users amongst the adult "hidden" non-problematic community', *Drugs: Education, Prevention and Policy*, 12(4): 279–90.

Noy, C. (2008). 'Sampling knowledge: The hermeneutics of snowball sampling in qualitative research', *International Journal of Social Research Methodology*, 11(4): 327–44.

Nutt, D., King, L.A. and Phillips, L.D. (2010). 'Drug harms in the UK: A multi-criteria decision analysis', *The Lancet*, 376(9752): 1558–65.

Nutt, D., King, L.A., Saulsbury, W. and Blakemore, C. (2007). 'Development of a rational scale to assess the harms of drugs of potential misuse', *The Lancet*, 369(9566): 1047–53.

O'Donnell, J. (1969). *Narcotics addicts in Kentucky*. Washington, DC: United States Government Printing Office.

Office for National Statistics (2014). *Statistical bulletin: Annual mid-year population estimates, 2013*. Newport: Office for National Statistics. Available at http://www.ons.gov.uk/ons/rel/pop-estimate/population-estimates-for-uk-england-and-wales-scotland-and-northern-ireland/2013/stb-mid-2013-uk-population-estimates.html

Office for National Statistics (2015). *The effects of taxes and benefits on household income, historical data, 1977 to financial year ending 2014*. London: Office for National Statistics.

Oppenheimer, E., Stimson, G. and Thorley, A. (1979). 'Seven-year follow-up of heroin addicts in abstinence and continued use compared', *British Medical Journal*, 2: 627–30.

Oppenheimer, E., Tobutt, C., Taylor, C. and Andrew, T. (1994). 'Death and survival in a cohort of heroin addicts from London clinics: A 12-year follow-up study', *Addiction*, 89(10): 1299–308.

Orford, J. (1984). *Excessive appetites: A psychological view of addiction*. Chichester: Wiley.

Osborne, G. and Fogel, C. (2007). 'The normalization of marijuana use by adult Canadian users', *International Journal of Crime, Criminal Justice and Law*, 2(2): 201–25.

Osborne, G. and Fogel, C. (2008). 'Understanding the motivations for recreational marijuana use among adult Canadians', *Substance Use and Misuse*, 43(3 & 4): 539–72.

Parker, H. (2005). 'Normalization as a barometer: Recreational drug use and the consumption of leisure by younger Britons', *Addiction Research and Theory*, 13(3): 205–15.

Parker, H., Aldridge, J. and Eggington, R. (2001). *UK drugs unlimited: New research and policy lessons on illicit drug use*. Basingstoke: Palgrave.

Parker, H., Aldridge, J. and Measham, F. (1998). *Illegal leisure: The normalisation of adolescent recreational drug use*. London: Routledge.

Parker, H., Measham, F. and Aldridge, J. (1995). *Drug futures: Changing patterns of drug use amongst English youth*. London: Institute for the Study of Drug Dependence.

Parker, H., Williams, L. and Aldridge, J. (2002). 'The normalisation of sensible recreational drug use: Further evidence from the north west England longitudinal study', *Sociology*, 36(4): 941–64.

Pascarelli, B. and Fischer, W. (1974). 'Drug dependence in the elderly', *International Journal of Aging and Human Development*, 5(4): 347–56.

Patrick, J. (1973). *A glasgow gang observed*. London: Eyre Methuen.

Patton, M.Q. (2002). *Qualitative research and evaluation methods (3rd edition)*. Thousand Oaks: Sage.

Pearson, G. (2001). 'Normal drug use: Ethnographic fieldwork among an adult network of recreational drug users in inner London', *Substance Use and Misuse*, 36(1 & 2): 167–200.

Pennay, A. and Moore, D. (2010). 'Exploring the micro-politics of normalisation: Narratives of pleasure, self-control and desire in a sample of young Australian "party drug" users', *Addiction Research and Theory*, 18(5): 557–71.

Petersen, D. (1978). 'Drug use among the aged: Introduction', *Addictive Diseases: An International Journal*, 3(3): 305–9.

Phillipson, C., Leach, R., Money, A. and Biggs, S. (2008). 'Social and cultural constructions of ageing: The case of the baby boomers', *Sociological Research Online*, 13(3). http://www.socresonline.org.uk/13/3/5.html

Plant, M.A. (1975). 'Drug takers in an English town', *British Journal of Criminology*, 15(2): 181–6.

Plant, M.L., Plant, M.A. and Mason, W. (2002). 'Drinking, smoking and illicit drug use among British adults: Gender differences explored', *Journal of Substance Use*, 7(1): 24–33.

Pollok, M. and Schlitz, M.A. (1998). 'Does voluntary testing matter? How it influences homosexual safer sex'. Paper presented at the Fourth International Conference on AIDS, June 13 1998, Stockholm, Sweden.

Potter, G. (2009). 'Exploring retail level drug distribution: Social supply, "real" dealers and the user/dealer interface', in Demetrovics, Z., Fountain, J. and Kraus, L. (eds.), *Old and new policies, theories, research methods and drug users across Europe*, p. 51–74. Lengerich: Pabst Science Publishers.

Potter, G. (2010a). 'You reap what you sow: Profit, pleasure and pain in domestic cannabis cultivation', in Decorte, T. and Fountain, J. (eds.), *Pleasure, pain and profit: European perspectives on drugs*, p. 134–51. Lengerich: Pabst Science Publishers.

Potter, G. (2010b). *Weed, need and greed: A study of domestic cannabis cultivation*. London: Free Association Books.

Potter, G. and Chatwin, C. (2012). 'The problem with "skunk"', *Drugs and Alcohol Today*, 12(4): 232–40.

Potter, G. and Dann, S. (2005). 'Urban crop circles: Urban cannabis growers in the north of England', in Palacios, W. (ed.), *Cocktails and dreams: Perspectives on drug and alcohol use*, p. 89–109. Upper Saddle River, NJ: Pearson.

Potter, G.R., Barratt, M.J., Malm, A., Bouchard, M., Blok, T., Christensen, A., . . . and Wouters, M. (2015). 'Global patterns of domestic cannabis cultivation: Sample characteristics and patterns of growing across eleven countries', *International Journal of Drug Policy*, 26(3): 226–37.

Powell, J.L. and Wahidin, A. (2006). 'Rethinking criminology: The case of "ageing studies"', in Wahidin, A. and Cain, M. (eds.), *Ageing, crime and society*, p. 17–34. Cullompton: Willan.

Powell, J.L. and Wahidin, A. (2008). 'Understanding old age and victimisation: A critical exploration', *International Journal of Sociology and Social Policy*, 3(4): 90–98.

Power, R. (1994). 'Some methodological and practical implications of employing drug users as indigenous fieldworkers', in Boulton, M. (ed.), *Challenge and innovation: Methodological advances in social research on HIV/AIDS*, p. 97–109. Abingdon: Taylor and Francis.

Preble, E. and Casey, J.J. (1969). 'Taking care of business: The heroin street user's life on the street', *International Journal of the Addictions*, 4(1): 1–24.

Preston, A. (2014). 'Drug-taking fortysomethings with one foot in the rave', *The Guardian*, 5 October 2014, http://www.theguardian.com/society/2014/oct/05/-sp-drug-taking-fortysomethings-rave-middle-aged

Public Health England (2013). *Drug treatment in England 2012–13*. London: Health and Wellbeing Directorate, Public Health England.

Ramsey, M. and Partridge, S. (1999). *Drug misuse declared in 1998: Results from the British Crime Survey*. Home Office Research Study 197. London: Home Office.

Redback Films (2005). *Stoned in Suburbia*. [TV broadcast] Sky One, 17 October 2005.

Redhead, S. (1990). *The end-of-the-century party: Youth and pop towards 2000*. Manchester: Manchester University Press.

Reismann, C. (2008). *Narrative methods for the human sciences*. Thousand Oaks: Sage.

Reith, G. (2005). 'On the edge: Drugs and the consumption of risk in late modernity', in Lyng, S. (ed.), *Edgework: The sociology of risk taking*, p. 227–45. Abingdon: Routledge.

Reynolds, S. (2007). 'Changing marriage? Messing with Mr. In-Between?: Reflections upon media debates on same-sex marriage in Ireland', *Sociological Research Online*, 12(1). http://www.socresonline.org.uk/12/1/reynolds.html

Riley, M.W. (1971). 'Social gerontology and the age stratification of society', *The Gerontologist*, 11(1, part 1): 79–87.

Riley, M.W. (1973). 'Aging and cohort succession: Interpretations and misinterpretations', *Public Opinion Quarterly*, 37(1): 35–49.

Riley, M.W., Johnson, M. and Foner, A. (1972). *Aging and society: A sociology of age stratification (Vol. 3)*. New York: Russell Sage Foundation.

Robinson, G., Burke, L. and Millings, M. (2016). 'Criminal justice identities in transition: The case of devolved probation services in England and Wales', *British Journal of Criminology*, 56(1): 161–78.

Roe, S. (2005). *Drug misuse declared: Findings from the 2004/05 British Crime Survey*. London: Home Office.

Roe, B., Beynon, C., Pickering, L. and Duffy, P. (2010). 'Experiences of drug use and ageing: Health, quality of life, relationship and service implications', *Journal of Advanced Nursing*, 66(9): 1968–79.

Rosenberg, H. (1995). 'The elderly and the use of illicit drugs: Sociological and epidemiological considerations', *The International Journal of the Addictions*, 30(13 & 14): 1925–51.

Rosenberg, H. (1997). 'Use and abuse of illicit drugs among older people', in Gurnack, A.M. (ed.), *Older adults' misuse of alcohol, medicines, and other drugs: Research and practice issues*, p. 206–27. New York: Springer.

Roxby, P. (2010). 'Ageing drug addicts "face chronic health problems"', *BBC News*, 12 September 2010, http://www.bbc.co.uk/news/health-11262369

Royal College of Psychiatrists (2011). *Our invisible addicts (first report of the older persons' substance misuse working group of the Royal College of Psychiatrists)*. College Report CR165. London: Royal College of Psychiatrists.

Salganik, M. and Heckathorn, D.D. (2004). 'Sampling and estimation in hidden populations using respondent-driven sampling', *Sociological Methodology*, 34(1): 193–240.

Sampson, R. and Laub, J. (1993). *Crime in the making: Pathways and turning points through life*. Cambridge, MA: Harvard University Press.

Sampson, R. and Laub, J. (2005). 'A life-course view of the development of crime', *Annals of the American Academy of Political and Social Science*, 602(1): 12–45.

Sandberg, S. (2013). 'Cannabis culture: A stable subculture in a changing world', *Criminology and Criminal Justice*, 13(1): 63–79.

Sandbrook, D. (2005). *Never had it so good: A history of Britain from Suez to the Beatles*. London: Brown.

Schlaerth, K.R., Splawn, R.G., Ong, J. and Smith, S.D. (2004). 'Change in the pattern of illegal drug use in an inner city population over 50: An observational study', *Journal of Addictive Diseases*, 23(2): 95–107.

Schoenenberger, A.W. and Stuck, A.E. (2014). 'Inappropriate drug use among older persons: Is it time for action?', *Age and Ageing*, 43(6): 737–9.

Schuckit, M. (1977). 'Geriatric alcoholism and drug abuse', *The Gerontologist*, 17(2): 168–74.

Scott, M. (2015). 'Theresa May wants to ban pleasure', *The Telegraph*, 2 June 2015, http://www.telegraph.co.uk/news/general-election-2015/politics-blog/11645354/Theresa-May-wants-to-ban-pleasure.html

Semaan, S. (2010). 'Time-space sampling and respondent-driven sampling with hard-to-reach populations', *Methodological Innovations Online*, 5(2): 60–75.

Semaan, S., Lauby, J. and Liebman, J. (2002). 'Street and network sampling in evaluation studies of HIV risk-reduction interventions', *AIDS Reviews*, 4(2): 213–23.

Sheff, D. (2000). *All we are saying: The last major interview with John Lennon and Yoko Ono*. New York: St. Martin's Press.

Shewan, D. and Dalgarno, P. (2005). 'Evidence for controlled heroin use? Low levels of negative health and social outcomes among non-treatment heroin users in Glasgow (Scotland)', *British Journal of Health Psychology*, 10(1): 33–48.

Shewan, D., Dalgarno, P., Marshall, A., Lowe, E., Campbell, M., Nicholson, S., . . . and Thomson, K. (1998). 'Patterns of heroin use among a non-treatment sample in Glasgow (Scotland)', *Addiction Research*, 6(3): 215–34.

Shewan, D., Dalgarno, P. and Reith, G. (2000). 'Perceived risk and risk reduction among ecstasy users: The role of drug, set, and setting', *International Journal of Drug Policy*, 10(6): 431–53.

Shildrick, T. (2002). 'Young people, illicit drugs and the question of normalisation', *Journal of Youth Studies*, 5(1): 35–48.

Shiner, M. (2009). *Drug use and social change: The distortion of history*. Basingstoke: Palgrave MacMillan.

Shiner, M. and Newburn, T. (1996). *Young people, drugs and peer education: An evaluation of the youth awareness programme*. London: Home Office.

Shiner, M. and Newburn, T. (1997). 'Definitely, maybe not: The normalisation of recreational drug use amongst young people', *Sociology*, 31(3): 511–29.

Shiner, M. and Newburn, T. (1999). 'Taking tea with Noel: The place and meaning of drug use in everyday life', in South, N. (ed.), *Drugs: Cultures, controls and everyday life*, p. 139–59. London: Sage.

Shukla, R.K. (2006). 'Using marijuana in adulthood', *Journal of Ethnicity in Substance Abuse*, 4(3 & 4): 153–81.

Simpson, M. (2003). 'The relationship between drug use and crime: A puzzle inside an enigma', *International Journal of Drug Policy*, 14(4): 307–19.

Snow, M. (1973). 'Maturing out of narcotic addiction in New York City', *International Journal of the Addictions*, 8(6): 921–38.

Spencer, P. (1990). 'The riddled course: Theories of age and its transformation', in Spencer, P. (ed.), *Anthropology and the riddle of the sphinx: Paradoxes of change in the life course*, p. 1–26. London: Routledge.

Standing, G. (2011). *The precariat: The new dangerous class.* London: Bloomsbury.

Stephens, R. (1991). *The street addict role.* Albany: State University of New York Press.

Stevens, A. (2007). 'My cannabis, your skunk: Reader's response to "the cannabis potency question"', *Drugs and Alcohol Today*, 7(3): 13–17.

Stevens, J. (1987). *Storming heaven: LSD and the American dream.* New York: Atlantic Monthly Press.

Stimson, G.V. and Oppenheimer, E. (1982). *Heroin addiction: Treatment and control in Britain.* London: Tavistock.

Stone, J. (2015). 'More people have joined Labour since Jeremy Corbyn became leader than are in UKIP', *The Independent*, 22 September 2015, http://www.independent.co.uk/news/uk/politics/more-people-have-joined-labour-since-jeremy-corbyn-became-leader-than-are-in-the-lib-dems-10512815.html

Strauss, A. (1987). *Qualitative analysis for social scientists.* Cambridge: Cambridge University Press.

Sullum, J. (2003). *Saying yes: In defense of drug use.* New York: Tarcher/Penguin.

Sumner, C. (1976). 'Marxism and deviancy theory', in Wiles, P. (ed.), *The sociology of crime and delinquency in Britain (Vol. 2): The new criminologies*, p. 159–74. London: Martin Robertson.

Sumner, C. (1990). 'Rethinking deviance: Towards a sociology of censure', in Sumner, C. (ed.), *Censure, politics and criminal justice*, p. 15–40. Buckingham: Open University Press.

Sumner, C. (1994). *The sociology of deviance: An obituary.* Buckingham: Open University Press.

Sumner, C. (2004). 'The social nature of crime and deviance', in Sumner, C. (ed.), *The blackwell companion to criminology*, p. 3–31. Oxford: Blackwell.

Sumner, C. (2012). 'Censure, culture and political economy: Beyond the death of deviance debate', in Hall, S. and Winlow, S. (eds.), *New directions in criminological theory*, p. 165–80. Abingdon: Routledge.

Szakolczai, A. (1998). *Max Weber and Michel Foucault: Parallel lifeworks.* London: Routledge.

Szakolczai, A. (2000). *Reflexive historical sociology.* London: Routledge.

Taylor, I. (1999). *Crime in context: A critical criminology of market societies.* Cambridge: Westview Press.

Thomassen, B. (2009). 'The uses and meanings of liminality', *International Political Anthropology*, 2(1): 5–27.

Thomassen, B. (2014). *Liminality and the modern: Living through the in-bewteen.* Farnham: Ashgate.

Thomassen, B. (2015). 'Thinking with liminality: To the boundaries of an anthropological concept', in Horvath, A., Thomassen, B. and Wydra, H. (eds.), *Breaking boundaries: Varieties of liminality*, p. 39–58. Oxford: Berghahn Books.

Tobutt, C., Oppenheimer, E. and Laranjeirna, R. (1996). 'Health of cohort of heroin addicts from London clinics: 22 year follow up', *British Medical Journal*, 312: 1458.

Travis, A. (2014). 'Eleven countries studied, one inescapable conclusion—the drug laws don't work', *The Guardian*, 30 October 2014, http://www.theguardian.com/society/2014/oct/30/drug-laws-international-study-tough-policy-use-problem

Travis, A. (2015). 'Ban on legal highs would technically cover alcohol, cigarettes and coffee', *The Guardian*, 27 May 2015, http://www.theguardian.com/society/2015/may/27/legal-highs-ban-technically-cover-alcohol-cigarettes-coffee

Turner, V. (1967). *The forest of symbols: Aspects of Ndembu ritual.* Manchester: Manchester University Press.

Turner, V. (1969). *The ritual process: Structure and anti-structure.* London: Routledge & Kegan Paul.

Turner, V. (1982). *From ritual to theatre: The human seriousness of play.* New York: PAJ.

Vaillant, G. (1973). 'A 20-year follow-up of New York narcotic addicts', *Archives of General Psychiatry*, 29(2): 237–41.

Van Gennep, A.V. (1960) [1909]. *The rites of passage.* London: Routledge & Kegan Paul.

Van Gundy, K. and Rebellon, C.J. (2010). 'A life-course perspective on the "gateway hypothesis"', *Journal of Health and Social Behavior*, 51(3): 244–59.

Van Meter, K.M. (1990). 'Methodological and design issues: Techniques for assessing the representativeness of snowball samples', in Lambert, E. (ed.), *The collection and interpretation of data from hidden populations (NIDA research monograph series, no. 98)*, p. 31–43. Rockville: National Institute on Drug Abuse.

Vervaeke, H.K.E. and Korf, D.J. (2006). 'Long-term ecstasy use and the management of work and relationships', *International Journal of Drug Policy*, 17(6): 484–93.

Volz, E. and Heckathorn, D.D. (2008). 'Probability-based estimation theory for respondent driven sampling', *Journal of Official Statistics*, 24(1): 79–97.

Wachsmuth, W., Blonigen, D.M., Jacob, T. and Price, R.K. (2016). 'Course of drug use from early adulthood to mid-life among Vietnam-era veterans', *Journal of Substance Use*, 21(1): 57–64.

Wacquant, L. (1994). 'The new urban colour line: The state and fate of the ghetto in post-fordist America', in Calhoun, C. (ed.), *Social theory and the politics of identity*, p. 232–4. Blackwell: Oxford.

Wacquant, L. (2008). *Urban outcasts: A comparative sociology of advanced marginality.* Cambridge: Polity Press.

Wadd, S. and Galvani, S. (2014). *The forgotten people: Drug problems in later life (a scoping study commissioned by the Big Lottery Fund).* Luton: Substance Misuse and Ageing Research Team, University of Bedfordshire.

Wahidin, A. (2006). '"No problems—old and quiet": Imprisonment in later life', in Wahidin, A. and Cain, M. (eds.), *Ageing, crime and society*, p. 171–92. Cullompton: Willan.

Wahidin, A. and Aday, R. (2011). 'Later life and imprisonment', in Phillipson, C. (eds.), *Handbook of social gerontology*, p. 65–78. London: Sage.

Wahidin, A. and Cain, M. (2006). 'Ageing, crime and society: An invitation to criminology', in Wahidin, A. and Cain, M. (eds.), *Ageing, crime and society*, p. 1–16. Cullompton: Willan.

Wainwright, T. (2015). 'The war on the war on drugs', *The Economist: The World in 2016*, 2 November 2015, http://www.theworldin.com/article/10455/war-war-drugs?fsrc=scn/tw/te/bl/ed/thewaronthewarondrugs

Waldorf, D. (1973). *Careers in dope*. Englewood Cliffs, NJ: Prentice Hall.

Waldorf, D. and Biernacki, P. (1981). 'The natural recovery from opiate addiction: Some preliminary findings', *The Journal of Drug Issues*, 11(1): 61–74.

Wallace, M. (2014). 'Conservative party membership has risen to 149,800—up 11.7 per cent', *ConservativeHome*, 28 September 2014, http://www.conservativehome.com/thetorydiary/2014/09/conference-survey-and-membership-figures.html

Warburton, H., Turnbull, P.J. and Hough, M. (2005). *Occasional and controlled heroin use: Not a problem?* York: Joseph Rowntree Foundation.

Warwick, D. and Littlejohn, G. (1992). *Coal, capital and culture: A sociological analysis of mining communities in West Yorkshire*. London: Routledge.

Waters, J. (2009). *Illegal drug use among older adults*, PhD thesis, Sheffield: The University of Sheffield.

Waters, J. (2015). 'Snowball sampling: A cautionary tale involving a study of older drug users', *International Journal of Social Research Methodology*, 18(4): 367–80.

Waters, J. (2016). 'How biography influences research: An autoethnography', *British Journal of Community Justice*, 14(2).

Weatherby, N., Needle, R.H., Cesari, H., Booth, R., McCoy, C., Waters, J., . . . and Chitwood, D. (1994). 'Validity of self-reported drug use among injection drug users and crack cocaine users recruited through street outreach', *Evaluation and Program Planning*, 17(4): 347–55.

Weisheit, R.A. (1991). 'The intangible rewards from crime: The case of domestic marijuana cultivation', *Crime and Delinquency*, 37(4): 506–27.

Whalen, T. and Boeri, M. (2014). 'Measuring discontinuity in binary longitudinal data: Applications to drug use trajectories', *Sociological Methods and Research*, 43(2): 248–79.

Whyte, W.F. (1955). *Street corner society: The social structure of an Italian slum (2nd edition)*. Chicago: University of Chicago Press.

Williams, L. (2013). *Changing lives, changing drug journeys: Drug taking decisions from adolescence to adulthood*. London: Routledge.

Williams, L. and Parker, H. (2001). 'Alcohol, cannabis, ecstasy and cocaine: Drugs of reasoned choice among young adult recreational drug users in England', *International Journal of Drug Policy*, 12(5): 397–413.

Wilson, A. (2007). *Northern soul: Music, drugs and subcultural identity*. Cullompton: Willan.

Winick, C. (1962). 'Maturing out of narcotic addiction', *UN Bulletin on Narcotics*, 1(1): 1–7.

Winlow, S. and Hall, S. (2013). *Rethinking social exclusion: The end of the social?* London: Sage.

Wright, R., Decker, S., Redfern, A. and Smith, D. (1992). 'A snowball's chance in hell: Doing fieldwork with active residential burglars', *Journal of Research in Crime and Delinquency*, 29(2): 148–61.

Wu, L.T. and Blazer, D. (2011). 'Illicit and nonmedical drug use among older adults: A review', *Journal of Aging and Health*, 23(3): 481–504.

Young, J. (1971). *The drugtakers: The social meaning of drug use*. London: Paladin.

Young, J. (2007). *The vertigo of late modernity*. London: Sage.

Zinberg, N. (1984). *Drug, set, and setting: The basis for controlled intoxicant use*. New Haven: Yale University Press.

Index

Note: Italicized page numbers indicate a figure on the corresponding page. Page numbers in bold indicate a table on the corresponding page.

For Product Safety Concerns and Information please contact our EU representative GPSR@taylorandfrancis.com
Taylor & Francis Verlag GmbH, Kaufingerstraße 24, 80331 München, Germany

www.ingramcontent.com/pod-product-compliance
Ingram Content Group UK Ltd.
Pitfield, Milton Keynes, MK11 3LW, UK
UKHW011015180926
475701UK00004B/748
9780367595999